# Get the eBook FREE!
(PDF, ePub, Kindle, and liveBook all included)

We believe that once you buy a book from us, you should be able to read it in any format we have available. To get electronic versions of this book at no additional cost to you, purchase and then register this book at the Manning website.

Go to https://www.manning.com/freebook and follow the instructions to complete your pBook registration.

## That's it!
## Thanks from Manning!

# *Blockchain in Action*

BINA RAMAMURTHY

MANNING
SHELTER ISLAND

For online information and ordering of this and other Manning books, please visit
www.manning.com. The publisher offers discounts on this book when ordered in quantity.
For more information, please contact

    Special Sales Department
    Manning Publications Co.
    20 Baldwin Road
    PO Box 761
    Shelter Island, NY 11964
    Email: orders@manning.com

Manning Publications Co.
20 Baldwin Road
PO Box 761
Shelter Island, NY 11964

| | |
|---|---|
| Development editor: | Christina Taylor |
| Technical development editor: | Kyle Smith |
| Review editor: | Ivan Martinović |
| Production editor: | Deirdre S. Hiam |
| Copy editor: | Keir Simpson |
| Proofreader: | Melody Dolab |
| Technical proofreader: | Valentin Crettaz |
| Typesetter: | Gordan Salinovic |
| Cover designer: | Marija Tudor |

ISBN 9781617296086
Printed in the United States of America

*I dedicate this book to my grandmother, Thanjavur Avva,*
*for her unconditional love and affection to me,*
*and compassion and generosity to everyone.*

# brief contents

# contents

# *Preface*

I'm fortunate to have been a computer scientist during an era of phenomenal advancement in computing, from integrated chips to the internet. I have designed and developed a wide range of systems, from a dot-matrix printer driver to algorithms for fault tolerance in distributed systems. I have programmed in a variety of high-level languages, from PL/1 to Python. All these years, I have also been an educator, teaching courses on the leading edge of technology, from grid computing to data science. And of course, my current passion and fascination is blockchain technology.

I first heard about Bitcoin around 2013, but ignored it as being yet another attempt at cryptocurrency. In 2016, I went back to explore Bitcoin for its underlying technology: the blockchain. I searched for more information on blockchain, of course, but could not find much. At a local meetup in Buffalo on a cold January night in 2016, one of the speakers showed a few YouTube videos on the magic of the blockchain's distributed ledger. That was my "Aha!" moment. I was amazed. I went on to read the Bitcoin white paper; then I dabbled with open source blockchain code with Eris and (later) Monax. In the summer of 2017, I taught blockchain in a course on Emerging Technologies. This course was held at Amrita University, Coimbatore, India, for a select group of automotive engineers. I spent the next year (August 2017–May 2018) producing and releasing a four-course MOOC specialization, which is still running, with more than 140,000 enrollees from all over the world.

I had generated an enormous amount of content, video, original diagrams, and about 220 pages of script for the Coursera video production. I decided to turn the material generated into a book. Then, in the summer of 2018, I got a call from a Manning technical editor and began this book project: *Blockchain in Action*. The project took two years to complete. I realize that a print book project with hands-on examples is different from a MOOC—much more complex and challenging. But here it is: the completed product. I enjoyed every minute I spent writing this book, and the effort was worth it. I liked thinking about blockchain concepts, exploring them, discovering useful problems to solve, and then describing them to an audience that is not in front of me.

Because blockchain is an emerging technology, few resources are available to help practitioners get started with application development in this area. This book addresses that need. This book covers end-to-end development of blockchain-based Dapp. I chose to use the Ethereum blockchain platform because its code is open source. Tools such as the Solidity compiler for smart contracts, the Remix IDE for exploration, the Truffle suite of tools for Dapp development and testing, the test chains Ganache and Ropsten, Infura for cloud deployment of smart contracts, and the MetaMask wallet have worked well for my team for the past four years. These tools work in unison to provide seamless learning as well as a prototyping environment.

I hope you enjoy reading the book as much as I did creating its content.

# *Acknowledgments*

I'd like to thank my family for supporting me through this challenging project, especially my husband, Kumar, for his encouragement and unwavering support through the years. I also would like to thank our daughters Nethra and Nainita for being my cheerleaders throughout this project.

Next, I'd like to acknowledge the team at Manning: Christina Taylor, my development editor; Deirdre Hiam, my project editor; Keir Simpson, my copy editor; Melody Dolab, my proofreader; Kyle Smith, my technical development editor; Ivan Martinović, my review editor; and the reviewers, whose feedback made this contents of this book useful and technically sound: Alessandro Campeis, Angelo Costa, Attoh-Okine Nii, Borko Djurkovic, Christophe Boschmans, Danny Chin, David DiMaria, Frederick Schiller, Garry Turkington, Glenn Swonk, Hilde Van Gysel, Jose San Leandro, Krzysztof Kamyczek, Luis Moux, Michael Jensen, Noreen Dertinger, Richard B. Ward, Ron Lease, Sambasiva Andaluri, Sheik Uduman Ali M, Shobha Iyer, Tim Holmes, Victor Durán, and Zalán Somogyváry. Special thanks to the technical proofreader, Valentin Crettaz, who ran the code and gave me some valuable feedback on the Dapps and token standards.

I thank all my students and research team members, who have been my source of inspiration with their relentless eagerness to learn about blockchain.

# *About this book*

*Blockchain in Action* is a comprehensive resource for designing and developing blockchain-based decentralized applications (Dapps). The resources in this book will help you get started with smart contracts and blockchain application development. The book provides enough details to help you understand blockchain without going into theoretical material.

The design and development of smart contracts and Dapps are illustrated by seven applications, each focusing on a certain aspect of blockchain. Several essential tools (Remix, Ganache, MetaMask, Truffle, Ropsten, and Infura) and techniques (encryption and digital signing) are introduced to demonstrate the development and deployment of Dapps on the Ethereum test chain. The core ideas of blockchain—trust and integrity, security and privacy, on-chain and off-chain data, and operations—are covered in detail with examples. The blockchain concepts are explained with more than 150 annotated figures and screenshots.

The codebase provided for the six fully developed Dapps is a valuable resource for blockchain application developers. The development of smart contracts and Dapps is explained in an incremental fashion. A standard directory structure and single-page web UI help you quickly configure, migrate, and transact with the Dapps. You may find some of the chapters to be lengthy, because a new blockchain concept is introduced with a Dapp and explained further with a second Dapp. Special techniques (such as off-chain and on-chain data), design principles, and best practices round up the exploration to offer a clear roadmap to robust smart contract and Dapp development.

## Who should read this book

*Blockchain in Action* is for developers who want to learn about blockchain technology and 'develop smart contracts and decentralized applications. Any programmer, from beginner to advanced, who wants to get started with blockchain programming can do that by reading and running the applications discussed in the book. Business professionals and practitioners who wish to have an overview of the special use cases of blockchain can learn from the diverse applications and Dapps described. This book is ideal for educators who are looking for a textbook to teach blockchain in their undergraduate or graduate courses. Also, a self-learner, such as a high-school student with some programming background, should be able to learn blockchain programming by reading this book and practicing the examples given.

## How this book is organized: A roadmap

The book has three parts that cover 12 chapters.

Part 1 (chapters 1–4) covers blockchain basics and the design and development of smart contracts.

Chapter 1 introduces the 3 Ds of blockchain—decentralization, disintermediation, and distributed immutable ledger—and provides a high-level conceptual view of a blockchain.

Chapter 2 is a gentle introduction to smart contracts on the Ethereum blockchain, applying design principles to develop smart contracts, code them with the Solidity language, deploy them in a web-based Remix integrated development environment, and transact with them. Smart contracts for a decentralized counter (Counter.sol) and an airline consortium (ASK.sol) are developed.

Chapter 3 is about techniques for adding trust and integrity to the smart contract code. A ballot smart contract (Ballot.sol) representing voting in a digital democracy is introduced and developed in incremental steps.

Chapter 4 introduces the design and development of a decentralized application (Dapp) with smart contract logic and a web-based user interface. A Node.js-based Truffle suite of tools is introduced for developing and running the smart contract and the web application. The Ballot application (Ballot-Dapp) is used to illustrate Truffle-based development steps and deployment on a local Ganache test chain.

Part 2 (chapters 5–8) is about end-to-end Dapp development, with additional blockchain-specific features such as on-chain data, security, and privacy.

Chapter 5 introduces security and privacy in the context of blockchain programming. Cryptography and hashing algorithms and techniques are discussed at a high level. The concepts are illustrated by means of a blind auction smart contract (BlindAuction.sol).

Chapter 6 introduces the concept of on-chain and off-chain data, which is unique to blockchain programming. The blind auction and ASK smart contracts are extended into Dapps (BA-Dapp, ASK-Dapp) to demonstrate development with on-chain and off-chain data. Defining, emitting, and accessing blockchain events and logs are illustrated.

Chapter 7 focuses on the web3 API of Ethereum that enables web applications to access the underlying blockchain services. The blockchain side-channel concept is introduced to illustrate the use of web3 in a micropayment channel (MPC) application for massive plastics cleanup (MPC-Dapp).

Chapter 8 discusses deploying the smart contracts developed on a public cloudlike infrastructure called Infura. Infura is a web3 provider, and a gateway to public blockchains such as Ropsten (mainnet and IPFS). Public deployment on Infura and Ropsten is illustrated by deploying MPC and blind auction smart contracts.

Part 3 (chapters 9–12) is about expanding your view of the Ethereum Dapps ecosystem with tokens, Ethereum standards, automated testing, and a roadmap for real-world application development.

Chapter 9 is about the tokenization of digital assets. A RES4-Dapp, a real estate token, is developed based on the Ethereum standard for non-fungible token ERC721.

Chapter 10 is fully dedicated to writing test scripts and running them by using Truffle's JS-based testing frameworks. Automated test script writing is illustrated by three smart contracts already discussed in the book: counter, ballot, and blind auction.

Chapter 11 provides an end-to-end roadmap of all the concepts, tools, and techniques discussed so far and brings them together in an application for educational credentialing: DCC-Dapp.

Chapter 12 reviews the road ahead, which is strewn with challenges, and explores the fantastic opportunities for you to contribute.

Two appendices are provided to help you with the design process.

Appendix A offers a refresher on design representation using Unified Modeling Language (UML). It illustrates structural, behavioral, and interaction modeling and diagrams that are used in the design of smart contracts.

Appendix B captures the design principles introduced in the book for guiding blockchain application development.

In general, a reader should start with chapter 1 and move sequentially through chapter 8. The chapters in part 3 can be explored in any order of interest. Chapter 10 (on testing), for example, can be read any time after chapter 5. I encourage you to do so.

A developer who wants to be proficient in smart contract design and Dapp development should try to follow along with the code examples in the chapters and learn from them.

## About the code

This book contains many examples of source code, both in numbered listings and inline with normal text. There are six fully working Dapps, along with numerous pieces of code and smart contracts to explain various concepts. In many listings within the book, some lines are represented by … (ellipsis) for brevity when the code is lengthy, but the complete code is available in the codebase accompanying the book. Code annotations accompany many of the listings, highlighting important concepts.

Source code for the examples in this book is available for download from the publisher's website at https://www.manning.com/books/blockchain-in-action.

## liveBook discussion forum

Purchase of *Blockchain in Action* includes free access to a private web forum run by Manning Publications where you can make comments about the book, ask technical questions, and receive help from the author and from other users. To access the forum, go to https://livebook.manning.com/book/blockchain-in-action/welcome/v-8. You can also learn more about Manning's forums and the rules of conduct at https://livebook.manning.com/#!/discussion.

Manning's commitment to our readers is to provide a venue where a meaningful dialogue between individual readers and between readers and the author can take place. It is not a commitment to any specific amount of participation on the part of the author, whose contribution to the forum remains voluntary (and unpaid). We suggest you try asking the author some challenging questions lest their interest stray! The forum and the archives of previous discussions will be accessible from the publisher's website as long as the book is in print.

## Other online resources

I teach a blockchain course for undergraduates and graduates, using this book as a text. You can follow the happenings in this course and review the lecture presentations, slides, and other exercises at my website: https://www.cse.buffalo.edu/~bina/cse426.

# *About the author*

Dr. Bina Ramamurthy is a Teaching Professor in the Department of Computer Science and Engineering, University at Buffalo, Buffalo, New York. In 2019, she was awarded the State University of New York (SUNY) Chancellor's Award for excellence in teaching.

She is the director of Blockchain Thinklab at the University at Buffalo. In the summer of 2018, she launched a four-course blockchain specialization on the Coursera platform for a worldwide audience. The suite of courses has been ranked number 1 among the best courses on blockchain technology and has enrolled more than 140,000 learners from all over the world.

She has been the principal investigator on four National Science Foundation (NSF) grants and a co-investigator on six Instructional Innovative Instructional Technology Grants (IITG) from SUNY. She has given numerous invited presentations at prominent conferences in the areas of data-intensive and big data computing. She has also been on the program committees of prestigious conferences, including the High-Performance Computing Conference and Special Interest Group in Computer Science Education (SIGCSE).

Bina Ramamurthy received a BE (Honors) from Guindy Engineering College, Madras, India; an MS in Computer Science from Wichita State University, Kansas; and a PhD in Electrical Engineering from the University at Buffalo.

# *About the cover illustration*

The figure on the cover of *Blockchain in Action* is captioned "Fille de Bulgarie," or "Bulgarian Girl." The illustration is taken from a collection of dress costumes from various countries by Jacques Grasset de Saint-Sauveur (1757–1810), titled *Costumes de Différents Pays*, published in France in 1788. Each illustration is finely drawn and colored by hand. The rich variety of Grasset de Saint-Sauveur's collection reminds us vividly of how culturally apart the world's towns and regions were just 200 years ago. Isolated from one another, people spoke different dialects and languages. In the streets or in the countryside, it was easy to identify where they lived and what their trade or station in life was just by their dress.

The way we dress has changed since then, and the diversity by region, so rich at the time, has faded away. It is now hard to tell apart the inhabitants of different continents, let alone different towns, regions, or countrieis. Perhaps we have traded cultural diversity for a more varied personal life—certainly for a more varied and fast-paced technological life.

At a time when it is hard to tell one computer book from another, Manning celebrates the inventiveness and initiative of the computer business with book covers based on the rich diversity of regional life of two centuries ago, brought back to life by Grasset de Saint-Sauveur's pictures.

# Part 1

# *Getting started with blockchain programming*

Blockchain is poised to become an integral part of existing computing systems as a trust layer. So part 1 begins with an overview of a blockchain as decentralized infrastructure, disintermediator, and distributed ledger technology: the three Ds of blockchain. The three Ds together enable trust in decentralized applications with the help of an essential coding element called smart contracts. Part 1 focuses on the design and development of smart contracts in incremental steps. Design diagrams and design principles are introduced to guide the smart contract design. You'll learn to code smart contracts by using the Solidity language, and deploy and test them by using a web-based Remix IDE. Then you'll learn to code rules for trust and integrity in the smart contracts. Finally I introduce the Truffle suite of tools with detailed instructions on installing it. You'll be using Truffle commands throughout the book for deploying and testing smart contracts.

Chapter 1 is about blockchain basics. Chapter 2 introduces essential coding elements of a smart contract, using a counter (Counter.sol) application and an airline consortium (ASK.sol) for trading seats. Chapter 3 illustrates techniques for verification and validation of the smart contract, using a digital democracy application. Chapter 4 demonstrates the use of the Truffle suite of tools for migrating the smart contract to a test chain Ganache and testing the deployment (Ballot-Dapp) with a web UI.

# Blockchain basics

In the latter part of 2008 and early 2009, centralized systems of the world's financial markets—enabled by large intermediaries such as banks and investment firms—failed and began to crumble. Trust in these systems eroded, and panic set in all over the world with the collapse of financial markets. It was at this juncture that a mysterious person or persons introduced to the world a working model of a peer-to-peer decentralized digital currency system (with no central authority or administration) called Bitcoin. The trust intermediation in this system was realized via software that would later be named *blockchain*. Blockchain provided the software-based verification, validation, recording, and integrity essentials for currency transfers.

Even though Bitcoin appeared to have launched suddenly in 2009, the idea of a working digital currency has been a quest since the dawn of computing. Bitcoin's

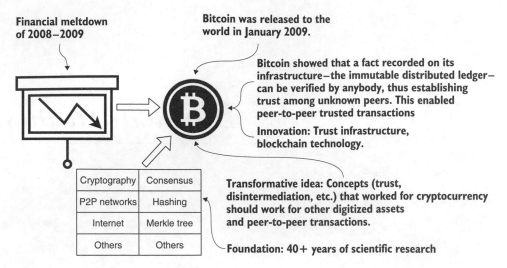

**Figure 1.1   The birth of blockchain technology**

blockchain technology stands on a strong foundation of more than 40 years of scientific research in cryptography, hashing, peer-to-peer networks, and consensus protocols. Figure 1.1 provides a brief history of blockchain, its innovation and robust scientific foundation, and its transformative effect on modern networked systems.

On completion of this chapter, you'll know the fundamental concepts of blockchain and decentralized applications, such as transactions, blocks, a chain of blocks, nodes, networks of nodes, and the protocol that ties all these elements together. With these many components, blockchain is indeed a complex system. An understanding of these foundational concepts is, therefore, imperative for the blockchain application design and development that you'll embark on in chapters 2–11.

## 1.1   *From Bitcoin to blockchain*

The initial excitement about blockchain technology was about enabling peer-to-peer transfers of digital currency to anybody in the world, crossing human-created boundaries (such as the borders of countries) without any intermediaries such as banks. This excitement was further heightened by the realization that this peer-to-peer capability could be applied to other, non-cryptocurrency types of transactions. These transactions involve assets such as titles, deeds, music and art, secret codes, contracts between businesses, autonomous driver decisions, and artifacts resulting from many everyday human endeavors. A transaction record may contain other details based on the blockchain protocol and the application.

> **DEFINITION**   A *transaction* recorded on a blockchain contains a peer-to-peer message that specifies the operations executed, data parameters used for the execution of operations, the sender and receiver of the message, the transaction fee, and the timestamp of its recording.

Bitcoin has been in operation continuously since its launch. At the time of this writing, according to Blockchain Charts (https://www.blockchain.com/en/charts), it is delivering more than 200,000 transactions per day. Following its initial success, people began to ask, "If you can transact digital currency, why not any other digital assets?" This question was answered around 2013 with the addition of an environment for code execution on another popular blockchain, Ethereum (https://ethereum.org). The innovation was that the verification, validation, and recording could be extended to other digital assets and to related transactions and systems. Therefore, blockchain can play a crucial role in implementing decentralized systems by providing software-based intermediation to other (non-currency) peer-to-peer transactions.

Let's take a look at a blockchain to give you an idea of what transactions, blocks, and chains of blocks look like. This example will help you visualize blockchain context and the problem space discussed in the next sections, which explore the transactions and blocks for the Ethereum public blockchain (https://etherscan.io). Figure 1.2 shows transactions (Tx and transaction#) that represent messages between two accounts (From and To) representing peer participants. These Txs enable the recording of information on the blocks of the blockchain.

Figure 1.2 also shows blocks of Txs. Each block (Bk) is made up of a set of transactions and is identified by a block number. Block #10163275 has 142 Txs, and block #10163274 has 60 Txs. You may see a different set of blocks when you visit the site. But

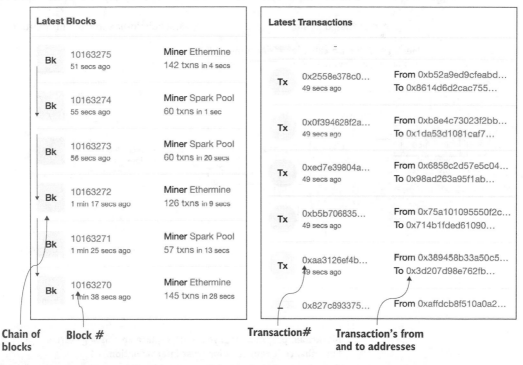

Figure 1.2  A snapshot of the Ethereum public blockchain

you can always search for a particular block number (#10163275, in this case) and verify the number of Txs. The block will have *the same number of Txs* shown here, exemplifying the immutable nature of blockchain technology. The blocks are linked to form a chain of blocks, or blockchain.

## 1.2   *What is a blockchain?*

A *blockchain* is a technology for enabling trust in a decentralized system of transacting peer participants. The purpose of a blockchain is to verify and validate (or reject, if not valid) a transaction initiated by a participant, and then execute the transaction and record the proof of these actions with the consensus of the peer participants. As shown in figure 1.3, the blockchain-based trust infrastructure exists within a larger system. Blockchain infrastructure contains software for a specific purpose: trust intermediation among a large number of (typically unknown) peer-to-peer participants. On the left side of figure 1.3 is a distributed (client/server) system performing routine operations. This system may send messages that contain data to be verified, validated, and recorded on the blockchain (on the right) to establish trust in that larger system. In blockchain programming, you don't replace an existing system; you enhance it with code for trust intermediation through validation and verification.

To help you further understand blockchain programming, let's examine the blockchain stacks for Bitcoin and Ethereum, shown in figure 1.4. These stacks represent the two models of blockchain in its short history. Bitcoin has only the wallet application,

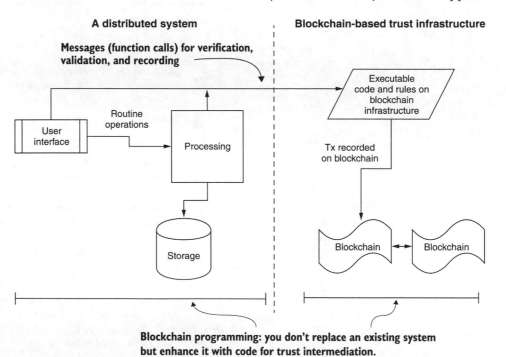

**Figure 1.3   Blockchain programming context**

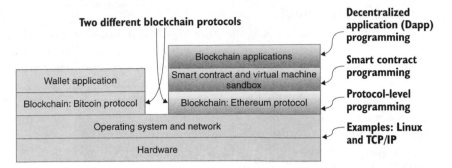

**Figure 1.4  Blockchain stacks and types of programming**

whereas Ethereum features programmable code called *smart contracts* (about which you'll learn more in chapters 2–4).

Figure 1.4 also shows the three levels of programming:

- *Protocol-level programming*—This level involves software that is needed for the deployment and operation of the blockchain itself. This software is similar to your operating system or networking software. If you are a systems programmer and administrator, you'll program at this level. This text does not cover protocol-level programming.

- *Smart contract-level programming*—One level above is smart contract (or rules engine) programming. It is at this level that you design and program the rules for verification and validation, and specify the data and messages that are to be recorded on the underlying blockchain. The smart contract is the engine that drives the blockchain on behalf of the user application. In chapters 2–4, you'll learn in depth about the design, development, and testing of smart contracts.

- *Application-level programming*—This level involves programming using web (or enterprise or mobile) application frameworks and user interface design concepts that are outside the blockchain protocol. In chapters 5–11, you'll be provided details on web programming to link to underlying smart contracts and to deploy end-to-end *decentralized applications (Dapps)* on the blockchain.

**DEFINITION** *Dapps* are web or enterprise applications that include application logic to invoke blockchain functions that implement trust intermediation.

Dapps embed a significant code element—that of smart contracts. For any given smart contract, an exact copy of the smart contract's code is transmitted through a special transaction and deployed in the participant nodes of a blockchain network.

**DEFINITION** A *smart contract* is an immutable executable code representing the logic of a Dapp. The data variables and functions defined in a smart contract collectively represent the state and operations for enforcing an application's (Dapp's) rules for verification, validation, and recording on the blockchain.

## 1.3    *Blockchain programming*

In the evolution from sequential programming to structured programming, functional programming, object-oriented programming (OOP), web and database programming, and big data programming, programmers experienced shifts in approaches, artifacts, and architectures (such as OOP with classes and objects, and Hadoop and Map Reduce for big data processing). Similarly, blockchain programming is yet another paradigm shift.

Four fundamental concepts play a significant role in making blockchain programming different. You need to understand these concepts before you start programming in chapter 2, just as you need to learn about class and object concepts before undertaking OOP (object-oriented programming). Given this context, the four key roles fulfilled by a blockchain are

- *Decentralized infrastructure*—Special computing hardware and software stacks support the blockchain protocol, smart contracts, and applications (Dapps). The main components of this infrastructure are the computing nodes and networks connecting the nodes (section 1.3.1).
- *Distributed ledger technology*—On top of the infrastructure is the ledger. Transactions and data are recorded simultaneously in all stakeholders' ledgers. The ledger is *distributed* because all the stakeholders record the same facts. It is *immutable* because each block is linked to the signature of the previous block, making it tamperproof (section 1.3.2).
- *Disintermediation protocol*—Participants in a decentralized system follow the same blockchain protocol to connect and to communicate and transact with one another. The protocol is a set of rules for everyone to follow. Ethereum and Hyperledger, for example, are two different blockchain protocols (section 1.3.3).
- *Trust enabler*—In a decentralized system of participants, there are no central authorities or intermediaries such as banks. You, therefore, need an infrastructure that implements the rules for governance, provenance, compliance, and the like automatically, without any intermediaries. Blockchain software assumes the role of a *trust enabler* (section 1.3.4).

### 1.3.1   *Decentralized infrastructure*

Blockchain infrastructure is inherently decentralized, like the railway tracks or roadways connecting cities. You can think of the Dapps that you'll deploy as being like the trains or vehicles that travel on the tracks and roads. With this picture in your mind, let's explore that infrastructure. I'll defer the technical details and coding of the applications to later chapters. Your aim in this chapter is to comprehend the crucial role played by blockchain infrastructure in supporting decentralized systems.

What is a decentralized system? A *decentralized* system is a type of distributed system in which

- Participants communicate peer to peer.
- Participants are in control of their assets, digital or otherwise (such as an audio file, a digital health record, or a piece of land).

- Participants can join and leave the system as they wish.
- Participants operate beyond the typical boundaries of trust (such as within a university or a country).
- Decisions are made by the distributed participants, not by any central authority.
- Intermediation is achieved by the use of automated software such as a blockchain.

Let's explore the architectural elements of blockchain that address the unique needs of a decentralized system.

### BLOCKCHAIN NODES, NETWORKS, AND APPLICATIONS

Consider air traffic. Flights have origins and destinations, and stopover airports and waypoints form the airline networks. Similarly, blockchain nodes host the computational environment that serves as endpoints of transactions and also performs other functions, such as relaying and broadcasting transactions.

> **DEFINITION** *Node* is a collective name for blockchain software and the machine or hardware on which it is installed for the participant of a decentralized system.

Figure 1.5 shows the logical architecture of a single blockchain node. A node can support many accounts to represent the identities of peer participants in the decentralized network. A 256-bit number represents an account. Compare this size with your traditional computer's address size of 64 bits!

> **DEFINITION** An *account* represents a unique identity for a transacting entity. An account is needed to initiate a transaction.

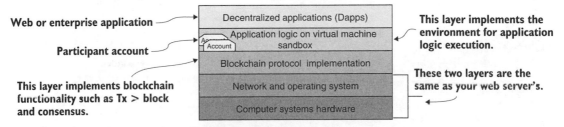

**Figure 1.5  Blockchain node and application stack**

A blockchain node hosts the elements represented by the stack in figure 1.5. It serves as a foundation for your blockchain application development.

Let's start from the bottom and move up. The lower two levels are the standard hardware and software of most computing systems. The next level up is the blockchain protocol level: it houses the components of the blockchain, but you won't program at this level. The next layer hosts the application logic. This layer is where you solve problems like access control to data and code functions for validation, verification, and recording. The top layer is the user-facing interface where web (or enterprise) programming is done, such as with HTML, JavaScript, and associated frameworks. These elements form the Dapp and its user interface (UI) layer.

A blockchain application is not a single-user application, unlike a handheld game or an income tax calculator. It typically connects a large number of participants through its network of nodes. Each node can host multiple accounts to identify the different customers it services. A node can also host more than one Dapp, such as one for a decentralized supply chain management system and another for a decentralized payment system.

Figure 1.6 shows a network of three nodes connected by a network. The network facilitates broadcast of the

- transactions initiated by users
- blocks formed out of the transactions

These transactions and blocks constitute the payload of the network and, eventually, after verification and validation, are recorded on the distributed ledger.

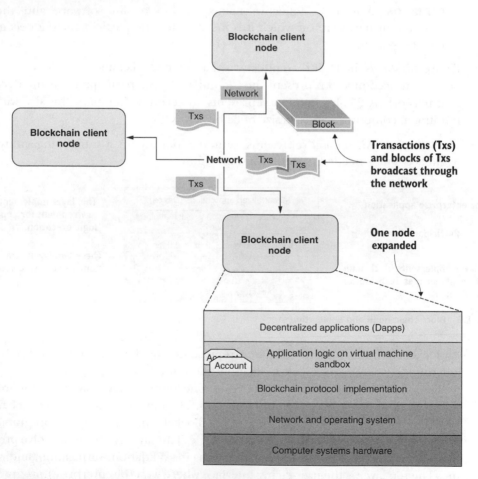

**Figure 1.6   A blockchain network of nodes broadcasting transactions and blocks**

A network identifier identifies a blockchain network of nodes. Network ID #1, for example, is the main Ethereum public network; network ID #4 is a public network called Rinkeby (https://www.rinkeby.io), and so on. You'll have to indicate the network by using its identifier while deploying your smart contract on the network. The participants on a given network will share a unified distributed ledger for recording their transaction details.

The smart contracts are deployed in a sandbox environment such as a virtual machine (VM) hosted by a blockchain node. The syntax of a smart contract is similar to a class in an OO (object-oriented) language. It contains data, functions, and rules for the execution of functions. Calling or invoking a smart contract function generates the transactions that are recorded on the blockchain, as shown in figure 1.7. If any of the verification and validation rules fails, the function invocation is reverted. But if the execution is successful, the generated transactions (Txs) are broadcast to the network for recording, as shown in figure 1.7. The figure illustrates how a function call is transformed into actions that are recorded on the blockchain.

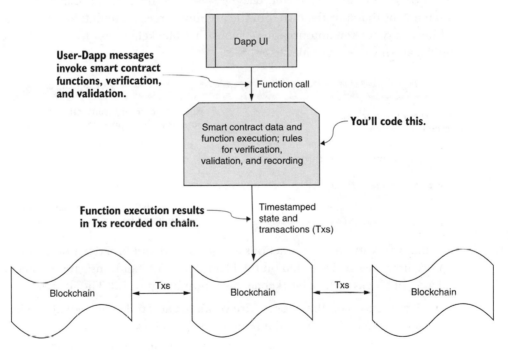

**Figure 1.7 From application messages to Txs on the blockchain**

## 1.3.2 *Distributed ledger technology*

Now that you've explored the infrastructure, let's focus on the technology that the infrastructure supports. This core blockchain technology is known as *distributed ledger technology (DLT)*. In this section, I'll dig deeper into this technology, exploring

- What constitutes the blockchain DLT
- The physical structure of the DLT for recording blocks of transactions
- The operational details of how an application gets to use the DLT for its intended purpose: verification, validation, and immutable recording for enabling trust
- The consensus algorithm (at a high level) for the integrity of the DLT

### TRANSACTIONS, BLOCKS, AND CHAIN OF BLOCKS

Applications initiate transactions and the execution of smart contract code. A simple cryptocurrency transfer between accounts, for example, generates a "send" transaction. The transactions generated are broadcast through the blockchain network and then gathered and recorded in the distributed immutable ledger. Listing 1.1 shows an example pseudocode for function calls for initiating two types of transactions. Tx1 is for the transfer of cryptocurrency. Tx2 is an application-specific transfer of ownership of an asset from one owner to another, probably to fulfill the sale of an asset. You can also observe the use of the rule `onlyByOwner` for the `transferOwnership` function, which means that only the owner of the account can execute that function. Such rules are necessary for the autonomous systems that blockchain controls. In chapters 3–5, you'll learn how to code rules like these.

> **Listing 1.1   Pseudocode for two functions initiating transactions**
>
> **Cryptocurrency transfer from one account to another**          **No-cryptocurrency transaction; current owner is the implied sender of this Tx.**
>
> ```
> /Tx1: */ web3.eth.sendTransaction(fromAccount, toAccount, value);
> /Tx2: */ transferOwnership(newOwner);
>
> function transferOwnership onlyByOwner (account newOwner)..
> ```
>
> **onlyByOwner rule validates that the sender is the owner; if not, Tx reverts.**

Now that you know how transactions are generated and broadcast on a network, let's explore how they get recorded on the blockchain. A set of transactions makes a block, and a set of blocks make a blockchain, as shown in figure 1.8. The process is as follows:

1. Transactions on the network are verified, gathered, and pooled. Nodes select a set of transactions from the pool to create a block.
2. Participant nodes use a consensus algorithm to collectively agree or come to a consensus on a single consistent block of transactions to be appended to the existing chain.
3. A hash or representative value of the current lead block of the chain is added to the newly appended block, creating a chain link.

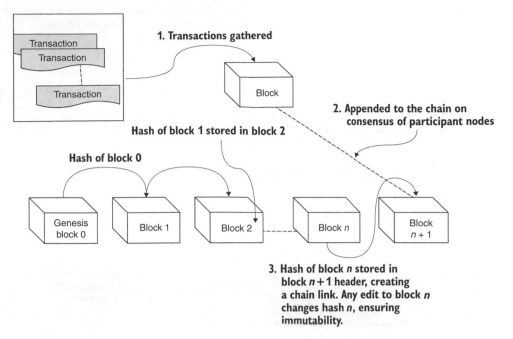

**1. Transactions gathered**

**2. Appended to the chain on consensus of participant nodes**

**Hash of block 1 stored in block 2**

**Hash of block 0**

**3. Hash of block *n* stored in block *n*+1 header, creating a chain link. Any edit to block *n* changes hash *n*, ensuring immutability.**

**Figure 1.8   Transactions to blocks and blocks to the blockchain**

As figure 1.8 demonstrates, a blockchain is an *append-only* distributed immutable ledger. Its creation begins with a single block called the *genesis block*. Every node of a stakeholder on the blockchain has an identical copy of the blockchain, starting with the genesis node. A blockchain DLT, therefore, is

- *Distributed*, because the blockchain protocol ensures that every distributed node involved has an identical copy of the chain of blocks.
- *Immutable*, because each newly created block is linked to the existing blockchain by the hash value of the current head of the blockchain, as shown in figure 1.8.

At this point, it is sufficient to know that a representative signature value of the block *n* is stored in the block *n*+1 to ensure immutability. Any inadvertent or deliberate change to a block's data at a node will change the block's hash value and render that node's chain invalid. (You'll learn more about the hash value and its computation in chapter 5.) The blocks of a blockchain are stored in the local file systems of the participant nodes, as shown in figure 1.9. The chain of blocks on each node is the distributed ledger recording Txs and related data in its blocks. Figure 1.9 depicts the fact that every node has an exact copy of the blockchain.

At the time of this writing (2020), Bitcoin block creation (or mining) time—and, hence, Tx confirmation time—is about 10 minutes. On Ethereum, block confirmation takes about 10 to 19 seconds, whereas transaction confirmation time on credit cards takes less than a second. Recall the speed of your internet connection 10 or 20 years back; blockchain technology is experiencing a similar situation in these early years of

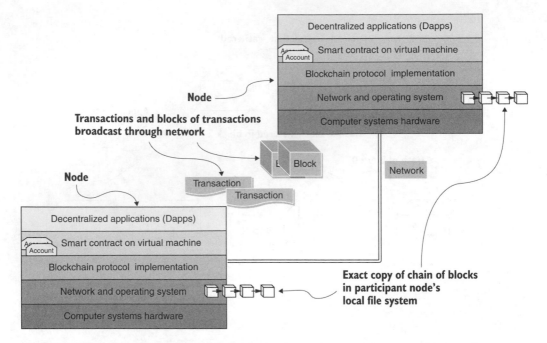

**Figure 1.9   Blockchains stored in local file systems**

its existence. The developer community at the blockchain protocol level is working on improving Tx confirmation times by using various consensus algorithms and by using relaying techniques at the network level.

### 1.3.3   *Disintermediation protocol*

Like any transportation infrastructure, a blockchain infrastructure has rules that you need to follow. If drivers don't follow the laws of the road, chaos and gridlock ensue. A protocol or a set of rules governs the structure and operation of a blockchain. A blockchain protocol defines the following, among other things:

- The structure of a blockchain (transactions, blocks, and chain of blocks)
- Fundamental algorithms and standards for encryption, hashing, and state management
- Methods for implementing consensus and a consistent chain of blocks
- Techniques for handling exceptions resulting in an inconsistent ledger
- The execution environment for code on the blockchain and rules for maintaining consistency, correctness, and immutability in this context

You get the idea. The structure of the blockchain and operations on it are not arbitrary, but well guided by a protocol. The implementation of the protocol establishes the base layer on which applications are written.

The framework for code execution introduced by the Ethereum blockchain proto-col has opened a whole world of opportunities in the decentralized realm. The smart contract is the centerpiece and the main contribution of the Ethereum protocol.

Consider the stack diagram in figure 1.10, which compares the Bitcoin and Ethe-reum blockchains. The Bitcoin blockchain is for the transfer of cryptocurrency, and it does that job well. It has only wallet applications for initiating transactions. Ethereum supports smart contracts and a VM sandbox called Ethereum VM (EVM) on which the smart contracts execute. Smart contracts in turn enable decentralized operation of applications.

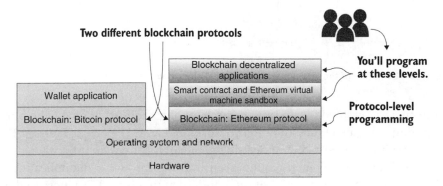

**Figure 1.10  Bitcoin versus Ethereum protocol stacks**

Currently, many blockchains (such as EOS, ZCash, and IOTA) exist, with different protocols, and the expectation is that they will consolidate to a few eventually. The goal of this chapter is to give you a general idea of the various features of blockchain, independent of any particular technology. This high-level knowledge will help you be a better blockchain designer and developer. You'll follow the Ethereum blockchain protocol for programming smart contracts and Dapps in chapters 2–11.

### 1.3.4  *Trust enabler*

Trust is critical for business and personal transactions, whether those transactions are trade, commerce, legal, medical, marital, interpersonal, or financial. Imagine a busi-ness transaction for transferring a million dollars. You have a secure channel for trans-fer, but are you sure you can trust the parties involved? You typically use an intermediary such as a bank to establish the credentials of the transacting parties. But in a decentralized system, there are no humans checking identities or banks verifying credentials. You need some other mechanism—a software mechanism. Blockchain addresses this need by enabling a trust layer over the internet, thus facilitating trust intermediation. The three Ds—decentralized infrastructure, distributed ledger tech-nology, and disintermediation protocol—collectively enable trust in a system.

**NOTE**   In a decentralized system, trust intermediation is achieved by the decentralized infrastructure (section 1.3.1), the DLT (section 1.3.2), and the disintermediation protocol (section 1.3.3).

Figure 1.11 shows the evolution of the protocols leading to blockchain-based trust, which has yet to become a standard in the internet context.

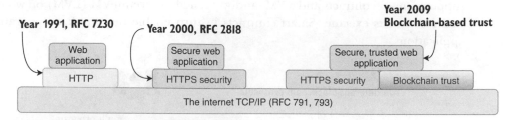

**Figure 1.11   Evolution of the internet and the blockchain-based trust layer**

The internet was created for sharing research among scientists. It enabled connectivity among computing machines and internetworking. Later, Hypertext Transfer Protocol (HTTP) was introduced as the underlying protocol for the web. It became a standard around 1991 and opened many commercial activities through web applications.

   Note that security was not part of the standard at that time. With increased digitization and adoption of online activities came rampant online fraud and security breaches. Security became critical for web applications, and it was retrofitted into HTTP as a standard (HTTPS) around 2000. This addition enabled secure web applications. Global standards were established with formal Request for Comments (RFC) documents from the Internet Engineering Task Force (IETF)—RFCs 7230, 2818, and so on. Blockchain, introduced in 2009, established a trust layer alongside the security layer of the internet. Trust is currently realized in centralized systems by ad hoc means (such as verifying credentials, recommendation systems, and reviews/ratings) and by human involvement in other situations, such as at airports and grocery-store checkouts. Blockchain enables the trust layer for Dapps through software-based verification, validation, and immutable recording of transactions and facts.

   Next, let's look at some compelling decentralized scenarios that can benefit from the blockchain's DLT and its trust layer.

## 1.4   *Motivating scenarios*

In this section, you explore several issues that are prevalent in the systems you may deal with in everyday activities. Consider the broad area of budgets and expense management in organizations small and large: governmental and nongovernmental agencies (NGOs), charities and disaster-relief agencies, and more. A significant issue is accountability. Is the allocated amount being spent on the designated item or service? Were the expected outcomes realized? Was the spending wasteful? Did the right people authorize it? Can you show the money trail in a disaster-relief effort? Is the process transparent? Are you able to collect the correct data for demonstrating the effectiveness of the effort? I'm sure you can think of several other similar concerns.

In the following sections, you'll explore some of these concerns and how they can be addressed by using smart contracts on an infrastructure enabled by the blockchain protocol.

### 1.4.1 Automatic and consistent data collection

The sustainable development goals of the United Nations General Assembly specify the purposes of UN programs. Your organization likely has similar goals that it hopes to achieve with the budget allocated, and it likely keeps track of the goals and related expenses through various reporting and data collection mechanisms. These are examples of decentralized scenarios in which many centralized computing systems are interacting, but often inefficiently. There is insufficient evidence of the effectiveness of many of the UN's interventions, for example, due to lack of data or ineffective data collection methods, such as surveys. In this situation, the items of interest could be recorded in the DLT ledger. These items include

- Funds allocated for each agency and dates of disbursement
- Start dates and amounts transferred from the agency to actual fund users
- Project completion dates and statuses

Smart contract-enabled code can help organizations to collect data automatically as the funds are disbursed and used. In this case, the user interface to the Dapp would be an intuitive mobile app that invokes smart contract functions to record a distributed and immutable copy of the actions in the ledger of the blockchain. All the stakeholders—say, UN agencies, local municipalities, and NGOs—automatically get a consistent copy of the ledger.

### 1.4.2 Timely information sharing

Another example is a significant issue in U.S. government agencies uncovered by experts who analyzed the 9/11 disasters: lack of sharing of information, in this case between the central office of the Federal Bureau of Investigation and local offices (one Minneapolis office in particular). In a blockchain setup, any update in a branch office would have updated the central office's ledger automatically. This information would have been readily available and could have prevented the terrorists from boarding the flights.

A similar lack of sharing of information with the FBI's central database enabled the slaughter of 24 people at a Texas church in 2017 (http://mng.bz/X0dY). A distributed ledger supported by smart contracts on the blockchain with proper user access to the data might have averted this massacre by preventing the sale of firearms to the gunman. These examples make a case for the importance of a distributed mechanism for timely information sharing. The sharing rules, conditions, and severity levels can be codified into a smart contract that will, in turn, enable recording of relevant metainformation in the distributed ledger of the blockchain.

### 1.4.3    Verifiable compliance

Let's examine another area with numerous potential uses for the smart contract. Health care is a vast domain that has many requirements related to regulations and laws. Blockchain-based compliance, provenance, and governance can address many inefficiencies in this domain. Consider the Health Insurance Portability and Accountability Act (HIPAA), which is meant to protect the privacy and confidentiality of patient and other health data. Violations of this act by health care organizations or individuals may result in fines of anywhere from $1,000 to $250,000, so it's in the best interest of everyone to keep track of how health care data is handled.

Compliance with HIPAA rules can be codified into smart contracts and recorded at the stakeholders' blockchain node automatically, preventing any unwanted leaks of sensitive data. Businesses can ensure verifiable compliance. And blockchain provides a mechanism to demonstrate compliance to regulators.

### 1.4.4    Auditable actions for provenance

In health care and other operations, such as disaster recovery, there's often a question of whether actions and interventions were undertaken at the appropriate time. You must have heard of cases in which a diagnostic test ordered at the right time would have prevented the untimely demise of a patient. In one particular case narrated by an expert in the field, the doctor did order the test, but the order was canceled by somebody else. This case ended up in a court of law. The doctor had to prove his side of the story—something that would have been helped by having the sequence of orders recorded in a distributed ledger. In this case, smart contracts could have been used for provenance, indicating that a particular treatment was ordered at the right time by a doctor.

The distributed ledger created by the smart contract can provide ready access to the audit trail of the actions taken for provenance in many other situations. I'm sure you can think of examples in your own organization in which important undertakings could be proved by an audit trail stored within the stakeholders' blockchain infrastructure.

### 1.4.5    Guidance for governance

Let's look at another use case from the health care domain. You must be aware of the rampant misuse of opioids in the United States and its disastrous consequences. Smart contracts could be used to prevent opioids from being dispensed to misusers while making sure that patients who need it get the medication. In this case, the rules for the governance of drug distribution could be codified into a smart contract shared by all stakeholders in the health care system, including doctors, pharmacies, and governing bodies. This blockchain-based governance approach could easily be expanded to cover the general distribution of any controlled substances and medicines.

### 1.4.6    Attribution of actions

In many situations, such as research and business workflows, it's important to know who did what and to whom to attribute the actions taken in a system. Suppose that a patient in a remote rural area with a medical emergency gets transported by ambulance to a major hospital for care. How does the medical insurer decide who gets paid and how much, based on the medical transportation process? The actions taken from the time the call for help was placed to the time when the patient was treated could be recorded in the stakeholders' ledgers. The payment settlement could be automated through rules governing the rates and services rendered. All this information could be coded in a smart contract.

The smart contract transforms the traditional distributed system into a decentralized system by implementing the rules for compliance, governance, provenance, and information sharing and by recording the necessary details on the blockchain.

### 1.4.7 Pandemic management

As I was finishing writing this book, the once-in-a-century COVID-19 pandemic descended upon us, engulfing the planet. Every one of us got firsthand experience with a decentralized planetary-level problem. Everyone and every community was isolated, resulting in a decentralized world.

Although blockchain is well suited to solving many problems in this type of situation, I feel that it is ideally suited to performing a crucial task in mitigating the spread of this virulent disease: that of contact tracing. According to the U.S. Centers for Disease Control (CDC), contact tracing identifies cases by testing and tracing the source and pathway to the affected patient. This task of contact tracing is similar to tracking a fraction of a Bitcoin cryptocurrency to its origin. This trace for a cryptocurrency is recorded automatically on the DLT of the blockchain. Thus, blockchain infrastructure and DLT, along with the smart contract code collectively, could provide an innovative solution for contact tracing in an epidemic.

Another area in which blockchain can help is the transparent management of distribution of trillion-dollar aid packages and resource allocations. A significant outcome of the pandemic is the decentralized world, in which people are managing the situation themselves. Blockchain infrastructure is ideally suited to solve many problems in this environment.

## 1.5 Retrospective

Computer systems are evolving toward decentralized systems, as shown in figure 1.12. In the progression shown in figure 1.12, blockchain provides the necessary trust layer for the operation of a decentralized network. These decentralized systems coexist with centralized and other distributed systems to provide a robust environment for innovative planetary-level use cases.

Think about learning to drive. Before you get started, you should know some details about the automobile you'll drive—essential parts such as the accelerator, brake, and clutch and their functions—and the rules of the road. Blockchain programming is similar. In this introductory chapter, you learned how to drive the blockchain machine by getting to know the motivating factors behind blockchain, its structural components and operational details, and the pioneering solutions for trust

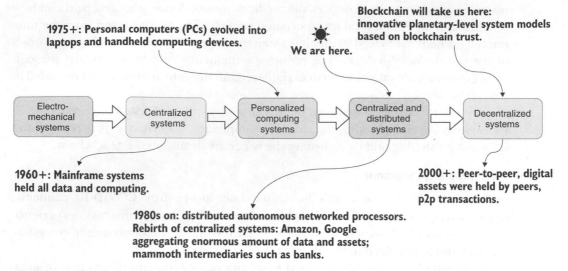

**1975+: Personal computers (PCs) evolved into laptops and handheld computing devices.**

**We are here.**

**Blockchain will take us here: innovative planetary-level system models based on blockchain trust.**

| Electro-mechanical systems | → | Centralized systems | → | Personalized computing systems | → | Centralized and distributed systems | → | Decentralized systems |

**1960+: Mainframe systems held all data and computing.**

**1980s on: distributed autonomous networked processors. Rebirth of centralized systems: Amazon, Google aggregating enormous amount of data and assets; mammoth intermediaries such as banks.**

**2000+: Peer-to-peer, digital assets were held by peers, p2p transactions.**

**Figure 1.12   Progression to decentralized systems**

and integrity in systems that it enables. You also explored blockchain as a means for supporting the three Ds: decentralization, disintermediation, and distributed immutable recording.

When you learn to drive, you can go places. Likewise, the basic knowledge you acquired by reading this chapter will pave your way toward an informed approach to problem-solving, designing, and coding with blockchain, helping you conceptualize creative use cases and discover new application domains for this technology.

In chapters 2–11, you'll learn how to problem-solve with blockchain and how to design, develop, and test smart contracts and Dapps. You'll learn about design principles for developing blockchain solutions, and you'll see how to tell when a blockchain solution will work and when blockchain is not the right choice. You'll also find ideas for disrupting your application domain and transforming the ongoing digitization and automation efforts in many application areas.

## 1.6   Summary

- Computing systems are trending from distributed, centralized systems to decentralized systems in which participants transact peer-to-peer and operate beyond the usual boundaries of trust.
- Blockchain makes decentralized operation possible by providing a trust layer, an infrastructure, and a protocol governing blockchain's operation.
- Blockchain enables decentralization, disintermediation, and a distributed immutable ledger for recording relevant information about an executing application.

- A blockchain protocol defines the rules governing the participants; the computing nodes; the networks connecting the nodes; the decentralized application stack on the nodes; and the transactions, blocks, and chain of blocks.
- The Ethereum blockchain application stack supports a computational framework called smart contracts and an execution environment for it.
- There are enormous opportunities to develop groundbreaking decentralized applications by using blockchain technology in numerous domains, thus disrupting and innovating ongoing digitization efforts.
- Businesses need thought leaders, designers, and developers to advance this innovation. It is imperative that application developers at all levels, from the Internet of Things (IoT) to the web, learn about blockchain. Providing you this blockchain knowledge and enabling related design and development skills is the overarching goal of this book.

# Smart contracts

2

## This chapter covers

- Understanding smart contracts
- Applying design principles to develop smart contracts
- Coding smart contracts with the Solidity language
- Running and transacting with smart contracts by using the Remix IDE
- Designing, developing, deploying, and testing smart contracts for two use cases

The smart contract is a significant component of the blockchain technology that has been instrumental in transforming a cryptocurrency framework into a trust framework enabling broad range of decentralized applications. This chapter provides details on the concept, design, and development of a smart contract, and also examines the power of executable code on the blockchain.

Structurally, a *smart contract* is a standalone piece of code similar to a class in an object-oriented program. It is a deployable module of code with data and functions. Functions serve the specific purposes of verification, validation, and enabling recording of the messages sent. A contract in the real world involves rules, conditions, laws, regulations to be enforced, criteria, contingencies, and items for provenance such as dates and signatures. Similarly, the smart contract in a blockchain context implements the contract rules for solving a decentralized problem. It functions as a rules engine as well as a gatekeeper, so understandably, the smart contract design requires careful consideration. Following is an explanation of a smart contract modified to include the code aspects.

> **DEFINITION** A *smart contract* is executable code on the blockchain intended to digitally facilitate, verify, validate, and enforce the rules and regulations of an application. Smart contracts allow the performance of credible transactions without third parties. These transactions are trackable and irreversible.

In this chapter, you'll learn a set of design principles that will guide you through the design and development of smart contracts and blockchain programming. You'll apply these design principles to design a smart contract for a simple use case (a decentralized counter) and a different larger use case (for a decentralized airline consortium). To implement the design in the form of code, you need the following:

- A blockchain platform
- A language to code the smart contract
- A suitable environment to develop, compile, deploy, and test it

You'll use the Ethereum (https://ethereum.org) blockchain as the platform and a special language called Solidity (https://solidity.readthedocs.io/en/v0.6.2) to code the smart contracts. Then you'll deploy the code in an integrated development environment (IDE) called Remix (https://remix-ide.readthedocs.io/en/latest) and test its operation. This trio of technologies provides a versatile development environment and helps you ramp up the blockchain programming learning curve quickly. Starting in chapter 6, you'll migrate from this initial environment to a production setup that will allow you to develop end-to-end Dapps and deploy them on public blockchains.

On completion of this chapter, you'll be able to analyze a problem, design a smart contract solution, implement it using Solidity, and deploy it on a test blockchain provided by the Remix IDE. You'll also have learned some best practices for blockchain programming.

## 2.1 The concept of a smart contract

A smart contract is a piece of code that improves on the basic trust enabled by the Bitcoin blockchain protocol. It adds *programmability* that in turn enables transactions for digital assets besides cryptocurrency. A smart contract addresses the need for application-specific verification and validation for blockchain applications. It opens the trust layer of the blockchain for general-purpose applications. Let's explore the smart contract in detail.

I've chosen to discuss Ethereum's definition of a smart contract because Ethereum is a general mainstream blockchain. Also, it has been used as a reference implementation for many other industry blockchains, such as JPMorgan's Quoram (https://www.goquorum.com) blockchain for large financial transactions and r3 Corda (https://www.r3.com/corda-platform) for business applications. Recall the layer diagram from chapter 1, shown again in figure 2.1, modified to include smart contract or application logic details. The smart contract is deployed in a sandbox environment and identified by a 160-bit account address like any other participants on the blockchain network. It executes on the virtual machine (VM) on the blockchain node and is identified by an account number, as shown in the figure.

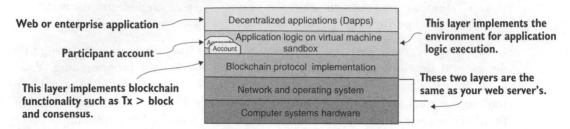

**Figure 2.1   Blockchain application stack and layers**

### 2.1.1   Bitcoin transactions versus smart contract transactions

Let's compare a Bitcoin transaction and a smart contract transaction, as shown in figure 2.2, to give you an idea of the difference between currency transactions and noncurrency, application-dependent function calls. As you can see, in Bitcoin, all the transactions are about sending value (Tx(sendValue)). In the case of a blockchain that supports smart contracts, a transaction embeds a function implemented by the smart contract. In figure 2.2, this function is a voting smart contract. The functions are validateVoter(), vote(), count(), and declareWinner(). The invocation of these functions results in the

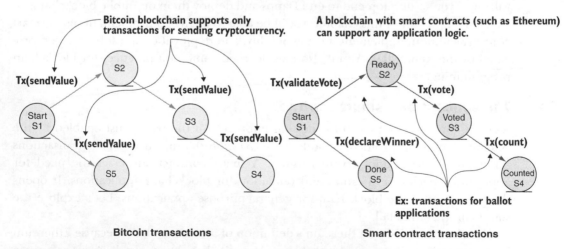

**Figure 2.2   Cryptocurrency transactions versus smart contract transactions**

transactions that will be recorded on the blockchain (Tx(validateVoter), Tx(vote), and so on). This ability to deploy an arbitrary logic on a blockchain significantly enhances its applicability beyond simple cryptocurrency transfers.

### 2.1.2 What does a smart contract do?

The smart contract acts as the brain of a blockchain application. Like the human brain, it is responsible for many vital functions, including the following:

- It represents a business logic layer for verification and validation of application-specific conditions.
- It allows for the specification of rules for operations on the blockchain.
- It facilitates the implementation of policies for the transfer of assets in a decentralized network.
- It embeds functions that can be invoked by messages or function calls from participant accounts or other smart contract accounts. These messages and their input parameters, along with additional metadata such as the sender's address and timestamp, result in transactions recorded in the distributed ledger of the blockchain.
- It acts as the software-based intermediator for decentralized blockchain-based applications.
- It adds programmability and intelligence to the blockchain through the specification of the parameters of its functions.

With all these crucial capabilities, a smart contract is indeed a core component of the decentralized blockchain application.

## 2.2 Design of a smart contract

Let's begin our exploration of smart contract design with a simple example that will take you through the entire process, from problem statement to code deployment. In this first example, you'll design a decentralized counter. Counters are common elements in everyday applications. Table 2.1 lists types of systems that use a counter. Turnstiles count the number of people entering and exiting an amusement park. A stock market index goes up or down based on the sales performance of stocks in a centralized system. A nation's trade deficit fluctuates depending on reports from the distributed entities representing the various trade sectors. The world we live in is an excellent example of a naturally decentralized system, with its population determined by the global number of births and deaths. Take a few minutes to reflect on these examples.

**Table 2.1  Examples of counters in diverse systems**

| System type | Counter example |
|---|---|
| Manual system | Turnstile for counting in an amusement park |
| Centralized system | Stock index |

**Table 2.1    Examples of counters in diverse systems** *(continued)*

| System type | Counter example |
| --- | --- |
| Distributed system | Nation's trade deficit |
| Decentralized system | World population |

The counter is a simple but versatile use case that illustrates the smart contract development. You may be tempted to jump in and start coding, but you must resist this temptation and instead design the contract first. It's important to have the correct design before developing the code. Moreover, a design representation is independent of the smart contract language, thus providing you a blueprint for different implementations.

A smart contract is deployed on the blockchain by a transaction. It is permanently recorded on the blockchain, irreversible and unchangeable, and part of the chain of blocks, as stated in design principle 1.

> **DESIGN PRINCIPLE 1**    Design before you code, develop, and deploy a smart contract on a test chain, and thoroughly test it before you deploy it on a production blockchain, because when the smart contract is deployed, it is immutable.

Your goal in the design process is to define the contents of a smart contract; specifically, its

- Data
- Functions that operate on the data
- Rules for operations

Design principle 2 initiates the design process by defining the users of the system that will be served by the application.

> **DESIGN PRINCIPLE 2**    Define the users of and use cases for the system. Users are entities that generate the actions and the input and receive the output from the system you'll be designing.

### 2.2.1   *A use case diagram for the counter*

Let's apply these principles and begin the design process for the counter problem with the standard Unified Modeling Language (UML; https://www.uml.org/index.htm) tools for design representation: the use case diagram and the class diagram. The UML design representation may be familiar to many advanced developers, but a beginner developer may not be familiar with this. You can refer to the UML description in appendix A to create these diagrams.

The UML use case diagram helps you think through the problem and decide how the smart contract—and, more specifically, its functions—will be used. Figure 2.3 shows just one actor: a stick figure representing a decentralized application that will use the counter.

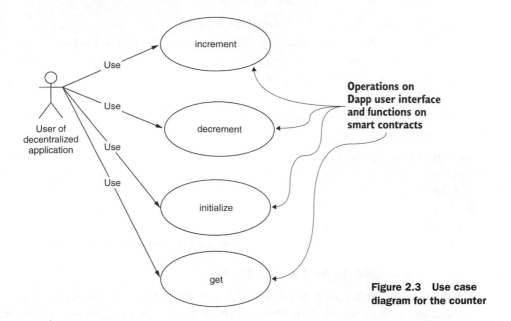

**Figure 2.3 Use case diagram for the counter**

First, let's think about the functions of a counter:

- `initialize()` to a value.
- `increment()` by a value.
- `decrement()` by a value.
- `get()` to access the value of the counter.

This diagram clearly articulates the intent of the smart contract. This diagram is a good starting point for the design process, providing an artifact for discussion among your team members and stakeholders who are interested in the problem. It also provides a systematic lead-in to the next steps in the design process. Note that this step of use case design representation is dependent on the problem specification; it does not require you to specify any coding or system dependencies.

Next, let's explore who uses these functions and what the rules (if any) are.

### 2.2.2 Data assets, peer participants, roles, rules, and transactions

Now that you've created the use case diagram, the next step is elucidating the various attributes of the blockchain-based component of the problem. We will refer to this step, outlined in design principle 3, as *data asset analysis.*

**DESIGN PRINCIPLE 3** Define the data assets, peer participants and their roles, rules to be enforced, and transactions to be recorded for the system you'll be designing.

For this decentralized counter problem, let's apply design principle 3 to arrive at the following items:

- *Data assets to track*—The value of the counter
- *Peer participants*—The applications that update the counter value
- *Roles of these participants*—Updating the counter value and accessing its value
- *Rules to be verified and validated, to be applied to data and functions*—None in this use case
- *Transactions to be recorded in the digital ledger*—`initialize()`, `increment()`, and `decrement()`

Note that you may decide to record only the functions or transactions that change the value of the counter. Thus, not all functions specified in the smart contract will result in transactions to be saved in the blockchain's distributed ledger. The `get()` function is to view the contents of the counter, and you may not want its invocation recorded on the blockchain. You can specify this characteristic by defining it as a *view-only* function. The transactions of view functions are not recorded on the blockchain.

### 2.2.3   *From class diagram to contract diagram*

In this step of the design process, you'll define the UML class diagram as a guide for the design of the solution to the counter problem. A class diagram defines the various structural elements of the solution. It draws upon the items discovered in the previous two steps (creating the use case diagram and digital asset analysis). The typical UML class diagram of traditional object-oriented programming (OOP) shown on the left side of figure 2.4 has three components:

- Name of the class
- Data definitions
- Function definitions

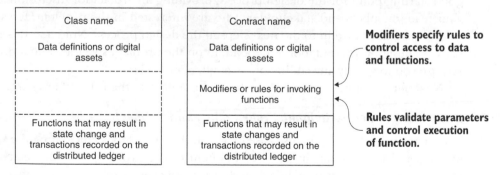

**Figure 2.4   Class diagram versus contract diagram templates**

The smart contract diagram on the right side of figure 2.4 has one additional component: the rules for accessing the functions and data. This component distinguishes a smart contract diagram from a traditional class diagram. Design principle 4 deals with contract diagrams.

**DESIGN PRINCIPLE 4** Define a contract diagram that specifies the name, data assets, functions, and rules for execution of functions and access to the data.

In the simple use case of the counter, no conditions or rules are used. That's fine; we don't need any rules, because this problem is a simple one used to illustrate the design process. The *contract diagram* for the counter is shown in figure 2.5. You'll use the camel-case convention for the identifiers of the various components (data variables and functions) of the contract. The diagram shows the name of the contract as Counter, the only data element as an integer called `value`, and the functions from the use case diagram in figure 2.3, which is replicated on the left side of figure 2.5. Besides the three functions—`initialize()`, `increment()`, and `decrement()`—the contract diagram includes a `constructor()` function and a `get()` function. The constructor, when invoked, deploys the smart contract code in the VM sandbox supported by the blockchain infrastructure. It also initializes the contract's state if the constructor has any parameters. The `get()` function is a utility function that returns the current value of the counter. This function is a view function; no transaction is recorded when it is invoked.

Conceptualizing the diagram in figure 2.5 is an essential step in the design of a smart contract. This representation in figure 2.5 is not much different from the routine object-oriented class design. You can create this contract diagram by using diagrams .net (https://www.diagrams.net) or any other UML tool you are familiar with. The contract diagram is a convenient artifact for design discussions with stakeholders and the development team.

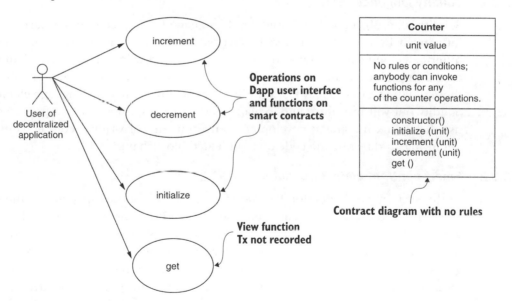

**Figure 2.5  Counter contract diagram**

## 2.3    *Development of a smart contract code*

You are now ready to develop the smart contract code in a high-level language. Although many languages are available—such as Java, Python, and Go—these are general-purpose languages with rich syntax and semantics, supported by extensive libraries. For smart contract development, you need a limited language customized for blockchain operations. Solidity is one such language. The Ethereum foundation introduced this language, but other blockchain platforms, such as Hyperledger, also support it. You will use Solidity to code your smart contracts.

It's important to understand that blockchain programming is not about porting or translating code written in a traditional high-level language to Solidity. Writing a contract code is about precise instructions for blockchain-oriented recording. Smart contract code does not need all the bells and whistles of a general-purpose language. On the other hand, it requires specific blockchain-oriented features for handling things like account addresses, rule specifications, and transaction reversals to be built into the language. Moreover, the smart contract code executes in a *restricted* sandbox environment to maintain consistency among the nodes of the blockchain. These are the justifications for using a special language for smart contract implementation. To summarize, Solidity is a custom language designed for smart contract development.

Let's explore some of the features of the Solidity language before coding the Counter smart contract.

### 2.3.1    *Solidity language*

Solidity is an object-oriented, high-level language for implementing smart contracts, influenced by C++, Python, and JavaScript. Solidity is statically typed and supports inheritance, libraries, and user-defined types; it also provides many useful features for developing blockchain applications. Because its syntax and semantics are similar to those of languages you may know, I will not explicitly discuss the language elements of Solidity but will introduce and explain them as we go, using code snippets. You will use the Remix integrated development environment for writing, editing, compiling, deploying, and testing the code on a simulated blockchain.

### 2.3.2    *Smart contract code for Counter*

In this section, you'll develop the code for the smart contract specified in the design diagrams of figure 2.5. The complete code in Solidity is shown in listing 2.1. The first line specifies the version of the language used for this code. It's mandatory to include this directive to ensure that you use the compiler version that matches the Solidity language version used in the code. In this case, you'll be using version 0.6.0 of the Solidity language. You specify the version number with the `pragma` directive. After the `pragma` directive, the `contract` keyword and the name of the contract (in this case, Counter) begin the definition of the contract code.

**NOTE** At the time of completion of this book, the latest version of Solidity was 6.0. This version is used for examples. You'll have to make any minor changes that may be required for later versions when you read this book.

Next, you define the data components of the smart contract. The data types in Solidity are similar to those in any high-level language. In this case, the `uint` (unsigned integer) data type is used to define the identifier that stores the value of the counter. The `uint` type in the blockchain realm differs significantly from the integer data in mainstream computing: it's a 256-bit value as opposed to 64-bit in a general-purpose language. `uint`, `int`, `int256`, and `uint256` are aliases of one another.

**Listing 2.1   Solidity code for Counter smart contract (Counter.sol)**

```
pragma solidity ^0.6.0;
// imagine a big integer counter that the whole world could share
contract Counter {
    uint value;
    function initialize (uint x) public {
        value = x;
    }

    function get() view public returns (uint) {
        return value;
    }

    function increment (uint n) public {
        value = value + n;
        // return (optional)
    }

    function decrement (uint n) public {
        value = value - n;

    }
}
```

**Shared data for the Counter value** → `uint value;`

**Functions of the Counter**

A function is defined by the `function` keyword and the name of the function, followed by the parameter type and name and the body of the function within curly braces. You can see the definitions of four functions in listing 2.1: `initialize()`, `get()`, `increment()`, and `decrement()`. You'll also observe that there is no definition for an explicit constructor. In this case, a default constructor is used for deploying the contract.

All the functions are declared `public` and therefore have public visibility (as opposed to private), which means that any valid participant (or account) on the blockchain can invoke these functions. The function definitions can end with a `return` statement, which is optional unless there is an explicit value to be returned, as is the case with the `get()` function. The `initialize()`, `increment()`, and `decrement()` functions receive a value as a parameter, and the function body uses the parameter value to update the variable `value`. Behind the scenes, each function invocation is recorded as a transaction on the distributed ledger. Any state change of `value` is also recorded.

Note that `get()` is a "view" function, and its invocation will not be recorded on the blockchain because it does not change the state or the value of the counter.

To create your smart contract, follow these steps:

1  Open the Remix web IDE in your browser.
2  Choose the language Solidity.
    (Vyper is the other language supported.)
3  In the IDE, click the + icon at the top of the left pane to create a new file.
4  In the pop-up window that opens, name the file Counter.sol.
    (.sol is the file type for programs written in Solidity.)
5  Type (enter) or copy the Counter code in listing 2.1 into the editor window.

## 2.4  *Deploying and testing the smart contract*

Are you ready to deploy the smart contract and explore its workings? You'll deploy the contract in the same Remix development environment in which you entered the smart contract code in Solidity (section 2.3.2). Let's explore the Remix IDE before you start testing the smart contract.

> **Remix**
>
> Are you curious about the development environment of the Solidity smart contract, editing it, compiling it, setting up and configuring a blockchain, deploying the compiled code on this chain, and testing it? Remix provides a cool web/cloud-based integrated development environment with no installation required. Not only that, but it also scaffolds a JavaScript-based simulated test chain environment where you can deploy your smart contract code and test it! This all-in-one environment also allows you to onboard your tested application to external blockchains other than the test chain supported by Remix.

### 2.4.1  *The Remix IDE*

The Remix IDE (figure 2.6) is directly accessible at https://remix.ethereum.org. You can open it and follow along as we discuss its features. This version is the latest version as of February 2020. The Remix IDE layout changes yearly to optimize user experience, but the concepts are the same. Be aware that the layout may change again next year and that the color schemes for the buttons also change frequently.

Figure 2.6 shows the seven features of the Remix IDE that you'll use in working with the development of a smart contract. Open the Remix IDE, identify the items indicated, and follow along with the explanation provided. (Note that I've chosen the light theme from the settings icon at the bottom corner, so that Remix appears better for print material.)

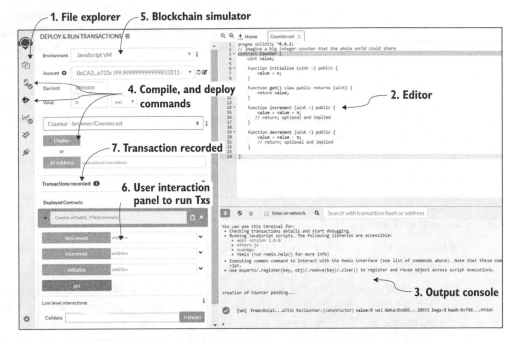

**Figure 2.6　The Remix IDE**

The main features of the Remix IDE include the following:

1　The *file explorer* on the left is where you create and manage your files: you can open, close, create, and delete files here. The files are automatically saved on the Remix (cloud) server. You can also synchronize them to your local drive and folder.

2　The *editor* space in the middle is where you enter your code and review files, such as the .sol files of the smart contract and the .json files of transactions recorded. It also features a just-in-time compiler (optional) that points out errors as you enter the code.

3　The *output console,* just below the editor window, is where you can view the transactions and see confirmation of their recording, as well as any errors and debugging details.

4　The *toolchain* on the left panel offers icons representing commands to compile and deploy the compiled code. After clicking the Compile and Deploy icons, click the Deploy button to deploy a smart contract.

5　The *blockchain simulator* offers an execution environment (JavaScript VM) as well as connections to live blockchain networks. The Remix IDE provides a set of account addresses and identities for the test blockchain. The account numbers identify participants. Few (10) accounts are available for testing purposes, but you can create more if you need them.

6 The *user interaction panel*, in the bottom-left corner, lets you interact with a deployed smart contract to run transactions. It exposes all the public functions and data, along with buttons to invoke the functions and text boxes for input parameters. The output of the invocation, if any, is displayed just below the function buttons.

7 All the transactions recorded on the blockchain are provisioned in a .json file for easy review. You can see the Transactions Recorded button in the middle of the panel on the left.

Now you are ready to test the smart contract code that you copied into Remix. Working with the simple Counter.sol contract will enable you to understand the smart contract's structure and development process, as well as the features of the Remix IDE.

### 2.4.2   *Deployment and testing*

It's time to deploy and test the Counter smart contract. In the Remix web IDE, follow these steps:

1 Open the file explorer icon, and click the dark + symbol. In the box that pops up, enter `Counter.sol` for the name of the contract. Copy the code from the Counter.sol file into the editor window, if you haven't done so already, and click the Compile icon. You should see a Compile button appear; when it does, click it. (You could also click the auto compile check box to skip this step.)

2 Make sure that the environment is set to JavaScript VM, and click the Run icon in the command menu. You should see a banner titled Counter.sol across the middle of the panel on the left.

3 You're ready to deploy and explore. Click the Deploy and Run Transactions icon. Click the Deploy button in the left panel. Then click the small down arrow next to Deployed Contracts, as shown in figure 2.7. You'll see an interaction panel at the bottom of the screen.

4 You're all set to interact with the smart contract and see it in operation. Here's a sample interaction: enter `456` in the Initialize box, click the Initialize button, and then click the Get button to view the value. Repeat the operation by entering values in the Increment and Decrement boxes and then clicking Get.

As you're testing these operations, make sure that you observe the output console at the bottom of the Remix IDE just below the editor. You'll see the transactions created by these operations (initialize, get, increment, and decrement) listed as pending at first and then showing successful execution. You can simulate different participants by changing the identity specified by the account number in the drop-down box in the top-left panel, as shown in figure 2.7.

You've now deployed and tested your first smart contract. This setup will be the rapid prototyping environment—the foundation on which you'll build a full-fledged Dapp. You'll explore other features of the Remix IDE in sections 2.5 and 2.7, as well as in later chapters when you design smart contracts for more complex use cases.

**Figure 2.7   Left panel of Remix IDE**

### 2.4.3   *Key takeaways*

Let's look back at what you've accomplished so far in the design process and compare it with traditional counter design.

You designed a Counter smart contract that was similar in appearance to the code for a conventional counter. You may think it's like a regular Java application that you run from the command line, but it is different.

When a smart contract code is deployed on a blockchain, it is accessible to anybody who has a defined identity on that blockchain. This identity could represent a participant (human or computer program) in Albany, New York, or in Bali, Indonesia; it is equally accessible as long as the participant has an account number and is connected to the same blockchain network. You may argue that this application is like any web application: a distributed system. But a distributed web application does not maintain a distributed immutable ledger. The blockchain does, and as a result, every participant records the same copy of the list of transactions that happened on the blockchain for this particular smart contract. This information is automatically logged with the agreement (consensus) of all the stakeholders on the network. Then the immutable ledger can be used to trace the provenance of the who, when, and what of the transactions. Thus, the distributed immutable ledger of the blockchain enables trust among unknown decentralized participant nodes, opening a whole world of opportunities for innovative Dapps, as you'll see next.

## 2.5    *What makes a blockchain contract smart?*

Here are some cool features of a smart contract that make it smart. A smart contract is equivalent to any participant in a blockchain network because it has

- A name
- An address
- A cryptocurrency balance (ether, in this case)
- Built-in features to send and receive cryptocurrency (ether, in this case)
- Data and functions
- Built-in features to receive messages and invoke functions
- The ability to reason out the execution of a function

These aspects distinguish and set apart a smart contract from a regular piece of code. A smart contract is indeed smart and different. Let's examine these features of a smart contract before we begin another application that uses some of these special features.

In a traditional computing system, a participant is identified by a username and an associated password. These elements are used for authentication. This <username, password> combination will not work in a decentralized system, because peers are beyond the usual boundaries of trust (as in the relationships university–student or country–citizen). The solution is to provide a unique identifier for each participant based on cryptographic algorithms. (You'll learn more about this topic in chapter 5.) All the participants interacting with the blockchain, including a smart contract, have an account number or address that uniquely identifies them:

- Ethereum supports two types of accounts: externally owned accounts (EOAs) and smart contract accounts. Both types of accounts are identified by addresses that are 160 bits, or 40 bytes, long. You can view the account numbers in the Remix IDE.
- Both types of accounts, EOAs and smart contracts, can hold a balance of ethers. Thus, every account has these two *implicit* attributes: address and balance. You may not find these attributes explicitly declared in your smart contract; address(this).balance will get you the balance held in your smart contract.
- An EOA or a smart contract account can invoke a smart contract function by sending a message. This message has two *implied* attributes: msg.sender and msg.value. Yes, a message can carry a value that is added to the balance held by the smart contract when one of its functions is invoked. The function has to be declared with a payable modifier to be eligible to receive funds.

These concepts are captured in the AccountsDemo.sol smart contract shown in listing 2.2. Copy this smart contract, and deploy it in the Remix IDE. You'll see the screenshot shown in figure 2.8. In the left panel of the Remix IDE, you'll see EOAs on the simulated VM. You can also see the smart contract address in the bottom part of the left panel, as indicated. Choose an Account in the left panel of the Remix IDE, and specify an ether value in the Value box before clicking the Deposit button. Then click the `accountBalance`, `depositAmt`, and `whoDeposited` buttons to view the AccountsDemo smart contract's attributes. Repeat with a different account (EOA) and ether value. You'll notice that the smart contract's balance is automatically and cumulatively updated. Explore more with this smart contract to get an idea of these powerful features. You can see that a smart contract can receive, keep, count, and send cryptocurrency autonomously! These special characteristics of a smart contract open a whole new world of opportunities.

**Listing 2.2　AccountsDemo.sol**

```solidity
pragma solidity ^0.6.0;
contract AccountsDemo {
    address public whoDeposited;
    uint public depositAmt;
    uint public accountBalance;
    function deposit() public payable
    {
        whoDeposited = msg.sender;
        depositAmt = msg.value;
        accountBalance = address(this).balance;
    }
}
```

deposit() function can receive payment (payable).

Every function invocation has an implied msg.sender.

Every function invocation can be sent a msg.value by the msg.sender.

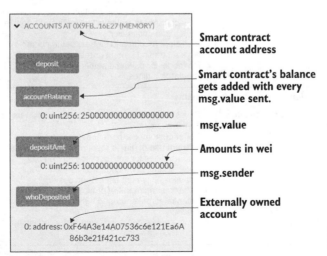

Smart contract account address

Smart contract's balance gets added with every msg.value sent.

msg.value

Amounts in wei

msg.sender

Externally owned account

**Figure 2.8　Interface for AccountsDemo smart contract**

## 2.6    *Decentralized airline system use case*

Let's apply what you've learned so far to another use case. The reason for introducing yet another Dapp is to highlight the importance of different types of accounts and to emphasize another important aspect of blockchain programming: keeping only minimal required information on the blockchain.

The *airline system consortium* (ASK instead of ASC) blockchain for the airline industry enables peer-to-peer transactions of flight seats among participating airlines. I'll use the acronym ASK to refer to this use case. You can think of ASK as being a peer-to-peer marketplace in which airlines that are not necessarily code-sharing partners can trade flight seats.

### 2.6.1    *ASK definition*

In the basic definition of the problem, airlines go about their routine business with their traditional centralized distributed systems and manual agents managing this system. Besides, they can participate in a permissioned, decentralized consortium of airlines. We'll refer to this consortium as ASK. This scenario is hypothetical and created especially for this exercise.

Unlike in traditional systems, airlines may join and leave this system as they wish. An airline joins ASK by depositing a predetermined minimum escrow used for payment settlement for seats used in ASK transactions. The consortium allows an airline to trade (buy and sell) flight seats under certain circumstances and conditions. The rules for the trades can be codified into the system so that there are no ambiguities and the outcomes are deterministic. The ASK problem statement, issues, blockchain-based solution, and outcomes are summarized in the quad chart in figure 2.9.

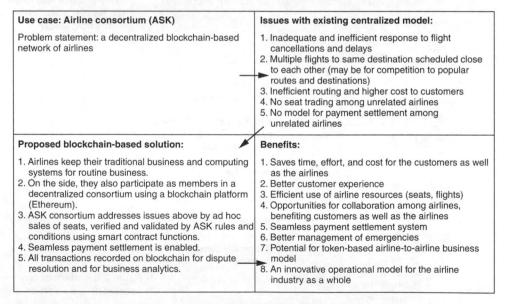

| Use case: Airline consortium (ASK) | Issues with existing centralized model: |
|---|---|
| Problem statement: a decentralized blockchain-based network of airlines | 1. Inadequate and inefficient response to flight cancellations and delays<br>2. Multiple flights to same destination scheduled close to each other (may be for competition to popular routes and destinations)<br>3. Inefficient routing and higher cost to customers<br>4. No seat trading among unrelated airlines<br>5. No model for payment settlement among unrelated airlines |
| **Proposed blockchain-based solution:** | **Benefits:** |
| 1. Airlines keep their traditional business and computing systems for routine business.<br>2. On the side, they also participate as members in a decentralized consortium using a blockchain platform (Ethereum).<br>3. ASK consortium addresses issues above by ad hoc sales of seats, verified and validated by ASK rules and conditions using smart contract functions.<br>4. Seamless payment settlement is enabled.<br>5. All transactions recorded on blockchain for dispute resolution and for business analytics. | 1. Saves time, effort, and cost for the customers as well as the airlines<br>2. Better customer experience<br>3. Efficient use of airline resources (seats, flights)<br>4. Opportunities for collaboration among airlines, benefiting customers as well as the airlines<br>5. Seamless payment settlement system<br>6. Better management of emergencies<br>7. Potential for token-based airline-to-airline business model<br>8. An innovative operational model for the airline industry as a whole |

Figure 2.9   ASK quad chart: use case, issues, blockchain solution, and benefits

The airline representatives (on behalf of the airlines) can initiate the trades proactively or reactively in response to customer demand or as warranted by circumstances such as weather-related cancellations. In this use case, you'll limit the scope to the elemental operation of peer-to-peer sales of flight seats among airlines. Enforcement of agreed rules of engagement and a seamless payment system is also enabled by the blockchain, alleviating the traditional business concerns of competing airlines. The participating airlines expose secure, standard APIs for simple queries about the availability of flight seats. These queries are like those you might post on a travel website like Kayak or Expedia (intermediaries), but with one significant difference: they are initiated programmatically by the software applications, and there are no intermediaries. An application requests trades from the airlines directly on your behalf.

### 2.6.2 *Sequence of operations*

Here are the steps followed by two airlines, A and B, that are not necessarily known to each other and that operate beyond the boundaries of traditional trust. In other words, they don't have a conventional business partnership such as code-sharing and alliances. How can the airlines trust each other to verify and record the transactions?

Consider this everyday situation: your sister wants to borrow $10, all in $1 bills. You take the bills out of your wallet, count them, verify there are 10 $1 bills, and hand them to her. She pockets the bills and leaves. She does not count them again because she trusts you.

Now imagine the same transaction at a checkout counter. You count out (verify) 10 $1 bills right in front of the checkout clerk and hand the money to her. In this case, the clerk verifies that you have given her the right number of bills by counting them again. Why? You two are decentralized entities that don't know each other well enough to trust each other.

That is the situation with airline A and airline B, which are not known to each other. In ASK, they rely on the trust established by the blockchain by verifying and recording the transactions. In addition to the two airlines, other stakeholders may verify the transactions and record the transactions as witnesses.

Let's analyze the operations indicated in figure 2.10 to understand the role that a blockchain plays in a decentralized system as a verifier, validator, and recorder. Figure 2.10 shows the numbered sequence of operations. Follow the operations in the sequence numbered to get the operational details discussed.

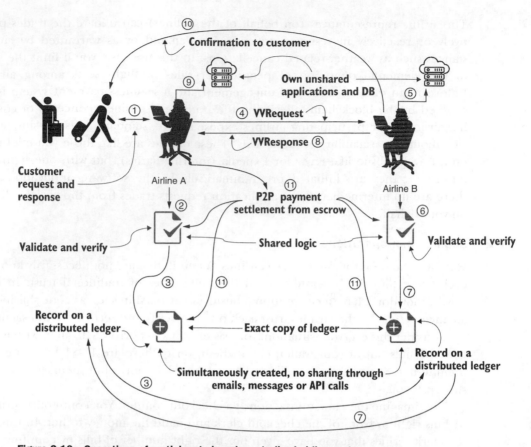

**Figure 2.10   Operations of participants in a decentralized airline system**

1   A customer initiates a change of flight seat that they hold on airline A.

2   An agent or application at airline A verifies and validates the request through smart contract logic shared among the ASK consortium members.

3   Once verified, the request Tx is confirmed and recorded in a distributed immutable ledger. Now everyone in the consortium knows that a legitimate request has been made.

4   In the simplest design, an agent at airline A sends the verified and validated request (VVRequest) to airline B. (Alternatively, we could use a broadcast model in which many airlines get the request, and any one of them could respond.)

5   An agent or application at airline B checks the airline's database to check for availability.

6   An agent at airline B responds through shared smart contract logic that verifies and validates the common interests and shared rules of the consortium.

7 Once verified, the response Tx is confirmed and recorded in a distributed immutable ledger. Now everyone in the consortium knows that a response has been sent.

8 Airline B sends the response (indicated by VVResponse) to the agent at airline A.

9 Airline A updates its database, noting that a change has been made.

10 An agent at airline B sends the customer the information for the flight seats and other details. (Note that airline B holds its data assets and transfers them directly to its known customer, not to airline A.)

11 Payments are settled through peer-to-peer Txs, using the escrow or deposit that participating airlines hold in their shared smart contract. The payment settlement can be embedded in other suitable operations in the system but will be handled by the shared smart contract and recorded in the ledger. This settlement is automatically carried out by the smart contract logic.

Note that the request, response, and payment settlement are simultaneously recorded by the stakeholders of the consortium. This concept is illustrated by two of each of steps 3, 7, and 11 in figure 2.10, which shows only two airlines: A and airline B. You can extrapolate this two-participant scenario to a larger-scale scenario with *N* airline participants.

Figure 2.10 is a dissection of one simplified operation. Still, you can imagine how this automatic verification and validation and the distributed ledger could solve other problems discussed in the airline scenario. These features can be further leveraged for other intelligent applications and token-based payment systems, as you'll see in chapter 10.

## 2.7 *Airlines smart contract*

Now let's design the use case model and contract diagram by applying design principles 1, 2, and 4 (design, use case, contract diagram). Figure 2.11 shows the ASK use case diagram and contract diagram. These diagrams will help you in structuring and developing the smart contract code.

**DESIGN PRINCIPLE 1** Design before you code, develop, and deploy a smart contract on a test chain, and thoroughly test it before you deploy it on a production blockchain, because when the smart contract is deployed, it is immutable.

**DESIGN PRINCIPLE 2** Define the users of and use cases for the system. Users are entities that generate the actions and the input and receive the output from the system you'll be designing.

**DESIGN PRINCIPLE 4** Define a contract diagram that specifies the name, data assets, functions, and rules for execution of functions and access to the data.

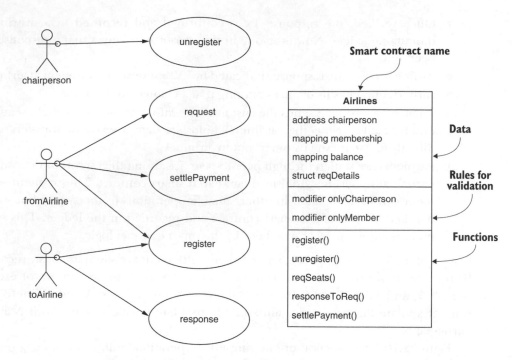

**Figure 2.11   ASK use case and contract diagrams**

Use the two design diagrams in figure 2.11 to discover the users, data assets, rules, roles, and functions.

### 2.7.1   *Peer participants, data assets, roles, rules, and transactions*

Now let's apply design principle 3 to code the smart contract's data structures and functions. Identifying the participants, their roles, the assets they control, and the related transactions is a common first step in any standard design process. This step is even more critical for users that do not necessarily operate in the same environment or within the business organization.

> **DESIGN PRINCIPLE 3**   Define the data assets, peer participants and their roles, rules to be enforced, and transactions to be recorded for the system you'll be designing.

#### USERS

You first identify the users of the system as peer participants. This term is used to emphasize that they interact with one another in a peer-to-peer fashion, without any intermediaries. In the ASK use case, the agents acting on behalf of their airlines are the peer participants. They act on a request from a customer to address the cancellation of a flight. The ASK consortium authority will have a monitor, whom you will refer to as the *chairperson* of the consortium. This consortium does not mean centralization, because this monitoring or chairperson role is periodically circulated among the consortium members. The chairperson does not manage any central database. The database of each airline is safe within their firewalls. The shared data is stored in the distributed ledger of the shared blockchain.

### ASSETS

The data assets are the flight seats and the funds held by the peer participants. We learned in chapter 1 that one of the fundamental tenets of a decentralized system is that peer participants—not an intermediary—hold their own assets.

### ROLES

The following are the roles:

- Agents acting on behalf of the airlines can enroll or self-register by using the `register()` function with an escrow/deposit; this action makes them (airlines) members of ASK.
- Agents (of members only) can request flight seats.
- Agents acting on behalf of the airlines can check their centralized databases for availability and reply.
- Peers settle the payment between themselves if seats are available.
- The chairperson of the consortium has the sole authority to unregister members and return leftover deposits.

The definition of roles is critical in an automated decentralized system, so you want to be certain that authorized participants initiate the requests. Agents can be human or software applications.

### TRANSACTIONS

A typical process of buying flight seats may involve many operations and interactions with various subsystems, such as databases. Let's refer to operations that need to be verified, validated, confirmed, and recorded by all parties as the transactions, or simply *Txs*.

### RULES

The contract diagram in figure 2.11 (section 2.7) shows new elements that did not appear in the counter use case: modifiers. *Modifiers* are special elements of a smart contract, representing the rules that act as gatekeepers to control access to data and functions. Only valid members (`onlyMember`) can transact on the system, and only the chairperson (`onlyChairperson`) can unregister any airline.

> **DEFINITION** *Modifiers* are a language feature that supports explicit specification of rules for validation and verification. These modifiers are the gatekeepers that do the verification and validation, and thus are specifically meant for realizing trust.

Recall from chapter 1 that the blockchain is a trust intermediator, which means that it automates the process of verification and validation for trust establishment in its code (smart contracts). Modifiers are features that enable this trust intermediation. Here's how it works:

- You specify the rules or conditions, using a control structure called a modifier. Solidity language provides the modifier feature to code the rules.
- Modifiers are used for specifying who can access the functions and who can access the data, and also for validating data uniformly.

The ASK codes demonstrate the use of modifiers in a smart contract with two modifiers: `onlyMember` and `onlyChairperson`. You'll learn more details about modifiers in chapter 3.

### 2.7.2  *Airlines smart contract code*

Now you're ready to enter the working code for a basic Airlines smart contract, provided in the Remix IDE (see the next listing). If the `pragma` line gives an error for the version, choose the correct version by looking at the compiler version in the top-right section of the Remix IDE window.

---

**Listing 2.3   Smart contract code for ASK (Airlines.sol)**

```
pragma solidity ^0.6.0;
    contract Airlines  {
    address chairperson;                    Airline data
    struct details{                         structures
        uint escrow; // deposit for payment settlement
        uint status;
        uint hashOfDetails;
    }

    mapping (address=>details) public balanceDetails;    Airline account payments
    mapping (address=>uint) membership;                  and membership mapping

    // modifiers or rules
    modifier onlyChairperson{
        require(msg.sender==chairperson);       Modifier for
        _;                                      onlyChairperson rule
    }
    modifier onlyMember{
        require(membership[msg.sender]==1);     Modifier for
        _;                                      onlyMember rule
    }

    // constructor function
    constructor () public payable  {

        chairperson=msg.sender;                                    Usage of msg.sender
        membership[msg.sender]=1; // automatically registered      and msg.value for a
        balanceDetails[msg.sender].escrow = msg.value;             payable function
    }

    function register ( ) public payable{
```

Functions
of the
contract

**Functions of the contract**

**Usage of msg.sender and msg.value for a payable function**

```
        address AirlineA = msg.sender;
        membership[AirlineA]=1;
        balanceDetails[msg.sender].escrow = msg.value;
    }

    function unregister (address payable AirlineZ) onlyChairperson public {
        if(chairperson!=msg.sender){
            revert(); }
        membership[AirlineZ]=0;
        // return escrow to leaving airline: verify other conditions
        AirlineZ.transfer(balanceDetails[AirlineZ].escrow);
        balanceDetails[AirlineZ].escrow = 0;
    }

    function request(address toAirline, uint hashOfDetails) onlyMember
    public{
        if(membership[toAirline]!=1){
            revert(); }
        balanceDetails[msg.sender].status=0;
        balanceDetails[msg.sender].hashOfDetails = hashOfDetails;
    }

    function  response(address fromAirline, uint hashOfDetails, uint done)
                        onlyMember public{

        if(membership[fromAirline]!=1){
            revert();   }
        balanceDetails[msg.sender].status=done;
        balanceDetails[fromAirline].hashOfDetails = hashOfDetails;
    }


    function settlePayment  (address payable toAirline) onlyMember payable
                                public{
        address fromAirline=msg.sender;
        uint amt = msg.value;
        balanceDetails[toAirline].escrow = balanceDetails[toAirline].escrow
                                                + amt;
        balanceDetails[fromAirline].escrow =
                balanceDetails[fromAirline].escrow - amt;

        // amt subtracted from msg.sender and given to toAirline
        toAirline.transfer(amt);
}}
```

**Functions of the contract**

**Functions of the contract**

**Smart contract account transferring amount to an external account**

Let's take a look at the new Solidity data types introduced by this smart contract. These data types include

- address to refer to the identity of the chairperson.
- struct to collectively define the data of the airlines, including the escrow or the deposit.

- mapping to map account addresses (identities) of members to their details. (A mapping is like a hash table.)
- modifier definitions for memberOnly and chairpersonOnly. (You'll learn about these definitions in chapter 3.)

These data types are followed by the function definitions: constructor(), register(), request(), response(), settlePayment(), and unregister(). It's important to note that the airlines have to execute their regular functions and checks by using their existing systems. Note the use of the msg.sender, msg.value, and payable features introduced in section 2.5. The smart contract only takes care of the extra functionality needed for the decentralized interaction with other airlines.

### 2.7.3  *ASK smart contract deployment and testing*

Before you start working with the Airlines smart contract, make sure that you've familiarized yourself with the Remix IDE, using the Counter use case discussed earlier in section 2.3. Now create a Solidity file called Airlines.sol, and enter the code from listing 2.3, available in the codebase of this chapter. Compile it, using the Compile command on the menu; select JavaScript VM as the environment; and click Deploy & Run transactions icon. Now you are ready to deploy and test the application on the simulated VM provided by the Remix IDE.

The chairperson is a legitimate peer airline, so choose the chairperson's address in the left panel below the VM simulator, enter a value for escrow of 50 ether, Click Deploy and Run transactions icon, and click the Deploy button at the center of the left panel. The bottom pane shows a deployed smart contract with its address and a down arrow. When you click the down arrow, you expand the web interface to the deployed application, displaying all the public functions and data for you to interact with, and you'll be able to observe the output from the function execution. All these items are shown in figure 2.12. In the Remix IDE, you'll observe that the functions of the user interface are color-coded:

- Orange for a public function with no validation rules.
- Red for functions with rules coded by modifiers.
- Blue for access functions that are for viewing any public data. All public functions are available for viewing through a blue button.

**NOTE**  Please note that the color scheme of the interface keeps changing. The colors may not be the same as the ones displayed here.

The constructor is used for the deployment of the contract when you click the Deploy button. The transaction created is displayed in the console of your Remix IDE, as shown in figure 2.13.

Now you're ready to test the other functions: register(), request(), response(), settlePayment(), and unregister(). You'll observe that the simulated VM has many accounts for testing purposes, which are listed in the Account drop-down box at the

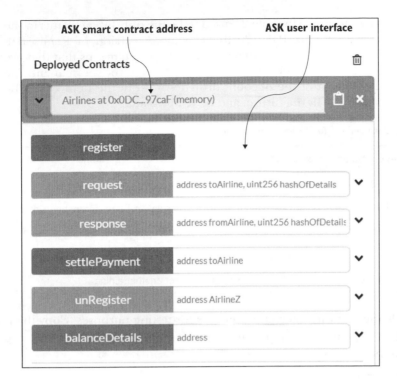

Figure 2.12   Deployed Airlines smart contract and its UI

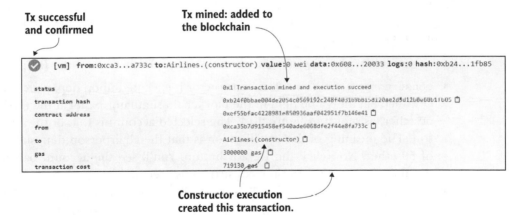

Figure 2.13   Transaction for Airlines constructor (recorded/mined)

top of the left panel. Some account numbers (five from the bottom) from the list are repeated in table 2.2, along with their allocations to the roles you identified: the chairperson of the ASK consortium, toAirline, and fromAirline.

**NOTE**    These five accounts in table 2.2 used to be the only five accounts in the previous version of Remix IDE (2019). The newer version of Remix IDE (2020) has 10 more test accounts that are random, which means that they are different every time you reload. I've chosen to use the permanent five accounts at the bottom of the Account drop-down list in the Remix IDE. Be aware of such changes in the future, and be ready to adapt.

Table 2.2    Account numbers for Airlines smart contract

| Account address or identity | Airline |
| --- | --- |
| 0xca35b7d915458ef540ade6068dfe2f44e8fa733c | ASK consortium chairperson |
| 0x14723a09acff6d2a60dcdf7aa4aff308fddc160c | `fromAirline` (for testing airline A) |
| 0x4b0897b0513fdc7c541b6d9d7e929c4e5364d2db | `toAirline` (for testing airline B) |
| 0x583031d1113ad414f02576bd6afabfb302140225 | Another airline |
| 0xdD870fA1b7C4700F2BD7f44238821C26f7392148 | Yet another airline |

You need only the first three account numbers for testing purposes. Copy them from the IDE, and store them in a notepad application so that it is easy for you to copy and paste them in the interface.

**TEST PLAN DESCRIPTION**

**NOTE**    I've described a test plan followed by actual instructions. If you're a beginner, review both, but if you're an advanced developer, you may choose to do either.

Here's a simple test plan to verify the execution of your functions in the IDE:

- `constructor()` *function*—The constructor is executed upon deployment of the contract. Set the Value field in the blockchain simulator panel at the top left to 50 ether, as shown in figure 2.14. The selected account is that of the chairperson. The meaning of this initialization is that the chairperson deposits a value of 50 ether. Now click the Deploy button. You'll see the account balance go down by this amount after the constructor is executed.
- `register()` *function*—Any airline can self-register with a deposit. Make sure that the `fromAirline` account is selected in the Account drop-down list in the top-left panel. This function needs two parameters: the account address and the escrow value. The account address is *implicitly provided* by `msg.sender`. Enter 50 ether for the escrow value; then click the Register button to execute the function. Repeat the same process for the `toAirline` address in the Account box.

**Figure 2.14   Before and after deployment of the Airlines smart contract**

- `request()` *function*—Make sure that the `fromAirline` account is selected in the Account box. Then, in the function parameter box, paste in the `toAirline` address, and supply any number (say, 123) to represent the hash of the off-chain details of data. (You'll learn about off-chain data and hash in chapter 5.) Click the Request button.

- `response()` *function*—Make sure that the `toAirline` account is selected in the Account box. In the function parameter box, paste in the `fromAirline` address, and supply any number (say, 345) to represent the hash of off-chain details of data and a third value to indicate whether the request was accepted (1) or declined (0) (based on the availability of seats, of course). Click the Response button.

- `settlePayment()` *function*—Make sure that the `fromAirline` account is selected in the Account box. In the function parameter box, paste in the `toAirline` address, and specify an amount to be paid (say, 2 ether) for settlement. Click the settlePayment button.

- `balanceDetails()` *function*—Click the balanceDetails button, with the `fromAirline` address as a parameter. You see all the details you entered there, but with the escrow reduced by 2 because it paid for seats. If you repeat this process for the `toAirline` address, you'll see 2 more ethers in its (`toAirline`) escrow, which verifies that all your functions worked as expected. You should see this verification reflected in the balances in the blockchain emulator panel's accounts.

- `unregister()` *function*—Unregistering can be done only by the chairperson, because there may be conditions to be checked before the escrow is returned to the airlines.

### TEST INSTRUCTIONS

Following are step-by-step instructions for the test sequence discussed in the previous plan. This list tests all the items of the Airlines smart contract that you see in the (Remix) UI. The execution details are displayed in the output console. You should be able to see whether the function executed successfully (a green check mark on the console) and many other details related to transaction execution and confirmation. Follow these steps to run the tests:

1   Restart the Remix IDE. This action resets the blockchain environment to its starting point. You can restart any time you make a mistake during the learning process. Clear the console, using the O symbol in the top-left corner of the console (bottom panel).

2   Copy listing 2.3 (Airlines.sol) into the editor window. Make sure to use the correct version of the compiler in the `pragma` line.

3   Click Compile in the menu in the top-right corner; then click Deploy.

4   Configure the following settings in the blockchain emulator panel and then click Deploy:

  a   *Environment*—JavaScript VM

  b   *Account*—the first address (the chairperson's account, such as 0xca3 . . .)

  c   *Value*—50 ether (not Wei)

      Refer to figure 2.14 for details.

5   Open the smart contract by clicking the down arrow next to Deployed Contracts.

6   (Self-)Register airlines A and B:

  a   Set Account to the `fromAirline` (airline A) address (0x147 . . .).

  b   Set Value to 50 ether (not Wei).

  c   Click Register.

  d   Repeat this process for the `toAirline` (airline B) address (0x4b0 . . .).

7   Transact one request and one response from Airline A to Airline B and back:

  a   With airline A's address (0x147 . . .) selected in the Account box, in the `request()` function's parameter box, paste in the address of airline B (0x4b0 . . .), enter 123 for the hash details, and click Request.

  b   With airline B's address (0x4b0 . . .) selected in the Account box, in the `response()` function's parameter box, paste in the address of airline A (0x147 . . .), enter 123 for the hash details and 1 for success, and then click Response.

8   To test the `settlePayment()` function, with the address of airline A in the Account box, enter `2 ether` in the Value box, paste the address of airline B in the function's parameter box, and click settlePayment. Figure 2.15 shows the updated account balances when this step is complete.

9   Unregister, using airline B's address (0x4b0 . . .) as a parameter. The address of the chairperson (0xca3 . . .) must be selected in the Account box; otherwise, it will revert.

10   Click balanceDetails, and use airline B's address (0x147 . . .) as a parameter to see the internal balance of this account. You can also check all the account balances in the top-left panel.

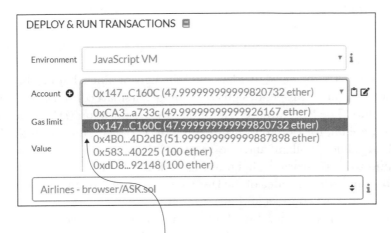

Account addresses and balances after a request/response/payment Txs
Airline A has 47.99 . . . because it paid 2 ethers to Airline B for seats.
Airline B has 51.99 . . . ethers.
The small amounts missing from these balances are the Tx fees.

Figure 2.15   Account balances after completion of step 8

Here ends our end-to-end discussion of smart contract design, deployment, and testing in the Remix IDE. Make sure that you review and understand the code and the design. In chapter 3, we'll further develop the core blockchain concept of the smart contract, and you'll see how to enhance it to make it a complete Dapp.

### Where's the immutable ledger?

If you're wondering where the blockchain's immutable recording is, click Transactions Recorded in the middle of the left panel, and then click the icon for storage (the floppy disk). A .json file opens in the editor space. This content of this file shows the immutable recording with timestamps of transactions recorded and all the details. You can use this file for any data-analytics applications, as well as for verification and review.

## 2.8   *Smart contract design considerations*

Smart contracts are immutable code, like the hardware integrated circuit chips in laptops, smartphones, and computers. In hardware chips, the code is etched in the silicon circuits. Similarly, when smart contracts are deployed, their code is final and cannot be updated unless special provisions or escape hatches are built in. You'll learn about these escape methods in later chapters.

We've also seen that smart contracts are shared with all the stakeholders so that they can independently verify, validate, and reach consensus on the transactions to be recorded in the distributed immutable ledger of the blockchain. Therefore, you must design and test a smart contract thoroughly before deploying it for production use. Though a smart contract is a software module, you cannot change its contents (unlike the weekly updates you get for many apps and operating systems). All these characteristics of a smart contract demand careful design as a precoding step and thorough testing as a postcoding step.

The smart contract is the good, the bad, and the ugly of blockchain technology. It is a powerful feature, but improper design and coding of a smart contract have resulted in significant failure. The Decentralized Autonomous Organization (DAO) hack in the early days of Ethereum, for example (http://mng.bz/yrYJ), culminated in the loss of several hundred million dollars, and the recent Parity wallet lockup (https://blog .zeppelin.solutions/on-the-parity-wallet-multisig-hack-405a8c12e8f7) resulted in funds getting locked up by code. The idea of the DAO was to raise cryptocurrency funds from investors through a smart contract and invest them in various instruments decided by the smart contract. In this case, a vulnerability in the smart contract code was exploited to funnel funds into a hacker's account. In the case of the Parity wallet, the accidental deletion of a function resulted in locking up the funds held by a smart contract. The former was a hack, and the latter was a careless accident. An important lesson to learn from these high-profile failures is that smart contracts require meticulous design and testing before deployment. These mishaps further emphasize the importance of following the best practices in the design and development of a smart contract.

## 2.9   *Best practices*

Now that you've been introduced to smart contract design and development, and to the features specific to blockchain application development, this is an appropriate time to review some best practices:

- *Make sure that your application requires blockchain features.* Blockchain is not a solution for all applications. In other words, blockchain-based solutions and smart contracts are not panaceas for any problem you have. So what are they good for? Recall from chapter 1 that blockchain solutions are most suitable for applications that
  - Are decentralized, meaning that participants hold the assets and are not necessarily co-located

- Involve peer-to-peer transactions without intermediaries
- Operate beyond the boundaries of trust among unknown peers
- Require validation, verification, and recording in a universally timestamped immutable ledger
- Have autonomous operations guided by rules and policies

- *Make sure that you need a smart contract for your application.* Understand that the smart contract will be visible to all the participants in the chain and will be executed on the full nodes. You need a smart contract when you need a collective agreement based on rules, regulations, or policies enforced and when the decisions (and the provenance for them) must be recorded. A smart contract is not for single-node computations. It does not replace your client/server or inherently stateless distributed solutions. Smart contracts are usually part of a broader distributed application—the part that requires the services provided by the blockchain.
- *Keep the smart contract code simple, coherent, and auditable.* The state variables and functions specified in a smart contract should each address a single problem. Do not include redundant data or unrelated functions.
- *Be aware that Solidity is updated frequently.* Solidity is still in its infancy, and its features and versions change much more frequently than those of more mature languages like Java. Be sure to change the compiler version to the one that matches your smart contract code.

## 2.10 *Summary*

- Blockchain-based peer-to-peer interaction will eliminate the overhead of intermediaries by enabling scalable automatic direct transactions.
- A smart contract is an executable code on the blockchain that allows for the realization of transactions other than cryptocurrency transfers.
- The design flow of a smart contract begins with a problem statement, followed by the user and asset analysis, design of use case and contract diagrams, and pseudocode.
- A particular high-level language is used for smart contract development for a specific blockchain. In this book, we'll use the Solidity and Ethereum blockchains.
- Unlike in regular programming, smart contracts on blockchain require a particular blockchain environment for testing. A one-stop integrated web-based development environment called Remix IDE can be used to deploy and test your contracts.
- Thanks to blockchain advancements, new disruptive business models may emerge that result in improved customer benefits and experiences, cost-cutting, and better management of emergencies, not only for airlines, but also for many other consumer-facing businesses.

# Techniques for
# trust and integrity

3

**This chapter covers**

- Establishing trust through verification, validation, and recording
- Enabling trust using Solidity language features
- Using finite state machine diagrams to characterize application phases
- Incremental development of smart contracts using the Remix IDE
- Tips for testing smart contracts

Trust and integrity are essential requirements for any system, but they are especially critical in a decentralized system where the peer participants operate beyond the traditional boundaries of trust. In this chapter, you'll learn how to add elements that establish trust and integrity to your blockchain-based solution, to support robust decentralized operations.

Imagine that your neighbors want to borrow your food processor. You know and trust them because of your prior interactions, so you don't hesitate to share your food processor with them. This action is a peer-to-peer transaction without an intermediary. What if you buy something online? You need a credit card and a bank account or some similar instrument whereby your credentials have been verified. The credit card company undertakes the responsibility of establishing trust in you for the online vendor. In this case, trust is quantified based on information like your credit rating and other credentials. Thus, building trust between the vendor and customer involves at least one intermediary and maybe more.

The cases I've described are just two of the many possibilities in the trust continuum, from simple peer-to-peer interactions between neighbors to complex financial systems. But how do you resolve the trust in a decentralized system in which no organizations or individuals act as intermediaries? Who or what fills this role in such systems? Blockchain can. It is ideally positioned to provide automated trust intermediation through its innovative infrastructure, unique protocol, and distributed ledger technology. It addresses trust and integrity by verification, validation, and protocol-level consensus, and through its distributed immutable recording.

In this chapter, you'll learn about trust and integrity in the context of blockchain-based decentralized systems. You'll learn to design smart contracts with additional techniques for improving trust in the system you developed in chapter 2. Often, the techniques for enabling trust, such as access control, encryption, and digital signatures, also address the integrity requirements of a system. We'll focus on the access control aspect in this chapter, and explore cryptography and hashing techniques in chapter 5.

The chapter introduces a new decentralized application for balloting in a digital democracy (Ballot), as well as a new design diagram in finite state machines (FSM). This chapter also illustrates the use of Solidity features including modifiers and `require()` and `assert()` declarations to implement verification and validation.

## 3.1 Essentials of trust and integrity

The constituents of trust and integrity are represented by the two quad charts in figure 3.1, one showing the components of trust and the other showing the elements of integrity. Spend a few minutes reviewing figure 3.1, and identify the various components of trust and integrity before we explore these concepts further.

### 3.1.1 Trust

Trust means different things in different contexts. Trust is an essential criterion for the success of any system. So let's first define trust in the context of blockchain-based decentralized systems.

> **DEFINITION** *Trust* is a measure of confidence in the credibility of a peer participant in a system. Trust in a blockchain-based system is established by verification and validation of relevant participant data and transactions, and by immutable recording of appropriate information done with the consensus of the stakeholders.

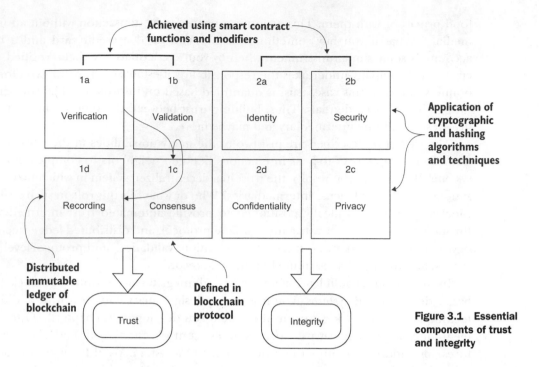

Figure 3.1 Essential components of trust and integrity

You establish trust by verification and validation; this aspect is shown in figure 3.2 as fundamental elements of trust (1a and 1b). Often, people use the terms *verification* and *validation* interchangeably. For smart contract development, we'll differentiate between these two terms. This clarification will aid in better design and development of smart contracts.

To understand the difference between verification and validation, let's consider these real-world examples:

- Verification (1a) is similar to a Transportation Security Administration (TSA) agent checking your identification at an airport security checkpoint. Verification is about general rules.
- Validation (1b) is similar to an airline's gate agent making sure that you have a valid boarding pass. Validation is about application-specific rules.

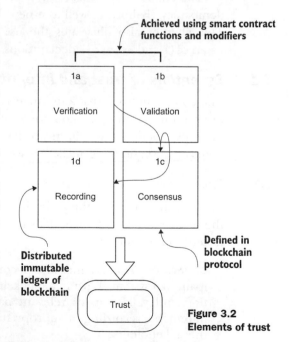

Figure 3.2 Elements of trust

- The recording (1d) is similar to TSA's and the airline's centralized database updated with the traveler's status. In the case of blockchain, the differences are that recording is on a distributed immutable ledger and the use of consensus protocol (1c).

You can think of verification as dealing with general or global requirements within a problem space and validation as being application- or data-specific. In the case of a blockchain application, the transactions are verified and validated according to general rules as well as application-specific rules and conditions.

The bottom two cells (1c and 1d) of the trust quad chart in figure 3.2, consensus and immutable distributed recording, are the responsibility of the blockchain protocol. The purpose of the consensus process is to make sure that a consistent set of transactions (a block) is recorded on the blockchain. As you'll recall from chapter 1, nodes form the blockchain network. An exact copy of each block, chosen by the consensus process, is recorded on all the distributed nodes. The chain of blocks is deemed to be immutable because each of the nodes or stakeholders has a copy; no one node can make changes without its copy going out of sync with the others. The blockchain protocol and infrastructure determine the necessary rules and software for these two cells (consensus and recording) of the trust chart. You can focus on these two aspects of trust when you develop and contribute at the protocol level. As an application developer, you'll design only the application-specific verification and validation (the top two cells, 1a and 1b).

### 3.1.2  Integrity

Integrity is about the truthfulness of the participants, the messages they send, the data, and the operations of the system under consideration.

> **DEFINITION**  *Integrity,* in the context of blockchain, means ensuring the security and privacy of data and confidentiality of transactions.

Integrity, shown in the second quad of figure 3.1, begins with a method for uniquely identifying the peer participant on the node. In a decentralized system, no username and password identify who you are, as in a centralized system. Blockchain account address is a simple way to specify a unique identity for a participant. The elements of integrity—identity, security, privacy, and confidentiality (figure 3.1, 2a to 2d)—are based predominantly on the private-public key pair concept. You'll learn in chapter 5 how to implement security and privacy aspects for participant data, using a combination of cryptography and hashing algorithms. Likewise, you'll learn about confidentiality (figure 3.1, 2d) and its implementation in a micropayment channel application in chapter 7.

In this chapter, you'll design a smart contract for application-specific trust and integrity. The ballot smart contract illustrates verification, validation, and identity and privacy aspects. Let's explore applying these features to solve a well-known problem. Digital democracy has been a quest ever since the advent of the internet. Balloting is an exciting topic that garners the interest of a wide range of people. We'll solve a balloting problem that allows for electronic voting by a set of decentralized participants.

## 3.2    Digital democracy problem

*Digital democracy* encompasses many things, from simple digital identity cards in India to e-residency in Estonia. In the context of this chapter, you'll be concerned with systems that enable democracy by using digitization, such as internet-based communication and information systems—in particular, using internet-based electronic voting systems instead of paper ballots or mechanical machines. Let's begin discussing the problem with a problem statement.

> **PROBLEM STATEMENT**   Consider an online ballot application. People vote to choose a proposal from a set of proposals. A chairperson registers the people who can vote, and only registered voters can vote (only once) on a proposal of their choice. The chairperson's vote is weighted twice (x2) as heavily as regular people's votes. The ballot process goes through four states (Init, Regs, Vote, Done), and the respective operations (initialize, register, vote, count votes) can be performed only in the corresponding states.

### 3.2.1    Designing a solution

We'll apply the design principles you learned in chapter 2, which are available in appendix B. Please review these principles before starting the design process.

Here are the recommended steps for solving the ballot problem:

1 Apply design principles 1, 2, and 3 to design the *use case diagram*; use that diagram to discover the users, data assets, and transactions.
2 Use design principle 4, design the *contract diagram* that defines the data, modifiers, or rules for verification and validation, and functions.
3 Using the contract diagram, develop the *smart contract* in Solidity.
4 Compile and deploy the smart contract in the Remix IDE, and test it.

This ballot problem offers an opportunity to add one more UML design diagram: that of a *finite state machine* (FSM) model to represent the phases of the voting process.

### 3.2.2    Use case diagram

Let's analyze the ballot problem using the UML diagram use case diagram. This diagram is the starting point for achieving the design principles of identifying the users, assets, and transactions. The use case diagram is shown in figure 3.3. The main actors and roles are as follows:

- The *chairperson* can register voters and also self-register and vote.
- *Voters* can vote.
- *Anybody* can request the winner or results of the ballot process.

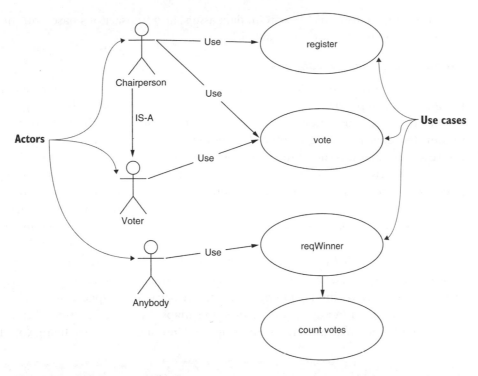

**Figure 3.3  Ballot use case diagram**

In this simple case, every call to the reqWinner() function will count the votes. Although this implementation is not efficient, you can leave it as such for now. In later versions, you can improve on this codebase. The diagram also captures one of the requirements of the problem: the fact that the chairperson is also a voter. The IS-A specialization relationship shows this: the chairperson *is a* voter, as shown in figure 3.3. The use cases are register, vote, and reqWinner; the function count votes is an internal function, as shown in the count votes use case of the diagram.

### 3.2.3  Incremental development of code

The code for the balloting problem will be developed in four incremental steps so that you can to learn the smart contract development process. Also, this process will allow you to learn Solidity language features by example. The four incremental steps in the development are as follows:

1  *BallotV1*—Define the data structures for the smart contract, and test them.
2  *BallotV2*—Add the constructor and the function to change the state of voting.
3  *BallotV3*—Add the other functions of the smart contract and a modifier to illustrate the use of Solidity features for enabling trust.
4  *BallotV4*—Add the trust elements require(), revert(), and assert(), and the function access modifier.

Let's now list the users of the system, data assets, and transactions based on the problem statement and the use case analysis.

### 3.2.4   *Users, assets, and transactions*

Now you're ready to apply design principle 3. Recall from the problem statement that the goal is for users to choose one of the many available proposals by voting on them. Based on the use case analysis in figure 3.3, the following are the users of the ballot system: the chairperson, the voters (including the chairperson), and anybody who's interested in the outcome of the balloting process.

The data assets, in this case, are the proposals on which the voters are voting. You also need to keep track of the voters, whether they have voted or not, and the weight of their votes. (Recall that the chairperson is also a voter and that the chairperson's vote counts as double, weight=2.) Let's use this analysis as a guideline and code the two data items identified: `voters` and `proposals`, as shown in listing 3.1. The phases of the voting specified in the problem statement are also coded into an `enum` or enumerated data type. `enum` is an internal data type provided by Solidity. A `Voter` type and `Proposal` type are defined using the `struct` construct, and a special voter, `chairperson`, is also defined. A `mapping` data structure maps the voter account address to the voter details, and an array defines the proposals (numbers) that are being voted on.

**Listing 3.1   Data items (BallotV1.sol)**

```
pragma solidity >=0.4.2 =<0.6.0;
contract BallotV1 {
                                    Type Voter contains
    struct Voter {        ⟵        the voter details.
        uint weight;
        bool voted;
        uint vote;
    }                              Type Proposal contains proposal
    struct Proposal {     ⟵        details: for now, only voteCount.
        uint voteCount;
    }

    address chairperson;
    mapping(address => Voter) voters;    ⟵  Mapping of voter
    Proposal[] proposals;                    address to voter details

    enum Phase {Init, Regs, Vote, Done}  ⟵
    Phase public state = Phase.Init;         Various phases (0,1,2,3) of voting,
    }                                        state initialized to Init phase
```

You can enter this code in the Remix IDE. This step allows you to check the syntax of the data items as well as the values of any public variables. Create a BallotV1.sol smart contract, and copy in the contents of listing 3.1. If you have the just-in-time compiler enabled (in the left panel of the Remix IDE), you see a red X mark next to any code line with a syntax error. Correct any errors; then compile the code. You'll see a check on the compile icon in the panel on the left, indicating that the compile process was successful. Make sure that the environment is set to the JavaScript VM, click the Deploy & Run Transactions icon, and then click the Deploy button (orange) in the middle of the left panel.

You should see the user interface with one button: state. Click that button, and you should see its value as 0 for the state value of Phase.Init. Now change the value of the state to Phase.Done in the code editor. Repeat the compile and deploy steps, and click the State button again. You should see the value of state as 3 for Phase.Done. Three test runs are shown in figure 3.4. Note that the variable state is available for user interaction (testing) because it was declared public in the code. If you remove the public visibility modifier from the state, you will not see the state button in the user interface.

You've completed a simple exercise to make sure that all the data definitions are syntax error-free. In the process, you also learned about a few more Solidity language types—enums and arrays—and used structs, mappings, and the public visibility modifier again. Note that the Remix IDE helps with incremental development of your code by allowing you to check the syntax of the data elements before you add functions. This step is useful for testing the data structures before you get into coding the functions.

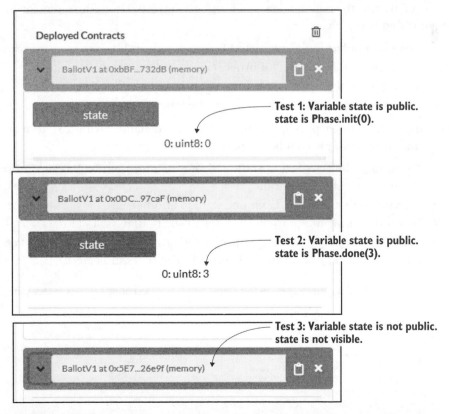

**Figure 3.4   Remix user interface for three runs (state = 0, state = 3, state is not public)**

### 3.2.5   *Finite state machine diagram*

The use case diagram in figure 3.3 provides only static details; it has no way to depict the dynamic timing and state transitions that the ballot process requires. Moreover, the diagram doesn't impose the order in which the operations should occur: registration period, voting period, and the determination of the winner. Do you now see the need for another design diagram that depicts the system dynamics?

To represent system dynamics, you'll use a UML finite state machine, or FSM diagram. The FSM is well founded in formal computer science and mathematics, but it is also a versatile UML design diagram. It is an important diagram because it represents the various state changes a smart contract goes through that are dependent on time and other conditions. Often, the conditions and rules are based on various phases of a real-world contract or process, which brings us to design principle 5.

> **DESIGN PRINCIPLE 5**   Use a finite state machine UML diagram to represent system dynamics such as state transitions within a smart contract.

In a voting process, voters are registered first, and there usually are deadlines for registration and voting. In some U.S. states, you have to be registered 30 days before the election day, and the voting takes place and is completed in a single day for in-person voters. If that is the case

- Registration has to be completed before voting and before a specific deadline.
- The functions for the ballot process proceed in a certain sequence.
- Voting is open only for a specified period.
- The winner can be determined only after the voting.

Let's apply this design principle and capture the dynamics with a state diagram, as shown in figure 3.5. This FSM is composed of

- *States*, including a starting state and one or more ending states, indicated by double circles by convention
- *Transitions* that take you from one state to another
- *Inputs* that bring about the transitions (T=0, T+10 days, T+11 days)
- Zero or more *outputs* during transitions. Registration (`Regs`), voting (`Vote`), and counting (`Done`), for example, happen in the states indicated.

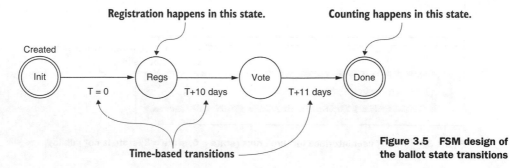

Figure 3.5   **FSM design of the ballot state transitions**

Earlier, we defined four phases or states representing the ballot problem. These four phases are `Init`, `Regs`, `Vote`, and `Done`. The system begins its operation after initialization in the `Init` phase and then transitions into the `Regs` phase, where registration can take place. After ten days (in this case) for registration, the system moves to the `Vote` phase, in which voting goes on for a day, and then enters the (ballot) `Done` phase, at which point the winning proposal can be requested. Transitions in this case are temporal, or time-driven; you can see this in figure 3.5, with T=0, T+10, and T+11 limiting the duration of each phase. These dynamic rules for transitioning through the balloting process have to be captured when you code the smart contract to enable trust.

Now let's translate these design representations into code, as shown in listing 3.2. This listing, BallotV2.sol, has all the contents of BallotV1.sol from listing 3.1, plus a constructor and an additional function: `changeState()`. The enumerated type `Phase` is used for setting the state variable `state`. Your goal is to effect and observe the state changes. Let's assume that the ballot process's chairperson is controlling when the transitions happen by calling the `changeState()` function with a parameter value of 0, 1, 2, or 3 (representing the four phases).

---

**Listing 3.2   Solution with voting states (Ballotv2.sol)**

```
// include the code from BallotV1.sol, not shown here

enum Phase {Init, Regs, Vote, Done}          ←——| Internally coded as 0,1,2,3
   // Phase can take only 0,1,2,3 values: Others invalid

Phase public state = Phase.Init;
                                                  Constructor makes contract
constructor (uint numProposals) public {          deployer the chairperson
      chairperson = msg.sender;
      voters[chairperson].weight = 2; // weight 2 for testing purposes
      for (uint prop = 0; prop < numProposals; prop ++)
            proposals.push(Proposal(0));          Number of proposals
                                                  is a parameter for the
   }                                              constructor
```

**State changer function** →
```
   // function for changing Phase: can be done only by chairperson
   function changeState(Phase x) public {
      if (msg.sender != chairperson) {revert();}   ←—— Only chairperson can change
      if (x < state) revert();               ←——        state; otherwise, revert
      state = x;         State has to progress in 0,1,2,3
   }                     order; otherwise, revert
   }
```

In listing 3.2, only the constructor for BallotV2 and the `changeState()` functions are shown. When you copy this code into the Remix IDE, be sure to preface it with the contents of listing 3.1. The complete BallotV2.sol is available in the codebase of this chapter.

Let's review the code. Initially, the `state` variable is set to `Init` by static initialization. The account (`msg.sender`) invoking the constructor is designated as the chairperson. More appropriately, we could say that the chairperson initiates the ballot process by deploying the smart contract. The number of proposals is initialized, and the chairperson's vote is given a weight of 2 (arbitrarily). Voting-phase changes are affected by the function `changeState()`; you can enforce that only the chairperson can change from one phase to another and that `Phase` can take only the values {0,1,2,3} for {Init, Regs, Vote, Done}. You want the phases to progress from `Init` to `Done` via `Regs` and `Vote`. Let's explore how all this works:

1. Enter the code for the BallotV2 smart contract into the Remix IDE, and check the state change functionality.
2. Compile and deploy the contract with 3 as a parameter when you click the Deploy button, indicating that three proposals are available to vote on. Every time you click Deploy, the value in the box to the right of it has to be set to the number of proposals to be voted on.
3. Click the `state` button in the UI to show 0 as the value of the `state`.
4. Now click `changeState`, using 1 as a parameter, and check the value of `state`, which will show 1 for `Regs`.
5. Repeat this test for the other parameter values.

You can also see functions reverting if invalid values are given for their parameters. The Ethereum VM itself will throw an error if you give a negative value as a parameter to the `changeState()` function.

The code in listing 3.2 provides a general pattern for any smart contract that transitions through state changes in its design. In listing 3.2, the rules (for validation) for the state transitions are stated as they are in any other common code, using `if` statements. It is desirable to separate the definition of rules from the actual code of the functions to emphasize the role of the smart contract as a trust intermediator. That's what we'll do next.

### 3.2.6 *Trust intermediation*

Typically, verification, validation, and exceptions in problems are specified by rules to be enforced and conditions to be checked. Additionally, in a blockchain-based application, you should revert or abort any transactions that violate trust (represented by a rule) to prevent bad or unauthorized transactions from becoming part of the immutable ledger of the blockchain. This aspect is a key difference between blockchain programming and a traditional distributed application development. How do you implement these rules and requirements?

Solidity provides various language features and functions that address these trust requirements. These language features are as follows:

- *Modifiers* specify access control rules to *verify* and manage who has control of data and functions to establish trust and privacy. (Perhaps only the chairperson can register members, for example.) These modifiers are also called *access modifiers* to distinguish them from the visibility modifiers (public and private) of functions and data.
- The `require(condition)` declaration *validates* the condition passed as a parameter and reverts the transaction if the check fails. This feature is commonly used for general validation of parameters (such as `age > 21`).
- The `revert()` statement allows you to *revert* a transaction and also prevent it from being recorded on the blockchain. This feature is commonly used in modifier definitions.
- The `assert(condition)` declaration *validates* the condition of the variable or data during the execution of a function and reverts the transaction if the check fails. This feature is used for exceptions when you don't want the condition to fail, such as to validate the head count in the middle of the ocean during a cruise! Another example is to stop your bill payment if there is not enough money in your bank account.

### 3.2.7 *Defining and using modifiers*

As you learned in chapter 2, modifiers are a special programming language structure offered by Solidity for implementing verification and validation rules in a smart contract. Let's first review how to define them and then dig into how to use them effectively.

Listing 3.3 shows the syntax of a modifier, which is somewhat like a function definition:

- It has a header line with a name and parameter list.
- It has a body that specifies the conditions to be checked within a `require` statement.
- This line is followed by `__;` , which represents the code that follows the modifier at the actual location where it would be used. This symbol represents the code that the modifier guards.

The next listing also shows an example use of a modifier. Here, it is verifying that the state of the ballot process is in the correct phase, as specified by the parameter `reqPhase`.

#### Listing 3.3 Modifier definition syntax and example

```
modifier name_of_modifier (parameters)    ⟵─── Modifier syntax
{ require { conditions_to_be_checked};
    _;
}

modifier validPhase(Phase reqPhase)    ⟵─┐
{ require(state == reqPhase);             │ Actual modifier definition
    _;                                    │ for validPhase rule
}
```

Why separate the modifier definition from the function definition? The idea is to separate the verification, validation, and exceptions so that the code clearly articulates the rules that are being enforced by the smart contract for implementing trust and integrity. The special keyword `modifier` can be used by a smart contract auditor (manual or automatic) to make sure that all the rules are defined up front and used as expected. When a modifier representing a rule is defined, it can be used any number of times, like a function call. This pattern allows you to review the code locations where rules are applied easily.

Now let's find out how a modifier is invoked within the code. Listing 3.4 shows an actual function, `register()`, using the modifier `validPhase`. The modifier is located in the header of the function. The traditional code for checking the condition is also shown in the listing's second line, commented out. You can see the elegance of the modifier as opposed to this line (the `if` statement). A review of the function header demonstrates that the state of the voting process is checked (it must be `Phase.Regs`) before anything is done in the function.

---

**Listing 3.4    Use of a modifier**

**Modifier in the header of function; if the
condition is not met, revert the transaction**

```
function register(address voter) public validPhase(Phase.Regs) {
        //if (state != Phase.Regs) {revert();}
        if (msg.sender != chairperson || voters[toVoter].voted) return;
        voters[voter].weight = 1;
        voters[voter].voted = false;
        ...
    }
```

**Equivalent
traditional
code**

---

The use of modifiers as trust implementers (intermediaries) results in design principle 6.

> **DESIGN PRINCIPLE 6**   Implement the verification and validation needed for trust intermediation by using modifiers specifying the rules and conditions in a smart contract. Typically, verification covers general rules about participants, and validation covers conditions for checking application-specific data.

Let's put all these concepts together in the next composite design representation: the contract diagram.

### 3.2.8    Contract diagram including modifiers

In this section, you'll use the analysis and design completed so far to develop a contract diagram (design principle 4; see appendix B) listing the data structures and functions needed for coding the Ballot smart contract. In the contract diagram shown in figure 3.6, you can see the definition of one modifier, `validPhase`, in the modifier box after the data definition. In this case, only one example of a modifier is defined to help you understand the modifier feature.

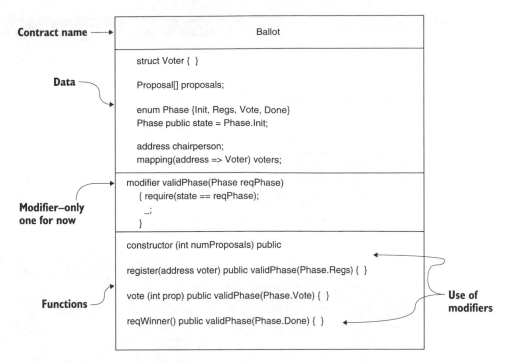

**Figure 3.6  Ballot contract diagram**

Note that the modifier validPhase has a parameter Phase reqPhase. In the functions box of the contract diagram, you see the repeated use of the validPhase modifier in the headers of three functions. Observe that the validPhase modifier is called with three different actual parameters—Regs, Vote, and Done—from the headers of the various functions, which illustrates the flexibility and reusability of the modifier. Before each function, the modifier is applied and executed with the actual parameter value. Inside the modifier, this actual parameter is compared with the current state of the voting process. If it does not match the state at the time the function is called, the function call is reverted, and it is not executed or recorded on the blockchain. This validation is the role of the modifier.

Now you can proceed to complete the Solidity code for the Ballot contract based on the details specified in the contract diagram.

### 3.2.9  *Putting it all together*

The complete code in Solidity is given in listing 3.5. Only the functions are shown because we already reviewed the data and modifier definitions in listings 3.1 through 3.4. Earlier, you saw only the templates of the functions; here, you see the completed code. Note that the Phase component is included in this code to illustrate the state transitions, the FSM-based design of dynamics, and the use of modifier-based validation.

**Listing 3.5   Solution with modifier `validPhase` (BallotV3.sol)**

```solidity
// include listing 3.1 data here

    // modifiers
    modifier validPhase(Phase reqPhase)
     { require(state == reqPhase);
       _;
     }

    constructor (uint numProposals) public  {
        chairperson = msg.sender;
        voters[chairperson].weight = 2; // weight 2 for testing purposes
        for (uint prop = 0; prop < numProposals; prop ++)
            proposals.push(Proposal(0));
        state = Phase.Regs; // change Phase to Regs

    }

    function changeState(Phase x) public {
        if (msg.sender != chairperson) {revert();}
        if (x < state ) revert();
        state = x;
    }


    function register(address voter) public validPhase(Phase.Regs) {
        if (msg.sender != chairperson || voters[voter].voted) revert();
        voters[voter].weight = 1;
        voters[voter].voted = false;

    }

    function vote(uint toProposal) public validPhase(Phase.Vote)  {

        Voter memory sender = voters[msg.sender];
        if (sender.voted || toProposal >= proposals.length) revert();
        sender.voted = true;
        sender.vote = toProposal;
        proposals[toProposal].voteCount += sender.weight;


    }

    function reqWinner() public validPhase(Phase.Done) view returns (uint
    ➥ winningProposal) {
        uint winningVoteCount = 0;
        for (uint prop = 0; prop < proposals.length; prop++)
            if (proposals[prop].voteCount > winningVoteCount) {
                winningVoteCount = proposals[prop].voteCount;
                winningProposal = prop;
            }

    }
```

Annotations:
- **Voting state change to be ordered by the chairperson**
- **Explicit validation using if statement**
- **validPhase modifier used in function headers**
- **View function, Tx not recorded on the chain**

### STORAGE VS. MEMORY VARIABLES

In the vote function, you'll find a local variable Voter struct. In Solidity, variables can be defined as storage (persistent and gets stored in the block) or memory (transient, does not get stored in the block). By default, simple variables are memory type, temporary, and do not get recorded in the block. The struct data structure is, by default, a storage variable, so you need to declare whether it is a memory or storage type when you use it. In the case of vote function, we've defined its local variable Voter struct as a memory type so that it does not waste storage in the block. When you define a struct inside a function as a local variable, you'll have to declare explicitly whether it is a memory or storage type.

### FUNCTION DETAILS

There are five functions, including the constructor:

- constructor()—The constructor function is called when the smart contract is deployed. The account number that deploys the contract is that of the chairperson. The constructor takes the number of proposals to be voted on as a parameter. It initializes the data elements and the state of the voting phase (to Regs from Init).
- changeState()—This function changes the state of the voting to the correct phase. It can be executed only by the chairperson, and the parameter value has to be in the correct order (1, 2, 3). Execute this function from the chairperson account's address before transitioning to register(), vote(), and reqWinner() for the first time. The statement if (x < state) revert(); works only for simple state advancement. This basic version of state change is improved to a generic version in chapter 4.
- register()—This function should be executed only by the chairperson account; otherwise, it will revert and won't be executed. It will also revert if the voted Boolean variable is true and if the state is not Phase.Regs.
- vote()—This function can execute only during the voting phase (Phase.Vote). This rule is enforced by the modifier (rule) validPhase(Phase.Vote). You can observe the validation of the "one person–one vote" rule and the proposal number. (When the voting period ends, the state is changed to Phase.Done by the chairperson.)
- reqWinner()—This function counts the votes and identifies the winning proposal by its number. It executes the counting every time it's called. During testing, this is okay because you might call the function once or twice, but for production, you may want to optimize it. (Also, in future designs, you'll move this function off-chain or out of the smart contract code.) Note that this function is a "view" function, so it's not recorded on the chain.

Review the roles of these functions before you move on to testing the complete Ballot in the Remix IDE.

## 3.3    Testing

Testing of smart contracts is a crucial step in the Dapp design process. Chapter 10 is fully dedicated to writing automated test scripts. In this chapter, you'll start learning about the basics of testing to lay the foundation for test-driven development.

Load the code for the ballot problem into the Remix IDE in a file named BallotV3.sol, and compile it. Click the Deploy & Run Transactions icon, and within the JavaScript VM, choose an account address in the Account box in the panel at the top left. To the right of the Deploy button, you'll see a box for the number of proposals. Enter the number of proposals (such as 3) in the text box next to it, and click Deploy. This action will invoke the constructor with number of proposals (in this case 3) as a parameter.

By now, you should be familiar with the various areas of the Remix IDE. Figure 3.7 shows a screenshot taken during the testing of the Ballot smart contract. During testing, you'll be working with the user interface provided by Remix at the bottom of the left panel. You can see the results of execution in the output console at the bottom of the middle panel, below the code. After you deploy the Ballot smart contract with 3 as the parameter for the number of proposals, click the State button. It should show 1, representing Phase.Regs (mapped to 1 in the enum). In this phase, you can start registering accounts (voters). Note that you won't use the Init state in this particular solution, even though it's defined in the problem.

To make testing easier, copy the account numbers for the chairperson and the voters (as shown in table 3.1) from Remix, and save them somewhere convenient (such as a digital notepad). These accounts are the bottom 5 of the 15 test accounts available in the Remix IDE. Recall from the problem statement (section 3.2) and use case

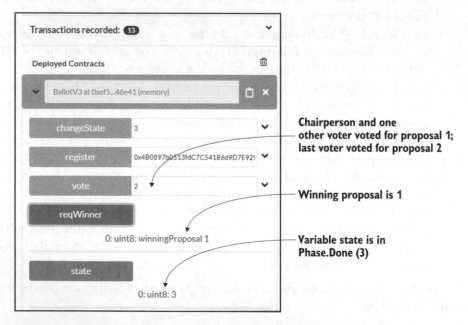

**Figure 3.7    Remix user interface after the execution of BallotV3.sol**

diagram (figure 3.3) that the chairperson is also a voter and that the chairperson's vote is weighted twice as heavily as that of a regular voter.

> **NOTE** The five accounts in Table 3.1 used to be the only five accounts in the previous version of Remix IDE (2019). The newer version of Remix IDE (2020) has ten additional test accounts that are random, which means that these accounts are different every time you reload. I've chosen to use the permanent five accounts at the bottom of the Account drop-down list of the Remix IDE. Be aware of such changes in the future, and be ready to adapt.

**Table 3.1  Accounts and their roles**

| Account addresses | Roles |
| --- | --- |
| 0xca35b7d915458ef540ade6068dfe2f44e8fa733c | Chairperson and voter (weight =2) |
| 0x14723a09acff6d2a60dcdf7aa4aff308fddc160c | Voter (weight =1) |
| 0x4b0897b0513fdc7c541b6d9d7e929c4e5364d2d | Voter (weight =1) |
| 0x583031d1113ad414f02576bd6afabfb302140225 | Voter (weight =1) |
| 0xdD870fA1b7C4700F2BD7f44238821C26f7392148 | Yet another voter |

A robust testing process includes two different types of testing:

- *Positive tests*—When given a valid set of data inputs, make sure that the smart contract performs correctly and as expected
- *Negative tests*—When given invalid data inputs, make sure that the smart contract catches errors during verification and validation and that functions revert.

### 3.3.1  Positive tests

Let's begin testing with the positive tests. In the Remix IDE, follow these steps:

1  Register three more voters (recall that the constructor already registers the chairperson). Copy and paste the second account number from the Account drop-down box (0x147 . . .) into the register() function's parameter box. You can copy it from your notepad or use the little copy button to the right of where the account number is displayed in the IDE. Make sure that the chairperson's account (0xca3 . . .) is selected in the Account box, and click the register button in the user interface. (Recall that only the chairperson can register voters.)

2  Repeat step 1 for two more voter accounts.

3  Use the stateChange() function to change the state to 2 or Phase.Vote. (Make sure that the chairperson's account is selected in the Account box before you click the stateChange button.) Click the state button representing the public variable state. If you see the number 2, you are ready to vote.

4  With the chairperson's account selected in the Account box, enter 2 in the vote() function's parameter box—that is, the chair is voting for proposal number 2—and click the vote button.

5  In the Account box, select the second account that was registered in step 1 of this test sequence. Enter 1 for the proposal number in the vote() function's parameter box, and click the vote button.

6  Repeat step 5 for the other two voter account numbers. Now you are set to test the results.

7  Change the state (from the chairperson's account) by using the state-Change() function with parameter 3. state should now be Phase.Done, or 3. Now you can call the reqWinner() function that does the counting. Click the reqWinner button, and the winner should show up as proposal number 1.

This step is the end of the positive test. If you like, you can do an exhaustive positive test for all the accounts in the test chain provided by Remix.

NOTE  Working with the user interface may take a little practice. Be patient. Account numbers may be different when you access the Remix IDE.

### 3.3.2  Negative tests

Now let's move on to the negative tests. These tests might be an exhaustive list of tests covering every possible scenario or a minimal set of tests covering only the most likely conditions. You can use the following test scenarios and action plans as guidelines to develop the other tests needed for your applications. Three representative negative test scenarios and the steps for executing them in the Remix IDE are given here:

- Account other than chairperson registers a voter. This transaction should be rejected in the register() function's regular code validation.

  From the Account drop-down list in the panel on the left, choose an account other than the chairperson's (say, 0x147 . . .). Recall that the first account is the designated account for the chairperson. Now copy and paste any of the voter accounts from the first column of table 3.1 into the register() function's parameter box, and click the register button. The function call should error out, as you can see in the console at the bottom of the central panel. Figure 3.8 shows the error and revert messages.

```
transact to BallotWithModifiers.register errored: VM error: revert.
revert  The transaction has been reverted to the initial state.
```

Figure 3.8  register() function error
and revert messages in the Remix console

- The smart contract is in the state Phase.Done, and an account tries to vote. The modifier validPhase should reject this transaction.

Make sure that you are in Phase.Done by clicking the State button in the user interface. It should show 3 for this phase. Choose the chairperson's account (0xca3 . . .) from the Account drop-down list in the left panel. Enter a number (0 to 2) in the vote() function's parameter box, and click the vote button. This transaction should error out and be reverted due to the modifier validPhase in the vote() function validating the correct phase. You should observe this error in the console.

- An account tries to vote for a proposal number that doesn't exist. This transaction is rejected by the condition in the vote() function.

  This test again concerns the vote() function. Close the current deployment by clicking the X button in the top-right corner of the user interface. Redeploy the contract by clicking the Deploy button and entering 3 as a parameter to the constructor. Register an account as a voter, and change state to 2 or Phase.vote. Now enter a number (>= 3) in the vote() function's parameter box, and click vote. Because the valid proposal numbers are 0, 1, and 2, this should error out as validated by the condition in the vote() function: toProposal >= proposals.length.

These examples should give you an idea about testing the smart contract. In this case, you are testing it manually in the interface provided by the Remix IDE, and you can review the errors in the console. In chapter 10, after you've developed the entire application stack, you'll learn to write test scripts, thus automating the manual test process.

## 3.4 *Using modifiers, require(), and revert()*

You've learned how to define a rule by using the modifier feature in Solidity. What if you have more than one rule for executing a function? You can apply a series of rules (access modifiers) to a function invocation. What if a condition is to be checked during or after the execution of the statements within a function? In this case, you can use a require() clause that reverts the function if the condition specified within it fails. The modifier validPhase specified in the Ballot smart contract uses a require() clause for checking the condition inside it and, if it fails, reverts the transaction. You also saw the use of revert() in the vote() function for validation that the voter has not already voted.

In the Ballot example, a single modifier was used in the function headers to validate the system parameters. Recall that the validPhase modifier enforces that all three functions—vote(), register(), and reqWinner()—are in the correct phase when they are invoked. Let's now define one more modifier to reinforce your understanding of modifiers. You'll do this for the validation within the register() function of the same smart contract. The modifier definition and use are shown in the next listing. Recall from the problem statement (section 3.2) that only the chairperson can register other voters. You can enforce this rule by using the onlyChair modifier.

Listing 3.6    Definition and use of `onlyChair` modifier

```
if (msg.sender != chairperson ..)          ◁─────  Statement to be replaced
                                                   by modifier onlyChair

   modifier onlyChair ()                    ◁─────  Modifier onlyChair
   { require(msg.sender == chairperson);            definition
   _;
}

function register(address voter) public validPhase(Phase.Regs) onlyChair  ◁──
{
                                                   Use of two modifiers in
                                                   register() function's header
```

You apply multiple modifiers to a function by specifying them in a whitespace-separated list. Modifiers are evaluated in the order in which they're presented, so if the outcome of one modifier depends on that of another, make sure that you order the modifiers in the right sequence. In Ballotv3.sol, which uses the access modifiers `validPhase` and `onlyChair`, the `validPhase` modifier may take precedence and be applied first. In other words, if the phase is incorrect, you don't have to check who is invoking the `register()` function. The header of the `register()` function, therefore, becomes

```
Function register(address voter) public validPhase(Phase.Regs)
                                          onlyChair
```

Here's another example from an online buying use case:

```
function buy(..) payable enoughMoney itemAvail returns (..)
```

A function call to `buy()` verifies whether enough money is available (with the `enoughMoney` modifier) before checking the availability of the item. If enough money is not available, the function reverts without checking the item's availability through the `itemAvail` modifier.

## 3.5    *Assert() declarations*

So far, our discussion of modifiers has involved two special built-in functions of Solidity: `require()` and `revert()`. In this section, you'll learn about one more special function, `assert()`, which asserts that a condition is met during the computation process inside a function.

Suppose that you would like at least three votes (or majority votes) to be cast for the winning proposal in the ballot problem we've been discussing. You can enforce this rule by using an `assert()` clause at the end of the `reqWinner()` function. You can validate the parameters not only on entry to a smart contract function, but also at various stages of computation inside a function. Using `assert(winningVoteCount>=3)` will cause the function to revert if a vote count of 1 or 2 is the highest or number of voters is less than 3.

**NOTE** The value of 3 is used here for quick testing. In a more realistic case, you could use the value for majority in the assert() function or some other exceptional condition that should be checked.

Listing 3.7 shows the Ballot smart contract code with these incremental improvements: another modifier, onlyChair, and the assert() function. The combination of revert(), require(), and assert() along with modifiers and their proper use will help you address exceptions through verification and validation, resulting in robust trust intermediation by the smart contracts. require() used instead of an if statement means that a transaction will be reverted if a condition fails. If the function call reverts, no Tx is recorded on the blockchain for this function call. It is critical to understand that revert() stops the Tx from happening.

**Listing 3.7  With all trust rules coded (BallotV4.sol)**

```
// modifiers
modifier validPhase(Phase reqPhase)         ◁────────┐
  { require(state == reqPhase);                       │  Two modifiers,
    _;                                                │  including onlyChair
  }                                                   │
  modifier onlyChair()                       ◁────────┘
   {require(msg.sender == chairperson);
    _;
   }

  constructor (uint numProposals) public  {
     chairperson = msg.sender;
     voters[chairperson].weight = 2; // weight 2 for testing purposes
     for (uint prop = 0; prop < numProposals; prop ++)
         proposals.push(Proposal(0));
     state = Phase.Regs;
  }
                                                            Use of onlyChair
                                                            modifier
  function changeState(Phase x) onlyChair public {  ◁──────┘

      require (x > state );
      state = x;                                        Use of two modifiers:
  }                                                     validPhase and onlyChair

  function register(address voter) public validPhase(Phase.Regs)
                                              onlyChair {   ◁───

      require (! voters[voter].voted);

      voters[voter].weight = 1;
      // voters[voter].voted = false;
  }                                              Use of memory instead of
                                                 storage type for local variables


  function vote(uint toProposal) public validPhase(Phase.Vote)  {

      Voter memory sender = voters[msg.sender];   ◁────────
```

*require() instead of traditional if*

```
        require (!sender.voted);                          require() instead
        require (toProposal < proposals.length);          of traditional if

        sender.voted = true;
        sender.vote = toProposal;
        proposals[toProposal].voteCount += sender.weight;
    }

    function reqWinner() public validPhase(Phase.Done) view
                            returns (uint winningProposal)
    {

        uint winningVoteCount = 0;
        for (uint prop = 0; prop < proposals.length; prop++)
            if (proposals[prop].voteCount > winningVoteCount) {
                winningVoteCount = proposals[prop].voteCount;
                winningProposal = prop;
            }
        assert(winningVoteCount>=3);              ◁——— Use of assert()
    }
}
```

The functions assert() and require() are similar in that both check conditions and revert the transaction if the check fails. You use require() for common validations such as checking the limits of a variable's value (such as age >= 18). You expect require() to fail sometimes; that is reasonable. assert() is meant for handling exceptions. You expect that this condition should not normally fail. To check the head count at a summer camp, for example, you might use assert(headcount == 44). You don't want this check to fail in the middle of the night! On a more serious note, an assert() failure costs a lot more in wasted blockchain gas (execution cost) than require() reverting, so be selective about what to use when. Use assert() sparingly for managing exceptions. Use require() for validation of data, computations, and parameter values.

At this time, you can load listing 3.7, Ballotv4.sol, into the Remix IDE. Review the code to see all the incremental improvements (modifiers, require(), revert(), and assert()), and explore its workings.

## 3.6   *Best practices*

Now that you've learned about some significant additional features specific to blockchain application development, it's an appropriate time to review some best practices:

- Keep your smart contract code simple, coherent, and auditable. Let each state variable and function specified in a smart contract address a single problem. Do not include redundant data or unrelated functions. Make the smart contract functions auditable by using custom function modifiers instead of inline (if/else) code for checking pre- and post-conditions of a function's execution.

- Use function access modifiers for
  - Implementing rules, policies, and regulations for data access for all the participants
  - Implementing common rules for all who may access a function
  - Declaratively validating application-specific conditions
  - Providing auditable elements to allow verification of the correctness of a smart contract
- Use the `memory` type as a qualifier for local variables that don't need to be stored on the blockchain. Memory variables are transient and are not stored. (You saw an example in listing 3.7.)
- Develop the smart contract in incremental steps, debugging each step.
- Be aware that the Solidity language updates frequently to improve performance and security. In this case, you have to adjust your code to meet the requirements of the latest version.

## 3.7   Retrospective

The design process you've learned in this chapter—creating a use case diagram; identifying users, data assets, and FSM state transitions; creating a contract diagram; and writing smart contract code—enables you to analyze a problem systematically and deliver a suitable smart contract solution. The smart contract syntax is similar to that of class in object-oriented programming, with the additional caveat that especially careful design is required for the trust and integrity elements.

You've also learned several special techniques for realizing these trust elements, including implementing trust intermediation through modifiers that enable validation and verification of conditions in a smart contract. Modifiers can also support privacy, security, confidentiality, and (thus) integrity by managing access to your data and functions.

## 3.8   Summary

- Trust and integrity are critical needs in a decentralized system, in which the participants operate beyond traditional boundaries of trust. In a decentralized system, no humans are checking your credentials, such as a driver's license, and no system is verifying your username/password combination for authentication.
- Trust in blockchain-based application development is achieved by verification and validation through a trio of features: modifiers, `require()`, and `assert()`.
- The `revert()` declaration reverts a function call and prevents transactions from being recorded in the blockchain's immutable ledger, thus preventing invalid information from accumulating in the ledger.
- FSM design provides another important design diagram, especially for the design of smart contracts with state transitions.

- The Remix web IDE gives you a one-stop web platform for blockchain-based application development, including account numbers, transactions, and recording. In chapters 6–11, you'll use this knowledge to develop Dapps in a desktop environment.

- Armed with your knowledge of design principles, the design process, and the techniques for trust, you are ready to solve blockchain problems, represent your solutions by using a variety of design diagrams, and code smart contracts in the Solidity language. You'll learn in chapters 5–7 about further strengthening trust in decentralized applications through algorithmic approaches using cryptography and secure hashing.

# *From smart contracts to Dapps*
# 4

---

**This chapter covers**

- Designing the directory structure and code elements of a Dapp
- Developing Dapps using the Truffle suite
- Connecting a Dapp front end to a smart contract
- Managing accounts with the MetaMask-enabled browser
- Deploying and testing an end-to-end Dapp

In the preceding chapters, you designed and developed the core component of a blockchain application: the smart contract. But the logic coded in a smart contract cannot act alone. You need user-facing applications that will trigger the smart contract functions and blockchain services. These applications invoke smart contract functions, which in turn verify, validate, and record the resulting transactions and data on the distributed ledger of the blockchain. In this chapter, you'll learn about the structure of this larger system, called a *decentralized application (Dapp)*, and

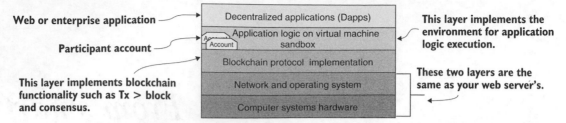

**Figure 4.1   Dapp stack**

explore the techniques and tools for developing Dapps. Recall the Dapp stack and the definition of a Dapp from chapter 1, shown in figure 4.1.

**DEFINITION**   *Dapps* are web or enterprise applications that contain decentralized smart contract logic to invoke blockchain functions.

Figure 4.2 depicts two nodes connected by a blockchain network. If you were to separate the second layer of the Dapp stack (figure 4.1) in these two nodes from its surrounding layers (as indicated by the dotted lines in figure 4.2) and take a peek, you'd see the APIs, ports, server code, and other scripts integrating the layers. These components are the ones you will work on while developing a Dapp.

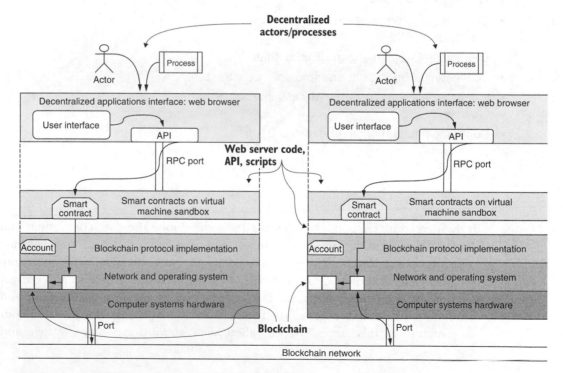

**Figure 4.2   Architectural model of a blockchain network**

Now let's follow the flow in the architectural model shown in figure 4.2. Starting at the top, the users (actors) or processes acting on behalf of users invoke the UI functions. These functions use web application software and blockchain APIs to connect to smart contract functions. Txs representing the smart contract function invocations are recorded on the blockchain. (Note that only some of the necessary Txs will be recorded.) You can follow the operational flow in a node from an actor to the consistent blockchain recording on both nodes via the blockchain network. This figure also illustrates how a blockchain-based Dapp is not a standalone application but is dependent on its host operating system's file system, ports, and network capabilities.

> **NOTE** The architecture in figure 4.2 shows just two nodes. In practice, many such nodes with the same blockchain configuration—the same network ID number and the same genesis block, for example—are connected to make up the blockchain network of a decentralized system.

In this chapter, you'll learn to develop and program the top two layers of the Dapp stack of a blockchain network. But before you start, be warned that blockchain programming is complex and that the Dapp stack is different from a traditional web stack. Following are some of the artifacts and techniques that you'll use for Dapp development:

- For every Dapp project, a `<project>-app` module for the web application and a `<project>-contract` module for smart contracts
- A web server and a package manager (Node.js and the Node Package Manager [npm])
- A blockchain provider (such as Ganache) called web3 provider
- A development tool, the Truffle suite (IDE) that provides an integrated environment to deploy and test a Dapp
- Account management using the MetaMask browser plugin

The end-to-end development process introduced in this chapter will be expanded in future chapters with various other Dapps.

## 4.1 Dapp development using Truffle

Truffle is an integrated development environment and testing framework that provides a suite of features and commands for end-to-end Ethereum-based Dapp development, including commands for

- Initializing a template or base directory structure for a Dapp (`truffle init`)
- Compiling and deploying smart contracts (`truffle compile`)
- Launching a personal blockchain for testing with a console (`truffle develop`)
- Running migration scripts for deploying smart contracts (`truffle migrate`)
- Opening a command-line interface to Truffle for testing without the Dapp UI (`truffle console`)
- Testing the deployed contract (`truffle test`) (discussed in chapter 10)

These are just a few of the core operations possible with Truffle, but they're sufficient to develop and deploy a Dapp.

You've already used an IDE, Remix, so you may be wondering why I'm introducing another one now. The Remix IDE is a learning environment for smart contract development. Truffle takes the Dapp development to the production level. It uses npm modules for project development, dependency management, and systematic migrations. The Truffle suite (IDE) supports scriptable deployment; it provides a migration framework for staging smart contracts and package management capabilities for portability and integration. Use of Truffle in this chapter requires familiarity with the command-line interface and working knowledge of an editor such as gedit or Atom.

### 4.1.1 *The development process*

Here are the major steps in the development process:

1 Analyze the problem statement; design and represent the solution guided by design principles and UML diagrams.
2 Develop and test the smart contract, using the Remix web IDE.
3 Code the end-to-end Dapp, test and deploy it on test blockchains, and migrate it to main networks using the Truffle IDE.

Ready to launch a Dapp development project?

### 4.1.2 *Installing Truffle*

You'll be developing an end-to-end Dapp with a web client for the user interface. The prerequisites for this project are

- *Operating system*—Linux Ubuntu 18.04, macOS (Sierra or later), or Windows 10 (or later)
- *Web server for the web client interface*—Node.js v12.16.0 or later
- *Package manager*—npm 6.13 or later
- *IDE*—Truffle 0.5.X or later
- *Smart contract language toolchain*—Solidity 0.5.16 or later (comes with the Truffle suite)
- *Browser/web client*—Chrome and the MetaMask (LTS) plugin
- *Editor*—Atom, gedit, VSCode or any other editor of your choice

In this list, Node.js serves as your web server for the Dapp front end, and MetaMask will hook into a specified blockchain to manage the accounts, acting as a pipe between the application front end and the blockchain node that hosts the accounts, as shown in figure 4.2.

> **NOTE**  All the commands shown here are to be typed or copied and pasted to the command line of a *terminal window*. Pressing Enter after entry will execute the command. Also, note that the version numbers may be different when you're running npm install. That's all right; npm pulls the right versions for the required modules.

Follow these steps to install the required software packages:

1 Install the operating system:

For Linux, download and install Ubuntu Linux LTS. You can also use CentOS, Arch Linux, OpenSUSE, or other distributions. The long-term support (LTS) version is recommended instead of the new releases for security and stability.

For macOS, download and install Homebrew (https://brew.sh).

For Windows, make sure that you have a 64-bit machine with the Windows 10 operating system.

2 Install the browser.

Download Chrome from https://www.google.com/chrome, and follow setup to complete the installation process. Google Chrome should start automatically when installation is complete.

3 Download and install Node.js and npm LTS from https://nodejs.org/en.

You can also install these packages from the repositories by running the following commands in a terminal window:

- Linux—`sudo apt-get install nodejs npm`
- macOS—`brew install node`

For Windows, download the 64-bit version installer, execute the .exe file, and accept all default options when installing

4 Check the installation and versions (node v12.16.0 and npm 6.13.4 and later) by running the following commands in a terminal window:

```
node -v
npm -v
```

5 Install the Truffle suite (IDE) from its GitHub repository at https://github.com/trufflesuite/truffle or via npm as follows, and verify that its version is 5.1.X or later:

```
npm install -g truffle
```

If errors result due to any version incompatibilities, try the LTS version of node:

```
npm uninstall -g truffle
npm install -g truffle@nodeLTS
```

The following command returns the versions of the software installed:

```
truffle version
```

The command produces output like the following (your version values may be higher):

```
Truffle v5.1.14 (core: 5.1.13)
Solidity v0.5.16 (solc-js)
Node v12.16.2
  Web3.js v1.2.1
```

At the point, you have completed the installation of the trio of development tools—Node.js, npm, and Truffle IDE—that you'll use for Dapp development in this book. Note that Truffle automatically installs the Solidity compiler.

> **NOTE**  These setup instructions are one-time only; this setup will be used for the Dapp development in chapters 5–11 and for any Dapps you may want to develop for your own projects. Go through each step carefully and completely before you start the next step. Understand that version numbers for the software may be higher and different from what are shown here. Seek the help of your IT administrator if you do not have admin privileges for software installation on your laptop or if you are working on enterprisewide installations.

### 4.1.3    *Building the Dapp stack*

The next steps focus on the upper levels of the Dapp stack (figure 4.3), and correspond to the following list of tasks (recall that this stack was introduced at a high level in chapter 1):

1  Install a local blockchain layer (section 4.2).
2  Develop a smart contract layer and deploy (section 4.3).
3  Develop the web application UI layer (section 4.4).
4  Configure the web server and develop glue code connecting the UI to the smart contract layer (section 4.4).

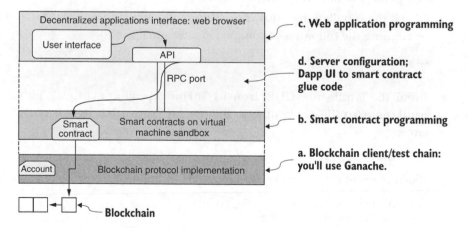

**Figure 4.3    Dapp development layers**

For a systematic organization of the many files and scripts of a Dapp, it's good to follow a standard directory structure. For the counter problem in chapter 2, for example, you'd store smart contract-related files in the counter-contract directory and the web application-related files in the counter-app directory, as shown here with the root directory of Counter-Dapp:

```
├── Counter-Dapp
│   ├── counter-app
│   └── counter-contract
```

## 4.2 Install Ganache test chain

For the blockchain layer, several options are available, from the simulated VM that you used in the Remix IDE to a full-blown Geth (Go Ethereum) client. In this chapter, you'll use a blockchain client (test chain) called Ganache that is part of the Truffle IDE suite.

Download Ganache from https://www.trufflesuite.com/ganache, and install it by clicking the downloaded file and clicking the Quickstart button. It is useful to pin the Ganache to the taskbar for quick access.

Ganache is also an Ethereum client, and by default, it is configured to run on the localhost. It's ideal for testing your Dapp prototypes; it provides ten accounts, each with 100 mock ether for paying for the gas points for execution as well as for transferring among accounts. Its blockchain interface is shown in figure 4.4. Toward the top, you'll see a set of seed words or *mnemonics*; copy and save them somewhere, because you'll need them to authenticate access to the chain during testing of the Dapp.

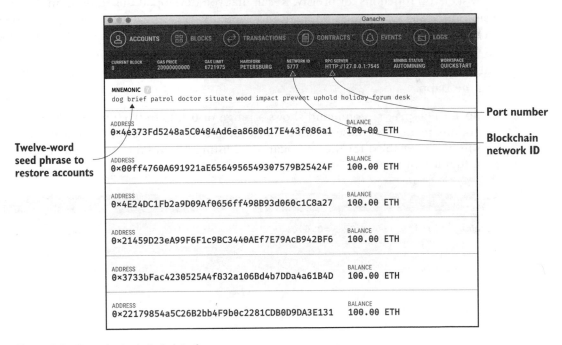

**Figure 4.4   Ganache test chain interface**

## 4.3    *Develop the smart contract*

To get you started quickly with the Dapp design process, we'll reuse the balloting problem introduced in chapter 3. The problem statement is repeated here for your convenience.

> **PROBLEM STATEMENT**    Consider an online ballot application. People vote to choose a proposal from a set of proposals. A chairperson registers the people who can vote, and only registered voters can vote (only once) on a proposal of their choice. The chairperson's vote is weighted twice (x2) as heavily as regular people's votes. The ballot process goes through four states (Init, Regs, Vote, Done), and the respective operations (initialize, register, vote, count votes) can be performed only in the corresponding states.

Voting phase transitions are usually dealt with outside the balloting process, so in this case, you can drop the code related to the states {Init, Regs, Vote, Done} from the smart contract of chapter 3. We'll assume that an authority (such as an election commission) outside the chain manages the voting stages.

The version of the Ballot smart contract in listing 4.1 omits the states and includes only skeleton functions for brevity. Recall that you developed this solution in Solidity, using the design principles outlined in chapter 3. One more modifier validates that the voter is registered before they vote. Now is a good time to download all the files for the Ballot-Dapp and review them. You can find the complete listing of Ballot.sol in this codebase for this chapter. You'll use that listing as the smart contract for developing the Dapp.

> **NOTE**    The pragma command shows a range of 0.4.22 to 0.6.0 to enable the Solidity features of these versions. For example, the features of 0.7.0 or 0.4.0 will not be enabled for the compilation of listing 4.1 and may throw an error if they are present.

---

**Listing 4.1    Smart contract for the ballot use case (Ballot.sol)**

```
pragma solidity >=0.4.22 <=0.6.0;
contract Ballot {

    struct Voter {

    }
    struct Proposal {

    }
    address chairperson;                          Use of address data type
    mapping(address => Voter) voters;             and mapping structure
    Proposal[] proposals;

    modifier onlyChair()            ◁────    Modifier definitions
      {require(msg.sender == chairperson);
       _;
```

```
    }
    modifier validVoter()          ◁──── Modifier definitions
    {
        require(voters[msg.sender].weight > 0, "Not a Registered Voter");
        _;
    }

    constructor(uint numProposals) public  { }

    function register(address voter) public onlyChair { }      Smart contract
                                                               function headers
    function vote(uint toProposal) public validVoter  {}       with modifiers

    function reqWinner() public view returns (uint winningProposal) {}
}
```

Our Ballot-Dapp will follow the directory structure discussed earlier, as shown here:

```
.
├── Ballot-Dapp
│     ├── ballot-app
│     └── ballot-contract
```

NOTE   ballot-contract will be the root or base directory for all the smart contract-related artifacts, and ballot-app will be the root directory for all the web UI-related artifacts.

Run the following commands in a terminal to create this directory structure:

```
mkdir Ballot-Dapp
cd Ballot-Dapp
mkdir ballot-app
mkdir ballot-contract
```

The next sections focus on Truffle-based development of the ballot-contract module.

NOTE   The steps in section 4.3.1 describe a detailed command-by-command assembly of a Dapp project. This chapter's codebase contains the pieces of code required for this process. A completed project with all the components and instructions on how to run it is also available.

### 4.3.1 Create a project folder

The first step is creating and initializing a standard directory structure to house your contracts. Truffle provides a template directory with the required structure. From the ballot-contract directory, run the following commands to initialize a basic project structure:

```
cd ballot-contract
truffle init
ls
```

The `ls` command lists the contents of the directory. You can use the `dir` command if you are working in the Windows OS. The output items should look like this:

```
contracts migrations test truffle-config.js
```

These items are the Ballot smart contract artifacts. Files and folders are as follows:

- *contracts/*—Solidity source files for your smart contracts. An important contract called Migrations.sol is here; this smart contract has the script for facilitating the deployment of other smart contracts of a project.
- *migrations/*—Truffle uses a migration system to handle smart contract deployments. Migration is an additional script (in JavaScript) that keeps track of changes in the contracts under development.
- *test/*—JavaScript and Solidity tests for your smart contracts.
- *truffle-config.js*—Truffle configuration file, containing, for example, configuration for the blockchain network ID, IP, and RPC port number.

The directory structure initialized by the `truffle init` command is shown in figure 4.5. You've got to be in the correct directory when executing Truffle commands; otherwise, the commands will result in an error. You'll use this directory structure as a guideline for Truffle-based development.

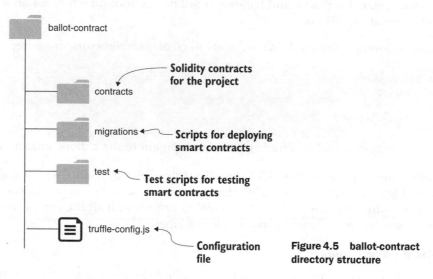

Figure 4.5  ballot-contract directory structure

In the following sections, when you enter Truffle commands from a (Linux, Mac, or Windows) command line, you'll prefix them with `truffle`: `truffle compile`, `truffle migrate`, and `truffle console`. This prefix enables the use of the default tools and techniques specified by the Truffle suite.

### 4.3.2 Add smart contract and compile

Now it's time to add the smart contract. The Solidity contract in this case is Ballot.sol from listing 4.1. Run the following commands to navigate to the contracts directory:

```
cd ballot-contract
cd contracts
```

Copy the Ballot.sol file into this directory. Then navigate back to the ballot-contract directory, check that you're in the right directory, ballot-contract, and run the compile command:

```
cd ..
truffle compile
```

You must run this command from the ballot-contract directory. If there are no errors, you should see outputs for the generation of compile artifacts for the contracts. The compiled code is saved in a newly created build/contracts directory. You see these messages upon successful compilation:

```
Compiling ./contracts/Ballot.sol...
Compiling ./contracts/Migrations.sol...
Artifacts written to ./build/contracts
Compiled successfully using: -- solc: 0.5.16+commit.id4f565a...
```

The build/contracts directory contains JSON files for the contracts that are used for (JSON-RPC) communication between the web client and blockchain server. Navigate to build/contracts after a successful compilation, and make sure that you see the Ballot.json file.

> **DEFINITION** The JSON file of the smart contract is called the *application binary interface (ABI)* of the smart contract code. This file is the interface that will be used by calls from the web application to smart contracts and also for data transfer between these modules.

During compilation, if there were any syntax errors in your code, you have two options for fixing them. (If you didn't get any errors but would like to try these options, open Ballot.sol in an editor, remove a semicolon [;] somewhere, and repeat the compile process; you'll see that `truffle compile` outputs the error.)

The first option is to open Ballot.sol in an editor such as Atom or gedit, debug the code, save it, and recompile using `truffle compile`. The second option is to use the Remix IDE introduced in earlier chapters. Recall that Remix has a just-in-time compiler. That compiler can catch syntax errors as you type in the smart contract code, as well as highlight errors in the code that you paste into it. Then you can transfer the smart contract code into the truffle contracts directory.

### 4.3.3    Configure blockchain network

Now edit the truffle-config.js file in the ballot-contract directory so that it matches listing 4.2. This file is the configuration file for the test blockchain you'll deploy next, and it's where you set the RPC port for connecting the web application to the smart contracts. In this case, you are using a test blockchain on the localhost, bound to the port 7545, and the blockchain network ID is 5777. (You learned in chapter 1 that the network ID of the Ethereum main network is 1.) Localhost and port number 5777 (http://127.0.0.1:7545) is the standard configuration for Ganache. You can also copy the prefilled file from the chapter's code.

Listing 4.2    Configuring the test chain (truffle-config.js)

```
module.exports = {
  // See <http://truffleframework.com/docs/advanced/configuration>
  // to customize your Truffle configuration for the RPC port
  networks: {
development: {
  host: "localhost",       <──  The server is your
                                local machine.
  port: 7545,              <──┐
  network_id: "5777"          │ This is the RPC port for the
}                             │ Ganache blockchain client.
  }
};
```

In your development, you are using your local machine as the server, as indicated by `localhost`, and the RPC port is 7545 for binding the local development test chain. You can identify the port number and network ID in the Ganache interface, below the top line of icons (see figure 4.4). You'll configure a different ID and port number when deploying contracts on other blockchain networks.

### 4.3.4    Deploy the smart contract

The last step before you deploy is adding a file to the migrations directory to deploy your smart contract. In this case, the smart contract is called Ballot, and to deploy it, you'll add a migration script named 2_deploy_contracts.js to the migrations directory. The file's contents are shown in the next listing. The name of the artifact should be the same as the smart contract name at the top—in this case, Ballot.

Listing 4.3    Deploy script for Ballot smart contract (2_deploy_contracts.js)

```
var Ballot = artifacts.require("Ballot");   <──  Specify the contract to be deployed.

module.exports = function(deployer) {
  deployer.deploy(Ballot,4);       <──┐  Ballot constructor is sent a parameter (4)
};                                     │  for number of proposals
```

The 2_deploy_contract.js file specifies the contracts to deploy and also the parameters to the constructor, if any. In this case, the parameter to the Ballot's constructor is initialized to 4, meaning that there are four proposals to vote on. You can deploy any number of contracts with this script; at this time, you only have the Ballot contract, but you can configure 2_deploy_contracts.js to deploy other smart contracts as you develop them. You'll see one additional file, 1_initial_migration.js, in the migrations directory; this is the script for deploying the initial migration, Migrations.sol, which is required by `truffle migrate`. The prefixes 1 and 2 in the names stand for the migration steps, 1 and 2. Do not change the filenames.

Navigate to the root of the ballot-contract directory (ballot-contract). Make sure that the Ganache chain is launched and ready (section 4.2). Type the following command to deploy your Ballot contract on the Ganache test chain:

```
truffle migrate --reset
```

The `reset` option will redeploy all contracts, including Migrations.sol. Without the reset option, Truffle will not redeploy an already-deployed smart contract. You should use this option only during the development phase when you are debugging and testing your smart contract because, during the production phase, a contract deployed is immutable and cannot be overwritten by a reset. The output will show you whether the deployments were successful and ends with a summary:

```
Summary
=======
> Total deployments:    2
> Final cost:           0.016526 ETH
..
```

Notice that it cost you some (test ether) ETH to deploy the smart contract. You can also observe this cost in ETH taken from the first account on the Ganache UI. The smart contract has been deployed and ready to be invoked. Next, let's build a web application to access the deployed smart contract.

## 4.4    *Develop and configure the web application*

Blockchain infrastructure hosts the smart contract and the Ethereum VM (figure 4.3) on which the smart contract code is run. A web application provides a convenient means for a user to interact with the smart contract. To build the web client front end, you'll need

- HTML, JavaScript, and CSS for rendering the server contents for user interaction
- A server to host the base entry script defined in index.js
- Server code (app.js) linking the web server and web client
- Additional wrappers and plugins for any frameworks such as Bootstrap and the web3 API
- A package configuration file, package.json

These items are organized in a standard project directory structure, as shown in figure 4.6. On the left is the ballot-contract directory, and on the right, you see the contents of ballot-app. ballot-contract was covered in chapter 3 and also in section 4.3.

Now let's get started on the web app (ballot-app) branch of the Dapp project. Your objective in this section is to understand the various components of the web application for the Ballot-Dapp. With this objective in mind, I've provided the complete code elements needed for the ballot-app to explore.

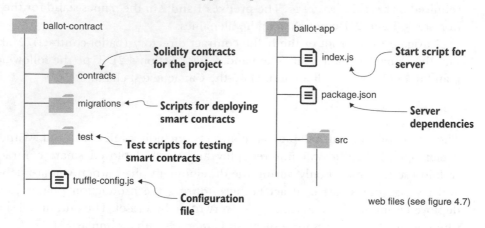

**Figure 4.6   ballot-contract and ballot-app directory structure**

### 4.4.1   *Develop ballot-app*

This structure is the standard directory format you'll use for Dapp development. To begin, navigate to the ballot-app directory, and initialize and configure the Node.js server.

> **NOTE**  npm is a convenient tool for managing JavaScript modules. It is the default package manager for Node.js modules.

Run the following commands from the base directory (Ballot-Dapp) of the ballot project to deploy the Ballot-Dapp on your Node.js server:

```
cd ballot-app
npm init
```

You'll be given a series of options about the server you are creating, including the main script file (index.js). Accept all the default values by pressing Enter. This process creates a file called package.json, listing the dependencies of the ballot-app server. You'll need to modify this file to add two items:

- The script for starting the Node.js server (index.js)
- A dependency on the express module for defining the web application

Modify your package.json file so that it looks like the following listing. You can also copy the prefilled package.json provided in the codebase of this chapter.

**Listing 4.4   package.json**

```
{
  "name": "ballot-app",
  "version": "1.0.0",
  "description": "",
  "main": "index.js",
  "scripts": {
    "start": "node index.js"        ◁——— Start script for Node.js server
  },
  "author": "",
  "license": "ISC",
  "dependencies": {
    "express": "^4.17.1"            ◁——— Dependency on express module
  }
}
```

Express is one of the many web application frameworks for the Node.js server; you'll use the express module to specify the script for the entry point of the server. (I'll refer to the web server as the Node.js server instead of the Node server to distinguish it from the blockchain node.)

    Let's examine the index.js file (listing 4.5) that defines the web application. It defines the request and response functions and the port number for the Node.js server. For subsequent deployments, you can use npm install (instead of npm init) to deploy all the required Node.js modules. You can use this file as a default index.js for your Dapps. Now you can create an index.js with the contents shown in listing 4.5, or use the one I've provided.

**Listing 4.5   Initializing express-based web application (index.js)**

```
var express = require('express');
var app = express();                              src is the directory for
app.use(express.static('src'));          ◁——┐    public web artifacts.
app.use(express.static('../ballot-contract/build/contracts'));   ◁——┐
app.get('/', function (req, res) {                                    Location
  res.render('index.html');      ◁——┐ index.html is the landing       of smart
});                                      page for the web app.         contract's
app.listen(3000, function () {                                        interface
  console.log('Example app listening on port 3000!');                 JSON file
});
```
3000 is the Node.js server port.

The only other directory in ballot-app is the src directory (figure 4.7), which contains

- The usual artifacts for a web page (CSS, fonts, images, JavaScript).
- The landing page for the web application (index.html).
- proposals.json, which holds details about the proposals being voted on. (Images for the proposals are in the images subdirectory.)
- app.js, the glue code connecting the web server layer and the smart contract layer.

You can review the files for the web app by unzipping src.zip in the codebase for this chapter and cloning it into the ballot-app folder, which contains

```
index.js package.json   src
```

The src directory contains the source for the web application part. Communication from the web client to the blockchain server is through JSON over RPC. Let's focus on analyzing app.js, which contains the handlers for the stimuli invoking the

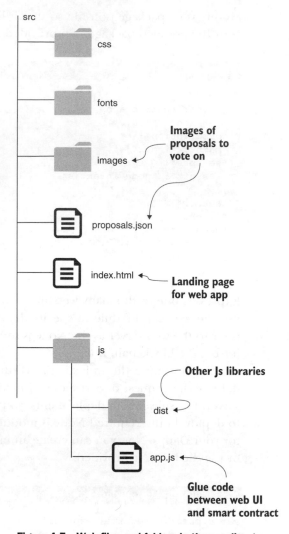

Figure 4.7   Web files and folders in the src directory

smart contract functions. I'll discuss this app.js code later for two reasons: this part will be different for different smart contracts and Dapp, and you'll have a better idea of the role of app.js after you run the Dapp and interact with it.

### 4.4.2   *Launch the ballot-app*

At this point, you have assembled all the components for the Ballot-Dapp. Navigate to the ballot-app directory, and type the following commands to start the Node.js server:

```
npm install
npm start
```

The first command installs all the required modules, and the second command starts the server on your localhost, launches the app.js, and starts listening for inputs from the port (3000) specified in the index.js file.

> **NOTE** As an alternative to the steps discussed above, you may use the ready-made modules for ballot-contract and ballot-app in this chapter's code (Ballot-Dapp), following the instructions given.

### 4.4.3 *Install MetaMask wallet*

You have one more step—installing MetaMask—to complete before you begin testing the Dapp. The account addresses are needed to identify the decentralized participants. Also, transactions have to be digitally signed and confirmed by the participant (sender of Txs). The balance of the account has to be verified to ensure that it has sufficient ether (gas points) to pay for the cost of execution of functions.

You need a mechanism for accomplishing all these important operations. For this purpose, you'll use a convenient browser plugin called MetaMask (https://metamask .io) that connects web clients to the web server and blockchain provider through the RPC port, as shown in figure 4.8. MetaMask is described as a crypto wallet and a gateway to blockchain applications; it is an intelligent digital wallet, and it acts as a proxy between the web client and the blockchain server. MetaMask securely manages the

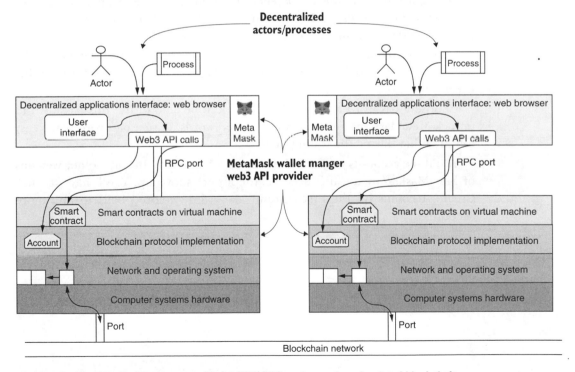

**Figure 4.8  Dapp Tx flow from a user via web API, RPC port, smart contract and blockchain**

accounts created on the blockchain and their balances in ether, and digitally signs the transactions issued by the participant accounts.

Add the MetaMask plugin to your Chrome browser by clicking MetaMask, select Chrome, and install MetaMask for Chrome.

Figure 4.8 traces the path from the decentralized user or a process to the block-chain network. The figure shows two nodes, each with its users interacting with the web client and to the blockchain node through smart contracts and contributing to the construction of the distributed ledger of the blockchain. The exact copy of the distributed ledger is in both nodes; can you spot it? (It is the one with three blocks in the network and operating system layer of both nodes.)

MetaMask uses Ethereum's web3 API to access the smart contract. Make sure that you've added the MetaMask plugin to your Chrome browser, as directed earlier. Now connect it to the Ganache blockchain by doing the following:

- *If this is your first time using MetaMask,* click the MetaMask icon (a fox) on your browser, which opens a screen with Get Started button. Click it. Then, on the screen that appears, click Import Wallet. On the next screen, click I Agree. After that, change the network by clicking the fox icon again and choosing Custom RPC from the drop-down list. Type a network name: Ganache or http://localhost:7545, network ID of 5777, and save.
- *For subsequent access to MetaMask,* click the MetaMask plugin on your browser and connect to the custom RPC at http://127.0.0.1:7545 or Ganache. (In some cases, MetaMask may link to your Ganache automatically.)

  Copy and paste the seed words or mnemonic at the top of your Ganache installation (figure 4.4) in the response screen, as shown on the left side of figure 4.9.

  Choose a password and type it; later, you'll be able to use this password to unlock MetaMask without entering the seed words. (Use a password that's easy to remember during the testing phase.)

  You'll see accounts on Ganache linked to MetaMask. In some older versions of MetaMask, only the first account (deployer) shows up. You'll have to click Create Accounts on the first account icon (little colored ball) to link more accounts.

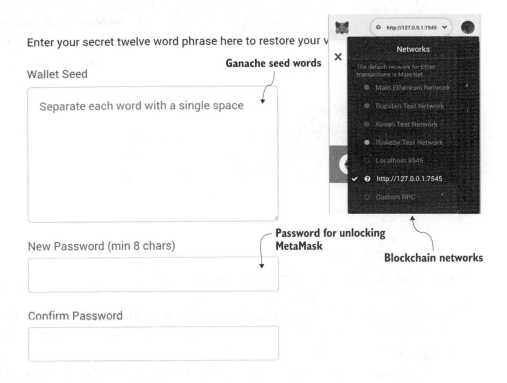

Figure 4.9   MetaMask configuration process

### 4.4.4   Interact with Ballot-Dapp

Now that you've deployed the Dapp, you are ready to interact with it. Start a web browser, and enter `localhost:3000` as the URL. You'll see that the proposals are for choosing one of four dogs (images). Locate and click the MetaMask symbol in the top-right corner of the browser window. A small window opens. The points of interest in figure 4.10 are indicated by 4A–4F. Make sure that you can locate these points on the web page and in the MetaMask window:

- 4A is the opening screen.
- 4B, 4C, and 4D are the Register, Vote, and Declare Winner buttons for contract functions.
- 4E is the MetaMask plugin's drop-down screen.
- 4F is the account icon on MetaMask.

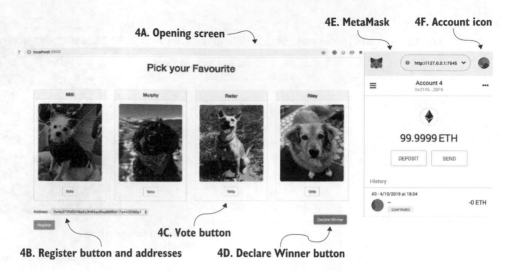

**Figure 4.10**   **Web client of Ballot-Dapp with MetaMask plugin**

The next step is connecting to the Ganache by using MetaMask, as instructed earlier. Then you'll be ready to interact with the application. Let's run some interactions that you can perform with the Dapp interface:

1. Register two accounts. Click the MetaMask icon, and click Account 1 in the list that opens. (Only the chairperson can register accounts.) Then, on the web page, choose the first address from the drop-down list (4B in figurr 4.11), and click Register. You'll see a response from MetaMask requesting that you confirm your choice, as shown on the right side of figure 4.11. Click Confirm.

    Choose the second address from the drop-down list on the web page, and click Register. Click Confirm when MetaMask requests a confirmation.

2. From Account 1, vote for the dog Milli by clicking the Vote button below her picture; then click Confirm. The right panel of figure 4.11 of MetaMask notification for the vote() function shows two addresses: the voter address and the smart contract address.

3. In MetaMask, navigate to Account 2 (shown on the left side of figure 4.11), and vote for any other dog other than Milli.

4. From any of the accounts, click the Declare Winner button on the web page. You should get a notification that Milli is the winner. (Recall that the chairperson's vote counts as two votes.)

You have completed the end-to-end exploration of the Ballot-Dapp. Don't hesitate to try other combinations of operations, including some incorrect ones, to see what happens. If an account that has not registered casts a vote, for example, that vote will be reverted. You can also involve more accounts just the two used in this example. This exploration is a demonstration of what you can expect when working with a Dapp.

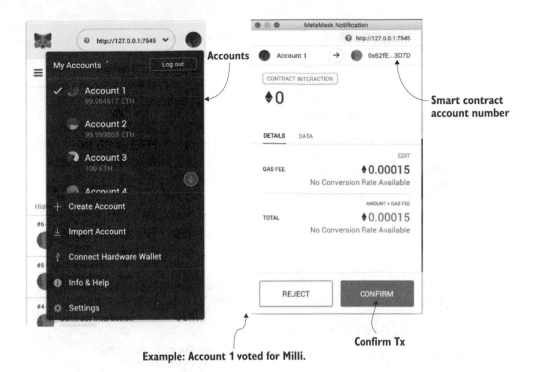

Figure 4.11   Network, accounts, and notifications from MetaMask

## 4.4.5   Connect web client to smart contract

One more piece of code is important for Dapp development: the piece that connects the web app to the smart contract. Recall from our discussion of the directory structure in section 4.4.1 that app.js is the glue that connects the web client to the smart contract through a set of handler functions. This code provisions the web3 and smart contract services for the web front end to call and invoke. The next listing shows the headers of the function scripts of app.js.

Listing 4.6   Glue code between UI and smart contract via web3 API (app.js)

```
App = {
 url: 'http://127.0.0.1:7545',          ◄── Web3 provider URL: IP
                                             address and RPC port

 init: function() {            ◄──
   return App.initWeb3();              Initialize app with
 },                                    web3 object

 initWeb3: function() {
                                              Configure web3 provider
     App.web3Provider = web3.currentProvider;  and the smart contract

   return App.initContract();
 },
```

```
initContract: function() {   ⟵──── Initialize contract object


  App.contracts.vote.setProvider(App.web3Provider);
  getJSON('Ballot.json', function(data) {

  return App.bindEvents();

},                                    Bind UI buttons to handlers
                                      for smart contract functions
bindEvents: function() {   ⟵──┘
  $(document).on('click', '.btn-vote', App.handleVote);
  $(document).on('click', '#win-count', App.handleWinner);
  $(document).on('click', '#register', ...  App.handleRegister(ad);
  ...
},


populateAddress : function(){ },
                                    Functions for drop-down list of
getChairperson : function(){ },     addresses and chairperson info


handleRegister: function(addr){ },
                                    Handler code connecting
handleVote: function(event){ },     front-end buttons to
                                    contract functions
handleWinner : function(){ };
```

The code in app.js initializes the web3 object of the Dapp with the port number, web3 provider, and smart contract JSON code (of Ballot.sol). It also binds the button clicks on the UI to the handlers for the functions register(), vote(), and reqWinner(). There are two support functions: getChairperson() and populateAddress(). The chairperson's address is needed because only the chairperson can register accounts. populateAddress() is a utility function that populates the drop-down list with account addresses for user convenience when registering accounts.

With this added knowledge, you can go back to the interface and explore the UI operations further as an informed user. Also, navigate to other directories and review the code. Note that the contents of app.js are application-specific and smart contract–dependent. You'll have to develop different codes for other Dapps and smart contracts. You'll get a chance to explore the app.js code for other Dapps in chapters 6–11.

## 4.5   Retrospective

The design and development process of a Dapp has three major components: smart contract design, front-end design, and development of the server-side glue code (app.js). For a blockchain developer, the focus is on the smart contract and the glue code in app.js to deploy the Dapp in a decentralized environment. As a blockchain developer, you'll typically work with a team of front-end and server-side developers to complete the design.

Smart contract development differs significantly from class design. A function invocation comes with the sender's identity and value (cost) for the execution of the statements within it. The sender's account has an address and a balance (of ether in Ethereum, for example). A Dapp developer must be aware of these attributes of a blockchain account when developing applications for the blockchain.

You can imagine blockchain as a ring road connecting all the peer participants and other autonomous entities of the world. This road is intended for the transportation not of people, but of useful transactions. Automatic rules verify, validate, and establish trust in the transactions and between peers, enabling them to transact with anyone connected by the ring road. Dapps provide the on ramps and exit ramps to allow anyone to transact with potentially everyone else, creating innovative opportunities.

## 4.6 Best practices

Here are some best practices specifically focusing on Dapp development:

- *Use a standard directory structure.* The Dapp ecosystem has many components, with the smart contract as the core. The use of a standard directory structure is important for organizing the components and automating the build process.
- *Use a standard naming convention.* Build tools such as Truffle create standard directories and use standard filenames, such as truffle-config.js and 2_deploy_script.js. Maintain these standard names to support dependencies and automatic build scripts. Build scripts like `truffle compile` and `truffle migrate` require specific filenames and execute actions based on the contents of certain configuration files, such as truffle.js. Don't rename 2_deploy_script.js as deployScript.js, for example; the 2_ prefix is required to preserve execution order. Accordingly, 1_initial_migrations.js executes before 2_deploy_script.js, and so on.
- *Be aware that Ganache provides a test chain, unlike the simulated environment provided by the Remix JavaScript VM.* The VM provides a controlled environment for debugging and testing during Dapp development. Later, you'll connect to real public blockchains, such as Ropsten and Rinkeby, and (if you own real ether) even to the Ethereum mainnet.
- *Be aware of the reset option in the migration of smart contracts.* During testing and development, the `truffle migrate --reset` command can be used to overwrite the deployed smart contracts on the blockchain server. In a real blockchain, when a smart contract is deployed on the server, the smart contract's code is recorded in the immutable of every stakeholder and is theoretically impossible to overwrite, according to the current Ethereum protocol. A general recommendation is to test the smart contract well in the development environment before moving to the production environment.

## *4.7    Summary*

- Truffle provides a suite of intuitive development tools and techniques (`truffle init`, `compile`, `develop`, `migrate`, `debug`, and `test`).
- The Truffle suite provides a convenient npm-based development environment for Dapps.
- The MetaMask browser plugin connects the web interface to smart contracts. It manages the accounts and allows you to confirm transactions.
- Ganache is a web3 provider with a simulated account addresses that is convenient for testing purposes.
- A blockchain Dapp identifies participants as well as smart contracts using account addresses.
- From the Dapp discussion in this chapter, it is apparent that a typical Dapp development team will have to include blockchain-based system developers as well as front-end and server-side developers, each with expertise in respective technologies and tools.

# Part 2

# *Techniques for end-to-end Dapp development*

A smart contract cannot act alone; it is a part of a larger application. A decentralized application, or Dapp, exposes the smart contract logic to enable users to transact and record on the blockchain. Part 2 introduces the design and development of Dapps, additional design considerations such as on-chain and off-chain data, and side-channel operations. You'll also learn about adding security and privacy to your applications by using cryptography and hashing functions. Two applications—a blind auction and a micropayment channel—are introduced to illustrate concepts for accessing blockchain services using the web3 API. You'll also develop the airline consortium smart contract introduced in part 1 into a full-fledged Dapp by adding a web UI. You'll learn to use a standard directory structure, and you'll use Truffle and Node.js (npm) commands to deploy the smart contract and the web application. Highlights of part 2 include migrating your smart contracts to public infrastructure Infura and a test chain Ropsten to allow potentially any decentralized user to access your Dapp. In short, part 2 shows you how to transform and code a smart contract into a full-fledged blockchain-based Dapp stack. This stack features a web frontend and a blockchain distributed ledger for recording transactions and relevant data.

Chapter 5 introduces security and privacy concepts. You'll learn about applying these concepts by designing and developing the blind auction smart contract. Chapter 6 is about on-chain and off-chain data. You'll develop the blind auction (BlindAuction-Dapp) and airline consortium (ASK-Dapp) applications, focusing on what data goes on-chain and what data stays off-chain. Chapter 7 discusses accessing blockchain services by using web API and a web3 provider and application-level concept called side channel. You'll see all these topics in action by using a micro-payment channel application (MPC-Dapp). Chapter 8 shows you how to migrate your smart contracts to a cloudlike infrastructure Infura.

# Security and privacy

## This chapter covers

- Understanding basics of cryptography and public-private key pairs
- Managing digital identity for decentralized participants using public-key cryptography
- Using cryptography and hashing for the privacy and security of blockchain data
- Illustrating security and privacy concepts using blind auction smart contract
- Deploying smart contracts on a public blockchain

Security and privacy are concerns in any system open to public access, from public buildings and highways to hardware and software systems. But they are especially serious concerns in blockchain-based systems. These systems operate beyond traditional boundaries of trust, such as the one established by a medical provider for its patients or by a university for its enrolled students. Security in these systems is typically established by verifying government-issued credentials, such as a driver's license and passport, authentication using usernames and passwords, and end-to-end encryption of messages and communications.

Advances in the digitization of health information, student records, and the like have led to regulations to ensure data privacy for the participants. The Health Insurance Portability and Accountability Act of 1996 (HIPAA) in the United States provides data privacy and security provisions for safeguarding medical information. The Family Educational Rights and Privacy Act of 1974 (FERPA) is a federal law that protects the privacy of student education records. The data records in these systems are typically housed in a centralized database, and its access is controlled by traditional methods such as those listed in the preceding paragraph. But blockchain is a decentralized system. In such a system, the participants typically are distributed, hold their assets themselves, can join and leave as they wish (within the rules coded in the smart contracts), have a self-managed identity, are loosely organized, and depend on the blockchain for the trust layer. Under these conditions, establishing identity and ensuring privacy and security are indeed challenging—but in this chapter, you'll learn methods for application of cryptography and hashing to address these issues in decentralized systems.

Remember the quad charts from chapter 3? In the diagram (repeated here in figure 5.1), the components of trust in the chart on the left—verification, validation, and recording with consensus—is addressed by smart contract modifiers and transaction recording on the blockchain (chapter 3). The issues in the quad chart on the right—identity, security, privacy, and confidentiality—are grouped (in the decentralized context) as contributors to the integrity of the system. Our focus in this chapter will be on addressing identity (2a), security (2b), and privacy (2c) concerns.

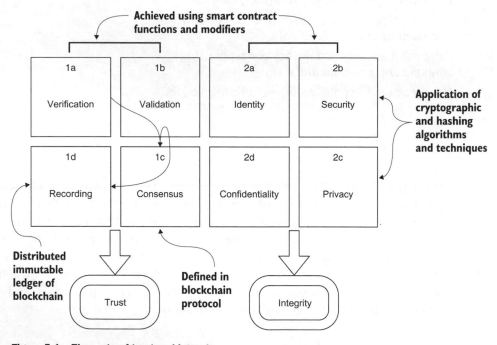

Figure 5.1  Elements of trust and integrity

We begin with cryptography, which is at the core of generating account addresses as an identity for the decentralized participants. Then we explore the hashing techniques to implement security and privacy. You'll learn how to apply these concepts, tools, and techniques in designing and developing smart contracts with security and privacy features.

We will explore an example application that solves a specific decentralized use case: a decentralized blind auction. Additionally, the blind auction example will reinforce the smart contract design principles you learned in chapters 2–4.

In this chapter, you'll see how to deploy smart contracts on a new tool: a public test chain called Ropsten. This approach is a first gradual step forward before deploying on a real production chain: the Ethereum mainnet, where operations cost real ether. The reason for introducing a public chain in this chapter is to highlight the importance of privacy and security when you deploy on a public chain. Let's begin with cryptography.

## 5.1 Cryptography basics

Bitcoin and its working cryptocurrency model are based on a strong foundation of cryptographic research and algorithms developed over more than 40 years. In most of your everyday programming projects, security is implicit. On the other hand, you'll find that cryptography plays an indispensable and explicit role in a decentralized blockchain-based solution, in which it is used for

- Creating a digital identity for the participants and other entities
- Securing data and transactions
- Ensuring the privacy of data
- Signing documents digitally

A quick review of cryptography fundamentals will help you understand the private-public key pair that is used in addressing the problem of decentralized identities for unknown participants. Unlike in a traditional system, in a decentralized system, you cannot use a username-and-password approach to identify and authenticate a user. Instead, the technique that is often used is similar to accessing a server instance on a cloud provider, using cryptographic key pairs.

### 5.1.1 Symmetric key cryptography

Let's start by taking a quick look at symmetric key cryptography so you understand the encryption process and also why this method may not be suitable for decentralized applications. It's called *symmetric key* encryption because the same key is used for encryption and decryption. Let's examine the common Caesar encryption. In this encryption, the individual letters of a message are alphabetically shifted by a fixed number (key). Consider the message in figure 5.2: Meet me at the cinema. You shift every letter by 3 to encrypt it; the receiver of your message decrypts it by using the same "key" and shifting each letter the other way by 3 to view the original message.

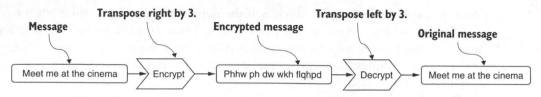

**Figure 5.2   Symmetric key encryption**

In this trivial example, 3 is the encryption key. Because the same key is used for encryption and decryption, it's symmetric key encryption. The key and the encryption and decryption functions are typically much more complex in a real application. Regardless, symmetric encryption has a significant issue: that of key distribution, or how to pass the key to the participants secretly. If you make it public, then anybody can decrypt the message. This issue is further exacerbated in a blockchain-based decentralized network, in which you're dealing with unknown participants. To address this situation, current networked systems use a method in which the keys used for encryption and decryption are different—*asymmetric*. Let's explore the asymmetric key solution and its relevance to the blockchain-based systems.

### 5.1.2   *Asymmetric key cryptography*

Asymmetric key cryptography is commonly known as public-key cryptography. This method uses two different keys instead of a single secret key (as in symmetric key cryptography):

- Let {b, B} be {private key, public key} for a participant in Buffalo, New York, USA.
- Let {k, K} be the key pair for a participant in Kathmandu, Nepal.
- Each participant publishes their public key but keeps their private key safe and secure, typically using a passphrase.
- Either participant can use the other's public key to encrypt a message that only that other person can decrypt, using the corresponding secret private key.

The key pair works as shown in figure 5.3. Input data (Data) is encrypted using function F and secret private key b, resulting in encrypted message X. The message X is decrypted using the same function F, but now with a different key—public key B—to extract the original data.

Thus, the public-private key pair has a unique property: when a message is encrypted with the private key, it can be decoded with the public key, and vice versa. The encryption and decryption keys are not the same; thus, the method is asymmetric. Now the key distribution problem is solved: you can publicize the public key for anyone to use, keeping the private key safe and secure. This property helps solve not only the key distribution issue, but also the issue of decentralized participant identity.

Next, let's explore how public-key cryptography is used to address many issues in blockchain and decentralized applications.

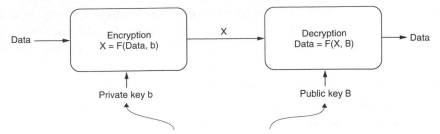

**Encryption and decryption keys are different.**

**Figure 5.3  Asymmetric key encryption and decryption**

## 5.2  *The relevance of public-key cryptography to blockchain*

Public-key cryptography is used for a range of operations on the blockchain, from account address generation to transaction signing.

### 5.2.1  *Generating Ethereum addresses*

As you learned in chapter 2 (section 2.5), there are two types of accounts in Ethereum: externally owned accounts (EOAs) and smart contract accounts. Open the Remix IDE, enter any smart contract, compile, and deploy. You'll see the addresses in the left panel, as shown in figure 5.4.

**Figure 5.4  EOAs and smart contract accounts**

Have you ever wondered how these account addresses (identities) are created? How is it that they are unique for the participants in the chain? To address these concerns, Ethereum uses a mechanism based in public-private key pairs to generate account addresses. Here is a high-level description of the mechanism:

1  A 256-bit random number is generated and designated as the private key.
2  A special algorithm called the *elliptic curve cryptography algorithm* is applied to this private key to derive a unique public key.

   These two form the {private, public} key pair; the private key is secured by a password, and the public key is open to the world.

3  A hashing function, RIPEMD160, is applied to the public key to obtain the account address:

   a  This address is shorter than the key: 160 bits or 20 bytes. This address is the account number you see in Remix and the Ganache environment and can be used as an address on a public blockchain network, as you'll do later in this chapter (section 5.2.3).
   b  The address is represented in hexadecimal for easy readability, as indicated by the 0x as the first two characters, as in the example 0xca35b7d915458ef540 ade6068dfe2f44e8fa733c.

You've been using EOA addresses to send messages to smart contracts, store ether, and transact on the blockchain. For obvious reasons, account addresses have the stringent requirement to be universally unique. This crucial requirement is addressed by choosing a large (256-bit) address space and by using a cryptographic mechanism to generate collision-free (unique) addresses.

## 5.2.2   *Transaction signing*

The cryptographic key pair is also used for Tx signing. The private key is used in the process of digitally signing transactions for authorization and authentication. Recall that in chapter 4, you used MetaMask to confirm your Txs. One of the operations performed at that time by MetaMask is signing the Txs by using your private key. Similar to how you secure and protect a credit card, you need to protect your private key to ensure the security of your assets on the blockchain. Thus, the two main applications of cryptography besides encryption are generating account addresses (the identity of decentralized participants and entities) and digitally signing transactions and messages. Let's apply these two concepts in deploying a smart contract on a public chain for the first time in this book.

## 5.2.3   *Deploying smart contracts on Ropsten*

So far, you've been developing smart contracts and Dapps and deploying them on a test chain, such as the Remix IDE's JavaScript VM or the Ganache local test chain, to gain experience in a controlled environment. Armed with the knowledge of cryptography basics, you can now graduate to deploying smart contracts on a public chain.

Ropsten is a public test network that implements the Ethereum blockchain protocol, but with mock ether. Ropsten is ideal for experimenting with your deployment after completing initial tests in Remix and other test networks. Before you deploy on Ropsten, you'll need a few items to set up the environment:

- A wallet for managing accounts and signing transactions. You can use MetaMask to manage your Ropsten accounts and their (test) ether balance.
- A method for populating this wallet with a deterministic set of test account addresses.
- A Ropsten faucet for depositing test ether into the accounts for Tx execution and ether transfer among peer participants.
- The Remix IDE's injected web3 environment for supporting the Ropsten accounts through MetaMask and interacting with the smart contract through its user interface.
- A smart contract ready to be deployed on the Ropsten network. You'll use the Counter smart contract (section 5.2.6) for this initial deployment.

### 5.2.4   Using the private key in mnemonic form

The 160-bit account addresses are cryptographically generated from the 256-bit private-public key pair. You need this private key every time you want to generate/recall your account addresses. It is simply impossible for you to remember this private key. Instead, a mnemonic is used to represent the private key.

> **NOTE**   *BIP39* (http://mng.bz/awoJ) stands for *Bitcoin Improvement Protocol 39*, which was developed to define a method to use a mnemonic to represent a private key. The mnemonic representation of a private key is equally applicable to any blockchain platform, including Ethereum.

You can obtain a 12-word mnemonic from a web tool called BIP39 (https://iancoleman .io/bip39). As shown in figure 5.5, use 12-word, ETH, and English as parameters, and click Generate. You'll get a unique 12-word mnemonic that's useful for any Ethereum-based blockchain.

Keep this mnemonic safe; do *not* share it. Treat it like your Social Security number. The mnemonic is used for cryptographically generating a deterministic set of account addresses. Using this mnemonic, you can populate a wallet with a deterministic set of accounts for operating on any Ethereum-based blockchain network.

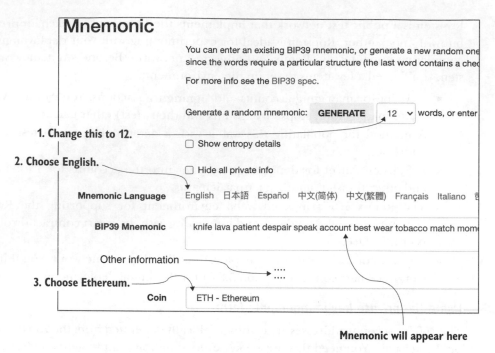

**Figure 5.5   BIP39 web tool for cryptographically generating a mnemonic**

### 5.2.5   *Populating a blockchain wallet*

Let's use the cryptographic key pair to generate a wallet so that we can operate on a public blockchain by generating the accounts from the mnemonic copied from the BIP39 tool (section 5.2.4) and by collecting ether as deposits in the accounts. Here is a way to use the cryptographic mnemonic you saved in section 5.2.4:

1   Open the Chrome browser where MetaMask is installed, and connect to Ropsten by choosing Ropsten Test Network from the Networks drop-down list. (You may have to click MetaMask, click the round account icon, and log out before completing this step.)

2   Click Import, using the account seed phrase, and in the text box that opens, enter the mnemonic you generated in section 5.2.4. This interface requires a password; enter the password twice and then click the Restore button. (This step is similar to connecting to the Ganache test chain from MetaMask in chapter 4.)

3   To create any number of accounts, click the Create Account button in Meta-Mask; copy one of the new account addresses that shows up to the clipboard. This account is a valid account of the Ropsten network. You'll notice that you have 0 ether balance.

4   Use the copied address to receive the test ether from a Ropsten faucet tool as shown in the next two steps.

To work on Ropsten, you need to receive some test ether, which you can do by accessing any Ropsten faucet. Follow these steps:

1   In your browser, navigate to the Ropsten faucet page (https://faucet.ropsten.be), shown on the left side of figure 5.6.
2   Paste in the address you created in MetaMask and copied to your clipboard, and then click the Send Me Test Ether button. After a short time, you'll receive 1.0 ether credited to the MetaMask account you created.

You can get 1 ether every 24 hours on this particular faucet, which is sufficient for making the initial deployment and learning about this public test blockchain. You'll have to repeat this operation to get more ether.

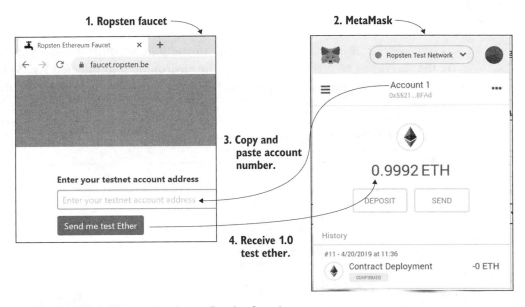

**Figure 5.6   Obtaining test ether from a Ropsten faucet**

### 5.2.6   *Deploying and transacting on Ropsten*

Let's use the simple Counter smart contract (listing 5.1) to demonstrate the deployment on Ropsten. By now, you must have realized that you need account balances in ether to deploy and operate on public blockchain networks. Every transaction costs ether, though typically only a fraction.

**Listing 5.1   Counter.sol**

```
pragma solidity >=0.4.21 <=0.6.0;
// Imagine a big integer counter that the whole world could share
contract Counter {
    uint value;

    function initialize (uint x) public {
```

```
        value = x;
    }

    function get() view public returns (uint) {
        return value;
    }

    function increment (uint n) public {
        value = value + n;
        return;
    }

    function decrement (uint n) public {
        value = value - n;
        return;
    }}
```

Save the code in listing 5.1 as Counter.sol in the Remix editor. Compile it, making sure that there are no errors, and then set the environment to Injected Web3 (instead of JavaScript VM). Figure 5.7 shows the setting of the Inject Web3 supported by MetaMask.

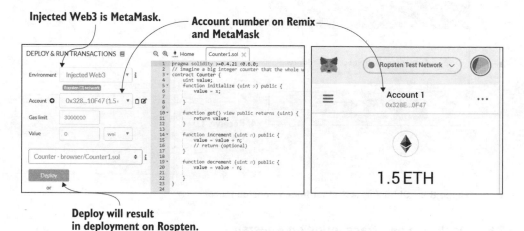

**Figure 5.7    Remix-MetaMask-Ropsten link via Injected Web3 environment**

Make sure that your account number in MetaMask shows up in the Account box in the Remix IDE, synchronizing the IDE with MetaMask and the Ropsten test network. If it does not, you will have to unlock MetaMask with your password and change the Privacy Mode setting to Off so that public participants can access your smart contract.

Now deploy the smart contract by clicking the Deploy button. You should see the deployment getting confirmed on the Ropsten network, with the transaction link on Ropsten Etherscan displayed in the console window:

```
https://ropsten.etherscan.io/tx/0xafeeb62d9a12a8d7ad08b38977040e795bd3d6f6d5e
      1d404c534aa28744e421d
```

Figure 5.8 shows the actual Tx scan I created when I wrote this chapter. It shows the Tx hash, the block number with many confirmations (because it was recorded a while earlier), the From address of the Tx, and the To address (a smart contract address). Isn't it cool that you can see the Tx I created a while ago on the scan in the future when you read this book? Don't miss this exploration. This is a foundation for many things that you'll do in later chapters.

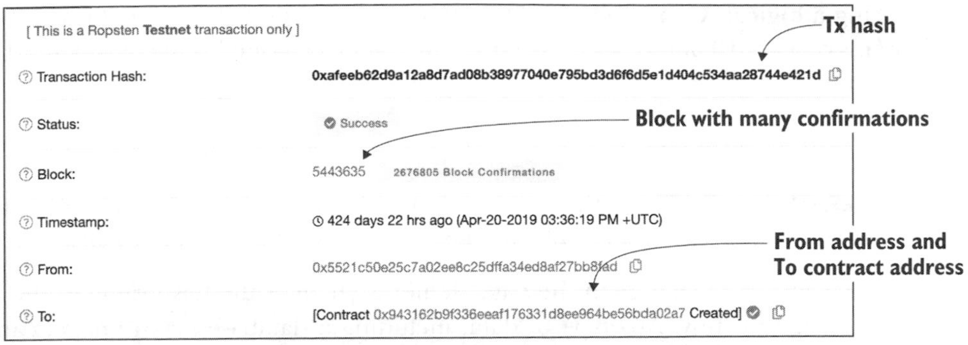

**Figure 5.8   Tx of contract deployment recorded on Ropsten as seen on Etherscan**

Now you can interact with the smart contract by using the user interface provided by Remix. Initialize the counter to 500, decrement it by 200, get the value (which should be 300), and increment it by 200. Then get the value again: it should be 500. You'll have to confirm each transaction in the MetaMask window that pops up. It takes longer to get the corresponding transaction confirmations for all these interactions on Ropsten than it does in the Remix local environment.

You have successfully deployed a smart contract on a public network for the first time. It's important to think about this: your contract is public to participants on Ropsten, so it is not private anymore. You'd better protect and secure any sensitive data that's transacted!

When you deploy a smart contract on a blockchain like Ropsten, where somebody else can interact with it, you have to realize that it's visible to everyone within the blockchain network on which it is deployed, whether that network is private, public, or permissioned. Although this concern is an obvious one for with decentralized public participation, in all these cases, you must be aware that data transmitted through the function parameters—such as bid values in a blind auction—has to be kept private and secure.

We'll examine in section 5.4 how a combination of cryptography and hashing is used to address these issues. Thus cryptography is used not only in establishing the identity of a decentralized participant, but also in secure hashing for privacy and security.

## 5.3    *Hashing basics*

*Hashing* is a transformation that maps data of arbitrary sizes to a standard fixed-size value. The *hash* of data elements are computed by using a hash function, as shown here:

```
hash = hashFunction(one or more data items)
```

Using a logical XOR (exclusive OR) function as a simple hash function and two data items of a =1010 binary, b= 1100 binary, you get the hashed value of the two data items as 0110:

```
hash value = xor(a=1010, b=1100) = 0110
```

> **DEFINITION**    *Hashing* is the process of mapping data of an arbitrary length to a fixed size by using a specially defined function called a *hash function.*

Even a single bit change in the data elements changes the hash value of the data elements significantly. Any type of data, including a database or an image, can be succinctly represented by a hash of fixed length, as shown in figure 5.9. A 256-bit data item and a strong hash function together provide a large, collision-free account address space. *Collision-free* means there is a high probability that no two values generated by the hash function will be the same and that you'll get a unique hash value when you apply the hashing function to the same data elements. This property is an important requirement of a hash function: you don't want to have the same identification number as your friend!

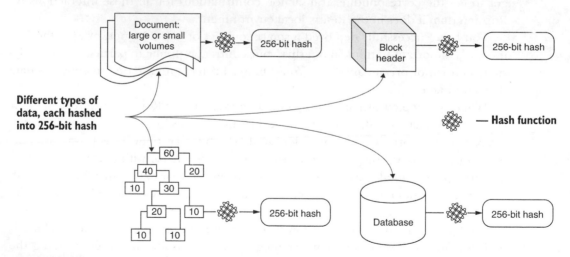

**Figure 5.9    Transforming different types of data to 256-bit hashes**

### 5.3.1 Digital signing of documents

For the digital signing of a document, a hash function is used to compute a hash of the document. This hash is used as the digital signature for the document and attached to the document by the sender. This signature can be verified later by the receiver of the document by recomputing the hash of the document and comparing it with the attached digital signature (hash).

### 5.3.2 Hashed data on distributed ledger

Blockchain is not your regular database; it stores only the minimal data needed in its distributed ledger. Hashing helps here too! The blockchain isn't overloaded by a large document because only the hash value (representation) of the document can be stored on the chain. You'll learn more about the versatility of hashing when we develop our decentralized system model further with on-chain and off-chain data in chapter 6.

### 5.3.3 Hashes in Ethereum block header

Recall from chapter 1 that the blockchain is a tamperproof immutable ledger consisting of blocks that contain records of transactions, mutable state, logs, return values (receipts), and many other details, as shown in the Ethereum block header diagrams in figure 5.10. Txs, state, logs, and receipts are stored in a Merkle tree (trie) data structure, and the hash of this tree is stored in the header. The header also stores a hash of the previous block's header, forming a link to the previous block, constructing the chain, and enforcing immutability. Even a single bit change in the block's contents will change its hash significantly, thus breaking the chain; so as you can see, the block hashes are instrumental in realizing the immutability and integrity of the chain!

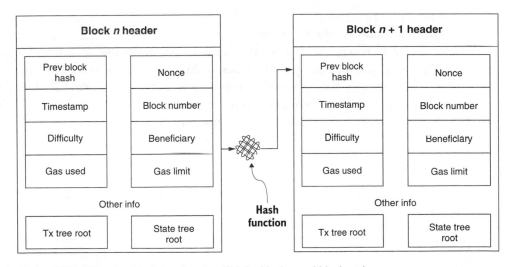

**Figure 5.10    Ethereum block headers (partial) for block n and block *n*+1**

Hashing is a core component of the consensus process for deciding the next block to be appended to the chain. Hashing is also a recommended preprocessing step for encryption of messages and digital signing of transactions. It plays an important role not only at the protocol level, but also at the application level.

### 5.3.4   *Solidity hashing functions*

Here are three hashing functions provided by Solidity: SHA256, Keccak (also a 256-bit hash function), and RIPEMD160. Recall from section 5.2.1 that RIPEMD160 is used in the generation of a 160-bit account address from the 256-bit public key of an Ethereum account. Keccak was developed for Ethereum based on the SHA3 (secure hash) algorithms. You'll use Keccak as your hash function for Dapp development because it was implemented for the Ethereum blockchain before SHA3 was finalized as a standard.

How can you compute a hash value for a set of data? Here is some simple Solidity code for the Keccak hash function. You can use this function to compute the Keccak hash, as shown in the next listing.

> **Listing 5.2   Smart contract for hashing (KHash.sol)**

```
pragma solidity >=0.4.22 <=0.6.0;

contract Khash {

bytes32 public hashedValue;
function hashMe( uint value1, bytes32 password) public
{
    hashedValue = keccak256(abi.encodePacked(value1, password));
}
}
```

The function `abi.encodedPacked` packs the parameters (any number) and returns byte representation of different types of parameters, and the `keccak256` function computes the hash. You can use this smart contract to compute the Keccak hash values for 20, 30, and so on with the password 0x426526. The only caveat is that you need to input all 32 bytes for the password, as this long hexadecimal number in the latest version of Remix. This representation is to be expected, because we are in the 256-bit realm when dealing with blockchain computing. Here are the 32 bytes of the password with the leading 0x, indicating that the string is hexadecimal:

```
0x4265260000000000000000000000000000000000000000000000000000000000
```

You can verify that with this password and values of 20 and 30, the hashes computed by the preceding code are (for 20)

```
0xf33027072471274d489ff841d4ea9e7e959a95c4d57d5f4f9c8541d474cb817a
```

and (for 30)

```
0xfaa88b88830698a2f37dd0fa4acbc258e126bc785f1407ba9824f408a905d784
```

Let's apply these concepts to solve a new decentralized application.

## 5.4 Application of hashing

Let's explore secure hashing for realizing privacy and security in a decentralized application. For this purpose, we'll consider the blind auction problem described in the Solidity documentation (https://solidity.readthedocs.io/en/v0.5.3). As with the voting and ballot problems, the requirements of this problem have been altered significantly to enable us to focus on privacy and security issues.

> **PROBLEM STATEMENT:** A beneficiary plans a blind auction for a piece of artwork. There may be many pieces to be auctioned off, but for this problem, you'll consider only one; you can always add others after this piece is sold. The beneficiary controls the various stages of the auction, {Init, Bidding, Reveal, Done}. After initiation by the beneficiary, the bidders bid one bid at a time during the Bidding phase, providing their bids securely and privately. Others, including the beneficiary, cannot see what each bid is. After a while, the beneficiary advances the stage to the Reveal phase. Now bidders openly send their bids, and the beneficiary opens the bids and identifies the highest bidder and highest bid. The beneficiary ends the auction by advancing the stage to Done, at which time the auction ends. The highest bid value is transferred to the beneficiary account. Nonwinner bidders can withdraw their deposits, and the winning bidder is returned the balance of their deposit.

Take a few minutes to review the problem statement and understand and play the steps in your mind or on paper before you proceed to design the solution.

### 5.4.1 Blind auction design

Let's study the problem and apply the design principles (DPs) you've learned, which are provided in appendix B. You'll use DP 2 and DP 3 to guide you in defining the data structures. You'll represent the design by using a contract diagram (DP 4) and the auction state transitions by using a finite state machine (FSM; DP 5), and you'll use modifiers for any rules (DP 6) to be implemented by the smart contract. Applying the DPs provides a structured approach to starting blockchain solution development.

Do you see the pattern in the states of the auction? They're similar to the states in the Ballot-Dapp. After all the DPs are applied, the contract diagram and the state transition diagram are as shown in figure 5.11. Before you start coding, make sure that you understand the process using the FSM on the left side of figure 5.11. In particular, note the Bidding and Reveal phases: blind bidding happens during the Bidding phase. A deposit is required for every bid; this deposit should be higher than the bid value. After all the blind bids are placed, the participants once again send their bid (open this time) during the Reveal phase. The winner is decided during the Reveal phase.

This problem is complex, but it exemplifies a pattern that is highly useful in many large systems, such as marketing and financial domains. Take your time to explore the ideas described here, and reuse them in your applications.

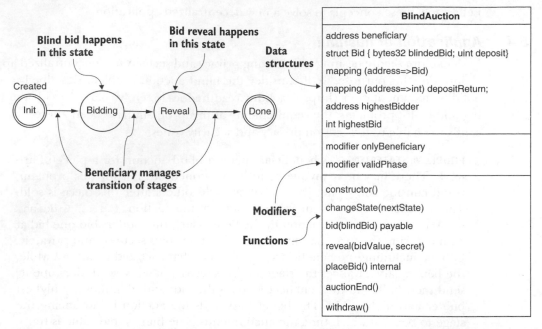

**Figure 5.11   State transition FSM and contract diagram for a blind auction**

### 5.4.2   *Blind auction smart contract*

The smart contract for the blind auction is a modified version of the code in the Solidity documentation, enabling us to focus on privacy and security concerning only one item: `blindedBid`. Let's review the code and then use the Remix IDE to test the smart contract. You can copy the listings to the Remix IDE as directed and explore it. Let's look at the following:

- Data elements (listing 5.3)
- Modifiers (listing 5.4)
- Functions (listing 5.5)

The data elements include data for the bid, an enumerated data type for the phases (states) of the auction, the beneficiary address, mappings for bids and deposit returns, and the highest bid details. These elements are defined in the next listing. Review the code, and load it into Remix.

---

**Listing 5.3   Data for blind auction (BlindAuction.sol)**

```
pragma solidity >=0.4.22 <=0.6.0;

contract BlindAuction {

    struct Bid {            <——  Bid details
        bytes32 blindedBid;
```

```
        uint deposit;
    }

    // state will be set by beneficiary     ◄──── Auction state details
    enum Phase {Init, Bidding, Reveal, Done}
    Phase public state = Phase.Init;
                                            ┌── Contract deployer
                                            │   is the beneficiary
    address payable beneficiary; // owner   ◄──┘
    mapping(address => Bid) bids;           ◄──┐
                                            Only one bid per address

    address public highestBidder;      │ Details of the
    uint public highestBid = 0;        │ highest bidder
                                            ┌── Returns of deposits
                                            │   for nonwinners
    mapping(address => uint) depositReturns;  ◄──┘
```

The blind auction problem has two main rules: the beneficiary decides on the timing of the starting, ending, Bidding, and Reveal phases of the auction, and only the beneficiary can change the phase from one to the next. These conditions are shown in the following listing, implemented as the modifiers validPhase and onlyBeneficiary. You can insert them into code (listing 5.3) already loaded in the Remix IDE.

**Listing 5.4   Modifiers for blind auction (BlindAuction.sol)**

```
// modifiers
modifier validPhase(Phase reqPhase)    ◄──┐
  { require(state == reqPhase);           Modifier for phases
                                          of the auction
    _;
  }

modifier onlyBeneficiary()                 ┌── Modifier checking
{ require(msg.sender == beneficiary);      │   beneficiary
                                        ◄──┘
    _;
  }
```

### 5.4.3   *Privacy and security aspects*

In a blind auction, during the Bidding phase, bidders place blind bids; thus, the contents of the bids (values) are private as well as secure. How do you guarantee privacy and security? You can achieve privacy by hashing the parameters. But although a hash may appear to human eyes to be indecipherable, it can be broken by brute force. The Keccak hash for the integer value (uint) 20, for example, is the same whether you're on the Earth, Moon, or Mars, in Lagos (Nigeria), or New York (United States), as follows:

```
0xce6d7b5282bd9a3661ae061feed1dbda4e52ab073b1f9285be6e155d9c38d4ec
```

This 32-byte hash value might look like gibberish to you, but a brute-force attack with knowledge of the approximate context and value of the auction item could easily decipher the bid value if so desired. So how do you secure it from such an attack? You can use a nonce or a secret password as the second parameter. This secret is like a personal identification number for your debit card. In this case, computing the Keccak hash of the value, packed up with the second secret password, makes it secure. These various forms of value 20 are shown in table 5.1. The first column is the plain data value, 20 (open); the second column is the Keccak256 hash of 20 (private but not secure); and the third column is the Keccak256 hash of 20 and the password (in this case, 0x426526) of choice from the decentralized participant (private and secure). In the table, the `abi.encodePacked()` function of Solidity creates a byte form of parameters before Keccak hashing. That's a simple hashing technique for privacy and security that you can apply in similar situations and, hence, another design principle that you can use in your applications to achieve these goals.

**Table 5.1   Keccak hashing for privacy and security**

| Open | Private for human eye (256 bits) | Private and secured by password (256 bits) |
|------|----------------------------------|--------------------------------------------|
| Plain data | keccak256(abi.encodePacked(20)) | keccak256(abi.encodePacked(20, 0x426526)) |
| 20 | 0xce6d7b5282bd9a3661ae061… | 0xf33027072471274d489ff841d4ea9e… |

**DESIGN PRINCIPLE 7**  Ensure the privacy and security of function parameters by secure-hashing the parameters along with a single-use secret password.

Finally, there's the utility function `changeState()`, which can be called only by the beneficiary. The functions `bid()`, `reveal()`, and `auctionEnd()` can be called only when the auction is in the correct phase, as specified by the `validPhase()` modifier defined in listing 5.4.

In the `Reveal` phase, all the (private and secure) valid bids are in by then. The bidder reveals the bid value as well as the secret password. It's okay to reveal the password because it is a one-time, single-use password decided by the bidder. The smart contract function `reveal()` computes the hash of the bid and the secret password, and verifies that it matches that of the blind bid sent earlier. If the hash does match, the contract accepts the bid (the `placeBid()` function) and evaluates it to see whether it is the highest. These checks for verifying the correctness of the blind bid are implemented with `if` statements.

You can add the code in the next listing to the code (listings 5.3 and 5.4) you added earlier to the Remix IDE. Review this code to explore these functions further before moving on to test this smart contract.

**Listing 5.5   Functions of the blind auction (BlindAuction.sol)**

```
constructor(  ) public {                    ◁───┐  Constructor sets
    beneficiary = msg.sender;                    │  the beneficiary
    state = Phase.Bidding;
}


function changeState(Phase x) public onlyBeneficiary {
```

```
        if (x < state || x != Phase.Init) revert();
        state = x;
    }

    function bid(bytes32 blindBid) public payable validPhase(Phase.Bidding)
    {
        bids[msg.sender] = Bid({
            blindedBid: blindBid,
            deposit: msg.value
        });
    }

    function reveal(uint value, bytes32 secret) public
            validPhase(Phase.Reveal)
    {
        uint refund = 0;
            Bid storage bidToCheck = bids[msg.sender];
            if (bidToCheck.blindedBid == keccak256(abi.encodePacked(value,
                    secret)))
            {
            refund += bidToCheck.deposit;
            if (bidToCheck.deposit >= value) {
                if (placeBid(msg.sender, value))
                    refund -= value;
            }}

        msg.sender.transfer(refund);
    }

    function placeBid(address bidder, uint value) internal
            returns (bool success)
    {
        if (value <= highestBid) {
            return false;
        }
        if (highestBidder != address(0)) {
            // Refund the previously highest bidder
            depositReturns[highestBidder] += highestBid;
        }
        highestBid = value;
        highestBidder = bidder;
        return true;
    }

    // Withdraw a non-winning bid
    function withdraw() public {
        uint amount = depositReturns[msg.sender];
        require (amount > 0);
        depositReturns[msg.sender] = 0;
        msg.sender.transfer(amount);
        }
    }
```

**Blind bid function** → (points to `{` after bid function)

**reveal() function checks blind bid** ← (points to reveal function)

**placeBid() is an internal function.** ← (points to placeBid function)

**withdraw() is invoked by losers.** ← (points to withdraw function)

```
// End the auction and send the highest bid to the beneficiary
function auctionEnd() public  validPhase(Phase.Done)
{
    beneficiary.transfer(highestBid);
}
}
```

**auctionEnd() function is invoked in the Done phase.**

Now it's time to test the blind auction smart contract. You can do that by using the Remix IDE or the Truffle console; you can even make it into a full-fledged end-to-end Dapp after developing the web front end. We'll implement an improved version of the blind auction smart contract and a full Dapp in chapter 6. In this chapter, let's focus on learning the secure hashing by exploring the application through the Remix IDE.

### 5.4.4  *Testing the BlindAuction contract*

You'll need a test plan (as discussed in chapter 3) to explore the operation of the smart contract code for the blind auction. Let's assume the following as preparation before testing:

- You need at least three participants: the beneficiary and at least two bidders. Let's choose the first three accounts of the Remix IDE: account[0], account[1], and account[2], with addresses that begin with 0xca3..., 0x147..., and 0x4b0..., respectively. You have to choose account[0], account[1], and account[2] from the drop-down list in the Remix simulated environment.
- account[0] will be the beneficiary, the one that deploys the smart contract, and the only one that can change the phase of the auction. For account[0], I've used the address 0xca3....
- account[1] and account[2] will be the two bidders for testing purposes. I used 0x147.. for account[1] and 0x4B0.. for account[2].
- account[1] will place a blind bid of 20 with a deposit (value) of 50 wei, and account[2] will place a blind bid of 30 with a deposit of 50 wei.
- The secret one-time password or the secret is  0x426526; the 0x indicates hexadecimal notation. You need the entire 32 bytes when entering it in the Remix UI. Here it is:

  0x4265260000000000000000000000000000000000000000000000000000000000

- The bid is computed by the Keccak function `Keccak256(abi.encoded-Packed(v, secret)`, where v=20 for account[1] and v=30 for account[2]. For your convenience, I provide the 256-bit password and the encoded values for 20 and 30 at the bottom of BlindAuction.sol. You can easily copy and paste when transacting in the Remix IDE.

### 5.4.5 Test plan

Compile and deploy the BlindAuction contract in the Remix IDE. Make sure that you're in account[0] when deploying. Click the state button representing the public variable state; it should be 1 for the Bidding phase. Here is a minimal test plan (refer to figure 5.12 to follow along):

1 Bidding phase.

From account[1], set the value (top-right panel of figure 5.12) to 50 wei. Specify the first blind bid value of 20 as

```
0xf33027072471274d489ff841d4ea9e7e959a95c4d57d5f4f9c8541d474cb817a
```

as the parameter for the bid() function, and click Bid. Repeat the process for account[2], but with the second blind bid value of 30 as

```
0xfaa88b88830698a2f37dd0fa4acbc258e126bc785f1407ba9824f408a905d784
```

as the parameter. Now the Bidding phase is over.

2 Reveal phase.

From account[0], the beneficiary account, enter 2 as the parameter for the changeState() function, and click the ChangeState button. Click the button for the state public variable to make sure that the value is 2 for the Reveal phase. From account[1], enter 20, 0x42652600000000000000000000000000000000000 00000000000000000000000000000

as parameters for the function reveal(), and click Reveal. Now click the High-estBidder and HighestBid buttons to check that they're correct. You'll see account[1]'s address and a bid of 20.

Repeat the reveal from account[2] but with 30, 0x4265260000000000000000 00000000000000000000000000000000000000000000000

as parameters. Then click the HighestBidder and HighestBid buttons again to verify that the bid of 20 has been knocked off by account[2]'s bid of 30. The Reveal phase is over.

3 Done phase.

From account[0], the beneficiary account, enter 3 as a parameter for the changeState() function; then click ChangeState. Click the button for the state public variable to make sure that the phase is Done. Now you can click the auctionEnd() button to pay the beneficiary the highestBid amount.

4 Check out the winner.

Click the HighestBidder and HighestBid buttons again to find the winner's values.

5 withdraw() function.

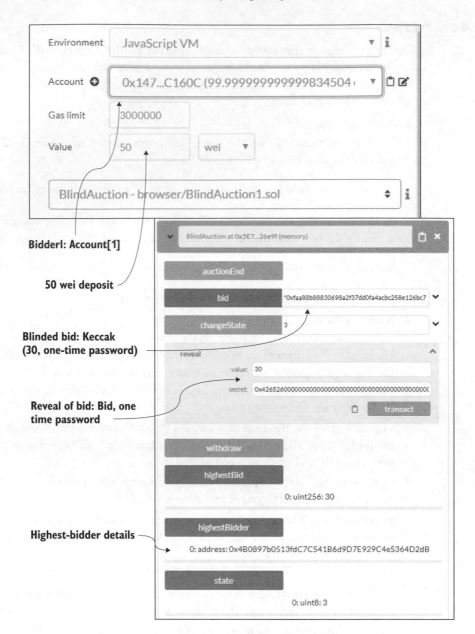

Figure 5.12   **Testing the BlindAuction contract in the Remix IDE (deploy panel and user interface)**

The nonwinning accounts can click this function button to be refunded the deposit they paid, in case they were not already returned by the bid() function, which itself returns any lower bid.

You have completed a walk-through of a basic blind auction with two bidders and a beneficiary. You can test other cases, such as when a bid is rejected during the Reveal phase because it was placed by an imposter who does not know the secret code used when hashing the blind bid. Recall that simple hashing of the parameter value can provide privacy, but hashing the parameters with a secret code provides security. The method used here is not a direct encrypt and decrypt, as you would see in traditional programming. The technique used for hashing in the blind auction illustrates a different approach to privacy and security—one that is appropriate for decentralized blockchain applications.

## 5.5    Retrospective

In the blind auction problem, the parameters (auction bid details) need to be kept private and secure in one of the phases but can be revealed to the public in another phase. Privacy and security are achieved during the Bidding phase by secure-hashing the parameters; when the parameters are revealed during the Reveal phase, the bid is verified by computing the hash from the revealed parameters and matching the hash sent during the Bidding phase. Thus, the approach used in the blind auction is not implementing security and privacy in the traditional sense of encrypting data with a private key and then decrypting it with a public key.

Other problems have similar hide-and-reveal phases, such as online quizzes and exams, requests for proposals (RFPs) in business contract bidding, and games such as poker (which has play, bet, and reveal phases).

Also, notice that the hashes and identities in the blockchain context use a 256-bit address space and 256-bit computations. This large address space ensures both the uniqueness of decentralized identities and an extremely low probability of collisions for hash values.

## 5.6    Best practices

Here are a few security-related best practices to keep in mind:

- Private-public key cryptography plays an indispensable role in uniquely identifying an account. As you secure and protect a credit card, you need to protect the private key for the security of your assets on the blockchain.
- Pay attention to the hashing technique used to achieve the privacy and security of data (parameters) transmitted in a decentralized blockchain-based system.

## 5.7    Summary

- This chapter demonstrated onboarding a smart contract on the Ropsten public chain and interacting with it, with truly decentralized access.
- You learned to use one more execution environment: Inject Web3.
- Cryptographic algorithms and techniques are used in the implementation of self-managed decentralized identity, with a unique 256-bit account number derived from a private key.

- Transactions generated by an account are digitally signed, using the account's private key. In this chapter, MetaMask facilitated this process, so you didn't observe it openly in the examples except when MetaMask asked for confirmation (via its Confirm pop-up screen).
- Using secure Keccak hashing, as was done for the blind auction problem, is a privacy and security technique that is suitable for decentralized applications.
- Using a secret code or password in the parameter list of the blind bid helps ensure the privacy and security of the data by obfuscating the bid value.

# On-chain and off-chain data

This is it. This is what distinguishes blockchain application development from that of non-blockchain applications: *on-chain data*. Do you wonder where the data associated with a Dapp is stored? Some are stored on the blockchain infrastructure (on-chain), and others in traditional databases and files (off-chain). In this chapter, you'll learn first about the concept of on-chain data introduced by the inclusion of blockchain features in an application. Then you'll learn to design and develop Dapps that deal with a combination of on-chain and off-chain data.

So what exactly are these two types of data in the context of blockchain programming? In general, any data stored on the blockchain is called *on-chain* data, and anything else is *off-chain*.

Let's analyze this concept further. In a traditional system, the results of function executions in an application are persisted in a local filesystem or a central database. A blockchain application stores the following on the blockchain node (on-chain):

- Transactions executed and confirmed
- Results of smart contract function execution
- State changes (changes in *storage* variable values)
- Logs of events emitted

These data are stored in designated data structures on a blockchain node and propagated to other stakeholder nodes as specified by a blockchain protocol.

> **DEFINITION**   *On-chain data* is a set of information generated by transactions initiated by blockchain-based applications and the items used during blockchain materialization. Most of this data is stored in a block and its header.

Figure 6.1 compares a traditional application and a blockchain-based application. The traditional system on the left has data stored in a filesystem or database. On the right is a blockchain application, with its familiar <Dapp>-app and <Dapp>-contract parts. In general, Dapp contract–generated data is stored on-chain, and data created and used by the Dapp app is stored off-chain. The function calls from a Dapp invoke a smart contract, the Txs are generated, and related artifacts are recorded on the blockchain. In figure 6.1, follow the arrows from the <Dapp>-app to understand the on-chain data. In this chapter, you'll explore this relationship between the on-chain and off-chain data.

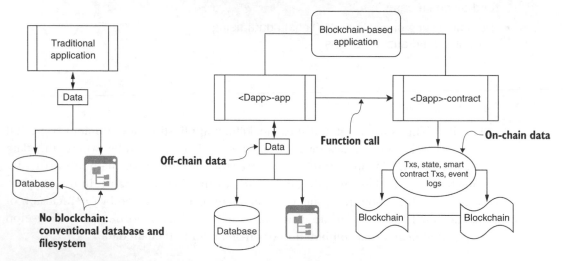

**Figure 6.1   Traditional application vs. blockchain Dapp with on-chain and off-chain data**

The left side of figure 6.1 shows a traditional application, with its conventional data stores. The right side of the figure shows the same system enhanced by blockchain recording of on-chain data. Thus, a blockchain-based system is a part of a larger system, which may be an enterprise system or a web-based system that stores data in a conventional database or on a local filesystem. An enterprise system, for example, may manage all its business data in a centralized private and secure database; it may also maintain a blockchain-based system for its decentralized operations. So in a typical business system, you'll have to deal with both categories of data: off-chain and on-chain.

> **NOTE** Understand that when you're developing a Dapp, you aren't porting your traditional system into the Solidity language; you're coding only the parts of a larger system that need blockchain support.

Given a decentralized scenario, a significant task in designing a Dapp is identifying the following:

- The activities that are the responsibility of the traditional part of the larger system
- The activities that are the responsibility of the blockchain application

Equally significant is the need for blockchain application designers and developers to decide the following:

- Which data will be stored on-chain
- Which data will be stored off-chain

These are the main issues that you'll see addressed in this chapter. In particular, you'll learn about event notification (on-chain data) and how to use it. You should already have an intuitive feel for what is on-chain data. You'll begin by examining different types of on-chain data in the Ethereum blockchain. Next, you'll explore the use of on-chain data in the blind auction Dapp introduced in (chapter 5). Then you'll learn to use both off-chain and on-chain data in the familiar example of the ASK airline Dapp (chapter 2). For each of these applications—blind auction and ASK airline—we'll design and develop an end-to-end application with a web UI.

## 6.1 On-chain data

Transactions are not the only data stored on the blockchain. A blockchain protocol determines the different types of on-chain data. In Ethereum protocol, as shown in figure 6.2, a block is made up of several elements, each serving a specific purpose:

- The blockchain header (6A) stores the attributes of the block.
- Transactions (6B) store the details of the Txs recorded in the block.
- Receipts (6C) store the execution results of Txs recorded in the block. Every transaction has a receipt; the 1:1 relationship in figure 6.2 depicts this fact.
- A composite global state (6D) stores all the data values or current state of the smart contract accounts and other regular accounts on the blockchain and is updated when Txs that use them are confirmed.

In addition to these items, observe the hash symbols in this figure, indicating that item 6A—the block header—contains (stores) the hashes of items 6B, 6C, and 6D. The hash of these items is the hash of the current block. The hash of the current block is stored in the next block added to the chain. Thus, the hash of a block stored as part of the following (newly added) block forms the chain link of the blockchain.

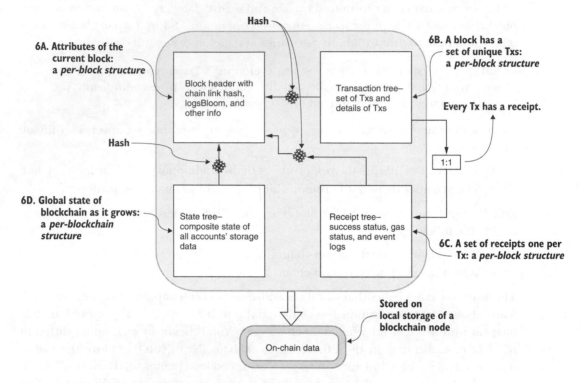

**Figure 6.2   Elements of on-chain data**

As shown in figure 6.2, the block header, Tx tree, and receipt tree are *per-block* data structures. That characterization means that for every new block added to the chain, there is a new instance of the block header, a new Tx tree, and a new set of receipts.

On the other hand, the state tree is a *per-blockchain* data structure: it stores the current state of all the accounts on the blockchain, starting from the genesis block. The state tree records the history of what happened on the blockchain as a whole and how it happened. Its state keeps changing as affected by the Txs executed. The state information is valuable information for verifying that certain Txs took place and for mining (or searching) for particular actions, changes, and events. You can analyze the on-chain data stored over a range of blocks to identify a pattern in transactions issued for a specific smart contract, for example.

I'm sure that you're eager to start coding, but a good understanding of these elements will help you design better Dapps. As you'll recall from chapter 3, the blockchain is not your regular database, and you'll want to keep only essential data in there. The information provided in this chapter will help you organize your on-chain data by designing the Txs, receipts, and state variables of your applications so as not to overload the chain. This knowledge will also be useful in extracting on-chain data records for offline analytics and decision-making.

## 6.2 Blind auction use case

The four items we've just examined—block header, Txs, receipts, and state storage—form the majority of the on-chain data. This data plays a significant role in ensuring the robustness and security of the blockchain, and also provides proof of existence for transactions and events. You can access the information stored on the blockchain to support operations at the application level. To illustrate these concepts, we'll explore an improved version of the blind auction application that was introduced in chapter 5.

As you've seen, the kinds of on-chain data are strictly controlled by the blockchain protocol, with the actual data values being determined by the Txs originating from the applications. You must be aware of this limitation when designing your blockchain-based systems. For the blind auction use case, we'll focus on one of the on-chain data elements: the event logs stored in the receipt tree. Let's begin by considering the following:

- What an event is
- How to define an event
- How to emit an event
- How to use event logs in the Tx receipts to provide notifications to the user via the UI

### 6.2.1 On-chain event data

*Events* are notifications that can be emitted from functions to indicate the presence of a condition or flag during a smart contract function's execution. Solidity provides features to define and emit an event with and without parameters. Events are logged on-chain, in the receipt tree, and can be accessed by their names.

You can define an event anywhere in the smart contract code before you use it. Still, it's a good idea to set aside a standard location to define the events in your design and coding so that they can be easily identified during the development and code review process. You can define events in the smart contract right after the type and variable declarations. Here is the syntax for an event definition:

```
event NameOfEvent (parameters);
```

Event names in Solidity begin with an uppercase letter and then use camel case. There can be three parameters at most. This limitation is set by Solidity to avoid overloading the chain and to enable efficient management of the event logs. Here's an example of an event definition for the blind auction smart contract introduced in chapter 5:

```
event AuctionEnded(address winner, uint highestBid);
```

Emitting an event involves calling it by its name and specifying any actual parameter values. Here's an example for triggering the `AuctionEnded` event:

```
emit AuctionEnded(highestBidder, highestBid);
```

You can also define events without any parameters by specifying them for different phases of the blind auction (here, `Bidding` and `Reveal`):

```
event BiddingStarted():
event RevealStarted();
```

The emit call triggers an event:

```
emit BiddingStarted();
emit RevealStarted();
```

All these examples look simple enough: define an event and then call (emit or trigger) it. Now let's see how you use these concepts and access a triggered event to notify users of what's happening in your application. We'll reuse the blind auction use case from chapter 5, but with the significant addition of events and related modifications to the code.

### 6.2.2   *Blind auction with events*

Online auctions and decentralized marketplaces are ideal use cases for blockchain. The blind auction introduced in chapter 5 has four phases: `Init`, `Bidding`, `Reveal`, and `Done` (auction ended). Wouldn't it be nice if you could notify users at the beginning of the `Bidding` and `Reveal` phases so that they were ready to act (bid or reveal) and didn't miss a deadline during any of the blind auction phases? In this chapter, you'll add three events: `AuctionEnded`, `BiddingStarted`, and `RevealStarted`.

Why are we discussing events in the context of on-chain data? As shown in figure 6.2, events are logged in the block's receipt tree, so events are good examples of on-chain data. Event logs can be used for near-real-time responses, as in the blind auction use case, and also for offline indexing, querying, searching, and analytics of on-chain data. Events (when triggered) create logs that can be indexed and searched by topic. The topics in this case are the event name itself and the individual parameters. This type of fine-grained access is useful for the analysis of a blockchain's historical data.

There are many ways to access emitted events, including using listeners (the push method) and using receipt logs (the pull method). In this example, we'll use the latter approach to illustrate the use of transaction receipts—another element of on-chain data. Let's redesign the blind auction contract diagram, which has a new element. The contract diagram, shown in figure 6.3, includes

- Data type (`struct`) definitions and data declarations
- Event definitions (the new section)
- Modifier headers
- Function headers

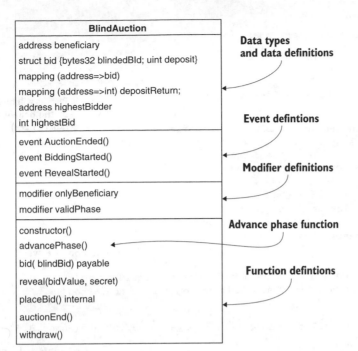

Figure 6.3   BlindAuction contract diagram with event definitions included

The design of the blind auction smart contract now features three events:

- `AuctionEnded` to announce the end of the auction
- `BiddingStarted` to announce the `Bidding` phase of the auction
- `RevealStarted` to announce the `Reveal` phase of the auction

Let's look at the smart contract code with the addition of these events and their triggers. The entire code (BlindAuction.sol) with events is available in the codebase for this chapter. You can download it into Remix to follow along with the discussion; the following listing shows only the parts that are relevant to events.

**Listing 6.1   Blind auction with events (BlindAuction.sol)**

```solidity
pragma solidity >=0.4.22 <=0.6.0;
contract BlindAuction {
    // Data types
    ...
    // Enum-uint mapping:
    // Init - 0; Bidding - 1; Reveal - 2; Done - 3
    enum Phase {Init, Bidding, Reveal, Done}
    ...
    Phase public currentPhase = Phase.Init;

// Events
    event AuctionEnded(address winner, uint highestBid);
    event BiddingStarted();
    event RevealStarted ();
```

Phases will be set only by the beneficiary (auctioneer).

Definition of events

```
// Modifiers
modifier validPhase(Phase phase) { ... }

modifier onlyBeneficiary() { ... }

constructor() public {
    beneficiary = msg.sender;
}

function advancePhase() public onlyBeneficiary {          ◄──┐  Phases will be set only
    // If already in Done phase, reset to Init phase             by the beneficiary
    if (currentPhase == Phase.Done) {                           (auctioneer).
        currentPhase = Phase.Init;
    } else {
    // Else, increment the phase
    // Conversion to uint needed as enums are internally uints
    uint nextPhase = uint(currentPhase) + 1;
    currentPhase = Phase(nextPhase);
    }                                             Emit appropriate event

    if (currentPhase == Phase.Reveal) emit RevealStarted();
    if (currentPhase == Phase.Bidding) emit BiddingStarted();
}

function bid(bytes32 blindBid) public payable validPhase(Phase.Bidding)
    { ... }
                                                    Internal function
function reveal(uint value, bytes32 secret) public  can be called
                validPhase(Phase.Reveal) { ... }    only from the
                                                    contract itself

function placeBid(address bidder, uint value) internal returns
                                    (bool success) {   ◄──
    ... }

function withdraw() public {
    ... }
                                                    Send the highest bid
function auctionEnd() public validPhase(Phase.Done) {  to the beneficiary;
    beneficiary.transfer(highestBid);                   announce the end of
    emit AuctionEnded(highestBidder, highestBid);  ◄──┘ the auction.
}}
```

### ADVANCEPHASE FUNCTION

A significant addition to the blind auction code is the function advancePhase(), which replaces a version of changeState() function that appeared in chapter 5. In this earlier version, repeated here for comparison, the beneficiary sets the state of the auction:

```
function changeState(Phase x) public onlyBeneficiary {
    if (x < state) revert();
    state = x;
}
```

The changeState() function as written here looks fine and will work well as long as the beneficiary explicitly and linearly advances the state value. It's appropriate for a traditional non-blockchain system in which you may redeploy the code from one auction to the next and as many times as you want. But a smart contract deployed with `changeState()` would be good for only a single use in a blockchain environment because the immutability requirement of the blockchain means that a smart contract, once deployed, cannot be overwritten! This limitation is significant.

Now consider the `advancePhase()` function from listing 6.1, which addresses this limitation of the earlier version by circularly advancing the state: `Init`, `Bidding`, `Reveal`, `Done`, and back to `Init`, ready for the next auction. It also emits the events `BiddingStarted` and `RevealStarted`.

> **NOTE** You must be aware of the immutable nature of smart contracts (and on-chain data) when you are designing blockchain-based systems. It's important to think of smart contracts as long-running programs and to make provisions for repeat runs through proper use of states.

### EVENT LOG ON-CHAIN DATA

Now you can upload the smart contract to the Remix IDE and check the events in operation. Compile, run, and deploy BlindAuction.sol; then take a look at the Tx recorded in the console window. The part of the recording called *logs* generated in response to the execution of the `advancePhase` function of the smart contract is shown in figure 6.4.

This action advances the phase from `Init` to `Bidding` and triggers an event announcing the `Bidding` phase, which results in the console output shown in figure 6.4. In this case, the phase is changed to `Bidding`, and an event `BiddingStarted` is emitted. When the Tx is confirmed, the event is logged in the block header as on-chain data. You can check this out in the Remix console when you click the `advancePhase` button. The numbers shown may be different, but the event will be `BiddingStarted`.

Let's analyze the on-chain log in figure 6.4. You can see the following information:

- The `"from"` address, identifying the account that deployed the smart contract.
- The `"topic"`, a hexadecimal representation of the signature (header) of the function called (in this case, `advancePhase()`).
- The `"event"` triggered (`BiddingStarted`) and its parameters. In this case, the event has no parameters, as indicated by the `length` value of 0.

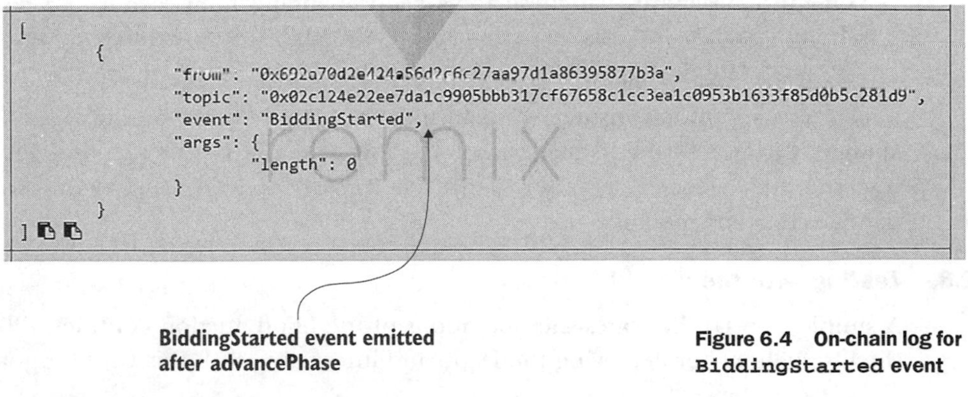

BiddingStarted event emitted after advancePhase

Figure 6.4   On-chain log for `BiddingStarted` event

This event log can be extracted from the receipt stored in the block corresponding to the Tx that deployed the contract. You can run through the phase changes to observe the events triggered in the console. These logs generated and stored on the blockchain ledger are indeed great information for postanalytics. Can you imagine some of their uses?

Figure 6.5 shows the BlindAuction contract in the Remix UI. In Remix, with the first account address selected (assuming it to be the beneficiary), click advancePhase, check the console logs to see the event that was triggered, and click advancePhase a few more times to complete the cycle from Init back to the Init phase. You should see the logs of all the events triggered after the Txs are confirmed.

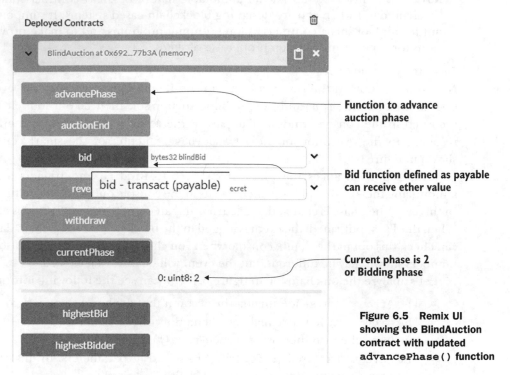

Figure 6.5   Remix UI showing the BlindAuction contract with updated advancePhase() function

**NOTE** Figure 6.5 depicts the latest version of Remix at the time of this writing. You must be aware that these tools keep changing their layout and color schemes to improve user experience. But the underlying features are mostly the same: edit, compile, deploy, and run interactions.

Let's now see how to consume (or use) these triggered events to notify users of phase changes through the blind auction web UI. You'll use the Truffle IDE to build the contract module, auction-contract, and Node Package Manager (npm) and Node.js for the auction-app module.

### 6.2.3   Testing with the web UI

A simple web UI illustrates the operations of the blind auction contract. I'll provide the instructions for deploying the Dapp and interacting with this UI. Our goal in this section is to access on-chain data to support the blind auction. In particular, you'll learn how to access the receipt logs. In the blind auction example, the code for accessing event logs is located in app.js, which serves as the glue code between the smart contract and the web UI.

Designing the web UI is a challenge. What goes in there? What are the functions of each role? Here is a solution to that challenge. Remix creates a UI that shows you the functionality needed. You can use this UI as a guideline for designing the contents of your web UI. Figure 6.6 shows a version of the web UI for the blind auction Dapp and

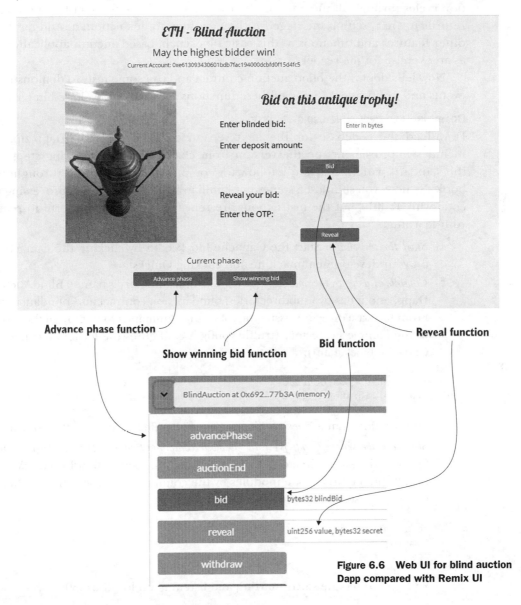

**Figure 6.6 Web UI for blind auction Dapp compared with Remix UI**

the corresponding Remix UI. This web UI is a combination of the beneficiary's interface and the bidder's interface. Examine figure 6.6 to see how the buttons (controls) for the blind auction in the Remix IDE have been rendered (mapped) as buttons and controls in the web UI. The code of this chapter is based on this UI but provides a separate interface for the beneficiary and bidders.

The Bid, Reveal, and Advance Phase buttons map one-to-one with the Remix controls (and smart contract functions). In the web UI shown in figure 6.6, I have not implemented an explicit auction-end button. Recall that the `advancePhase()` function cycles through all the phases: when you advance it from the last phase (`Done`), it returns to `Init`, setting the stage for the next item to be auctioned. Adding those or other features and functions to this basic blockchain-based auction application is left as an exercise for the reader.

Now let's deploy the blind auction contract and run some tests to demonstrate the events and notifications. Some of these functions are further developed in chapter 8.

### COMPILING AND DEPLOYING USING TRUFFLE

Download the codebase for the next version of BlindAuctionV2-Dapp.zip, which includes improvements on the version from chapter 5. The following steps reflect the standard pattern that you'll follow for compiling and deploying throughout this book. By now, you should be somewhat familiar with these steps for processing Dapp code with Truffle, but the instructions are repeated here in short form to reinforce your learning:

1 *Start the test chain.* Start the Ganache blockchain by clicking the Ganache icon on your development machine and clicking Quickstart.

2 *Compile and deploy the smart contract(s).* The base directory is named BlindAuctionV2-Dapp, and it has two subdirectories: blindauction-contract and blindauction-app. From the base directory, issue the following commands to deploy all the contracts in the contracts directory (truffle-config.js configures the local deployment on a Ganache blockchain):

```
cd blindauction-contract
truffle migrate --reset
```

You should see messages confirming the clean deployment of the contracts.

3 *Start the webserver (Node.js) and the web component of the Dapp.* Migrate to the blindauction-app directory from the base directory, BlindAuctionV2-Dapp; install the required node modules by the command npm install; and then start the Node.js server with the application's start script:

```
cd ../blindauction-app
npm install
npm start
```

You should see the server starting and listening on localhost:3000.

4  *Start a web browser (Chrome) with the MetaMask plugin installed.* Point the browser
to localhost:3000. Using your MetaMask password, make sure that MetaMask is
linked to the Ganache test chain. Restore accounts, using the mnemonic or the
12-word seed phrase of the Ganache test chain.

Now you can interact with the blind auction smart contract through the web UI
instead of the Remix IDE interface.

### TESTING THE BLIND AUCTION USING THE WEB UI

Restart your browser, and make sure that MetaMask has connected to Ganache on the
localhost. If MetaMask is already installed as a plugin and connected to the Ganache
chain, make sure that Account 1, Account 2, and Account 3 are visible. Be sure to reset
the nonce of all three accounts before you begin testing. The nonce maintains a running
count of the Txs issued from an account; it's persistent and may be stored from your earlier test runs, so it's good practice to clear it before you begin testing a new project.

To reset nonce, with Account 1 selected, click the account icon (the ball to the right
of the MetaMask icon); select Settings, Advanced option; and scroll down and click
Reset Account to reset the nonce of that account. Repeat this process for the other two
accounts. You need only these three accounts for minimal testing. In this test plan,
Account 1 is the beneficiary or auctioneer, and the other two accounts are the bidders.

For the first test, click the MetaMask icon, and choose Account 1 from the list that
opens. Then click Advance Phase at the bottom of the web UI. Keep clicking the button until you complete a full cycle from `Init` back to `Init`. You'll see notifications for
the various phases, including `Bidding` and `Reveal`, in the top-left corner of the UI, as
shown in figure 6.7. The notifications represent the logs in the Tx receipts that are

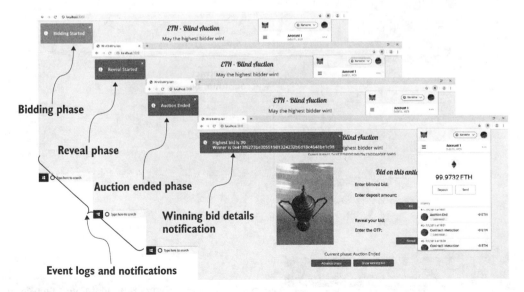

**Figure 6.7  Event notifications in the web UI and MetaMask confirmation on the right**

recorded in the block. In section 6.2.4, you'll see code snippets in app.js that access these event logs to notify users of the phase changes.

MetaMask requires confirmation from the user to go ahead with the transactions, as shown in figure 6.8. This process is similar to your accepting your credit card transaction at a checkout counter. Every time you click a smart contract operation in the UI, MetaMask opens a drop-down list with Tx sender and receiver details, and ether cost. This window also has two buttons: Reject and Confirm. Confirm proceeds with the Tx, and Reject stops them from executing. If the MetaMask drop-down box shown in figure 6.8 doesn't open automatically when confirmation is required, a little number appears on the MetaMask icon; click the icon to open the drop-down list. Click the Confirm button to go ahead with Tx execution and recording, or click Reject to cancel the transactions. Don't hesitate to click Reject if you made some mistake in your input or forgot something. The result of rejecting is that the Tx will be stopped and will not be recorded on the blockchain. It is good to have this control.

Now you're ready to do regular testing of the blind auction process. Recall the steps from chapter 5:

- During the `Bidding` phase, each bidder presents their blind bid and deposit.
- During the `Reveal` phase, each bidder reveals their bid and the secret one-time password (OTP) used for encrypting (Keccak hashing) or blinding (hiding) the bid.

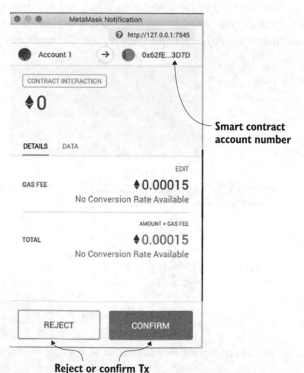

Figure 6.8   MetaMask drop-down box with Tx details, Reject button, and Confirm button

When the beneficiary ends the auction, the address of the highest bidder and the highest bid computed are emitted as parameters to the `AuctionEnded` event. When you click the Show Winning Bid button, your app.js code accesses these logs and displays them in the UI.

The test sequence from chapter 5 is repeated here for your convenience, so you can follow along and try it yourself. You can make the following assumptions for testing purposes:

1 Account 1 (in MetaMask) will be the beneficiary, which is the only user that can advance (control) the phase of the auction. You can also assume that the smart contract was deployed from Account 1.

2 Account 2 and Account 3 will be the two bidders. (Only two are needed for testing purposes.)

3 Account 2 will place a blind bid of 20 with a deposit of 50 ether, and Account 3 will place a blind bid of 30 with a deposit of 50 ether.

4 Each blind bid is computed by the Keccak secure hash function (the details of which are explained in chapter 5) `Keccak256(abi.encodedPacked(v, OTP)`, where v=20 for Account 2, v=30 for Account 3, and `OTP=0x426526` (the 0x indicates hexadecimal notation).

Here are the values you'll use for placing a blind bid. You can always compute them by using other methods, but for now, copy and use these:

0xf33027072471274d489ff841d4ea9e7e959a95c4d57d5f4f9c8541d474cb817a

0xfaa88b88830698a2f37dd0fa4acbc258e126bc785f1407ba9824f408a905d784

Here is a minimal test plan:

1 `Bidding` phase.

Use the `blindedBid` values in the preceding list. From Account 2 in MetaMask, copy the first `blindedBid` value (for v=20), set the deposit as 50 ether, set parameters for the `bid()` function, and click the Bid button. Repeat the process for Account 3, but with the second `blindedBid` value (for v=30). Now the `Bidding` phase is over.

2 `Reveal` phase.

From Account 1, the beneficiary account, advance to the `Reveal` phase by clicking AdvancePhase. From Account 2, enter 20, 0x426526 as parameters for the `reveal()` function, and click the Reveal button. Repeat this process for Account 3, but with 30, 0x426526 as parameters. The `Reveal` phase is over.

3 `Done` phase.

From Account 1, the beneficiary account, advance the phase by clicking the Advance Phase button.

4 Announcing the winner.

Click the Show Winning Bid button to find out the identity of the highest bidder and the highest bid value.

You can withdraw from the nonwinner bidder by choosing Account 2 and clicking the Withdraw button.

Then you can move back to the beneficiary and close the auction by clicking the Close Auction button.

You've completed a simple test of the blind auction. To explore the code further, you can try using other values and more accounts. This simple testing is all right for prototyping. For more thorough testing, you need automated test scripts. In chapter 10, you'll learn about automatic testing with test scripts.

### 6.2.4   *Accessing on-chain data using the web3 API*

There are two significant differences between the testing you've done here and what you did in chapter 5: in this chapter, you have a web UI, and you are accessing data logged for the events emitted. You explored the web UI in section 6.2.3. How about the event log data? How is it delivered as a notification to the user (figure 6.7)? Figure 6.9 shows the steps involved in processing on-chain logged events.

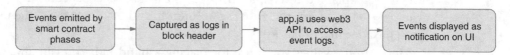

**Figure 6.9   Processing of event logs using web3 API**

Let's explore the app.js code for the new version of the blind auction (BlindAuctionV2-Dapp) and identify the snippets that access the logged events and notify the users. Of them, the first one shows how you access an event without parameters, and the second shows how you access an event with parameters. These examples show how you write code accessing event logs.

The following snippet is inside the `handlePhase()` function of app.js. The success of the function call execution is recorded in the blockchain receipt data structure and is checked by verifying that `status == 1`. If this statement is true, you can extract the indexed logs of the event(s) emitted as `logs[0]`, `logs[1]`, and so on. This snippet shows how the `BiddingStarted` and `RevealStarted` events are accessed and how the user is notified of these events. These two events do not have any parameters:

```
if(parseInt(result.receipt.status) == 1){
            if(result.logs.length > 0){
                App.showNotification(result.logs[0].event);
            }
```

The next snippet is inside the `handleWinner()` function of app.js. It executes the `auctionEnd()` function, which in turn triggers the `AuctionEnded` event with two parameters: `winner` and `highestBid`. These parameters are logged as on-chain data and returned as results that are extracted by the following code. (The `winner` argument of `logs[0]` and `highestBid` argument of `logs[0]` are extracted for display in the UI.)

Also note the `toNumber()` utility function that converts the `highestBid` argument (a 256-bit number) to a smaller 64-bit number:

```
return bidInstance.auctionEnd();
    }).then(function(res){
      var winner = res.logs[0].args.winner;
      var highestBid = res.logs[0].args.highestBid.toNumber();
```

These two snippets demonstrate how to access the event logs in transaction receipts and use them in your off-chain applications. This on-chain data is useful for real-time notifications, as illustrated in this demo, as well as for other purposes. The event logs are stored and indexed, and they can be extracted for offline data analytics based on topics and logs of immutable blockchain data.

## 6.3    *Off-chain data: External data sources*

Off-chain data is stored on a variety of data sources, some of which are shown in figure 6.10. A significant difference from on-chain data is that the types and uses of off-chain data are not determined by the blockchain protocol; this data is used by the non-blockchain part of the larger system. Off-chain data can be anything from the output of a medical device to data in cloud storage. The types and formats of data sources are limitless and application-dependent. A typical scenario, however, is a regular database

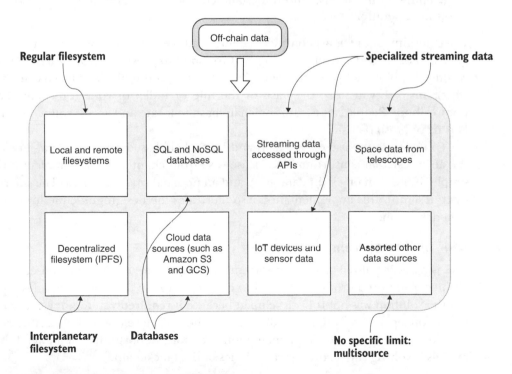

**Figure 6.10    Different types of off-chain data**

that works in tandem with the blockchain trust layer that is needed in a decentralized system of unknown peers.

Determining what goes on-chain and what stays off-chain is a significant design decision that makes blockchain application development different from traditional application development. In a traditional application, there is no on-chain data because *there is no blockchain.* The blockchain is a whole new concrete addition to enable trust. As we've seen, in a blockchain application, the data that will be recorded on-chain includes valid transactions, state changes, receipt values from Tx execution, logs of events emitted, and a few related details.

Do not define a traditional database in a smart contract. If you do, there will be multiple replicated databases, one in each node. Also, do not try to port a database of a centralized system into a smart contract. You don't explicitly say "Record this" and "Record that." The blockchain infrastructure in the background records most of the on-chain data.

So how should you store on-chain data? Because smart contracts facilitate on-chain recording, you'll design your contracts with only the functions and data needed for recording a hint of what happened off-chain.

> **DESIGN PRINCIPLE 8:**   Design smart contracts with only the functions and data needed for enforcing rules, compliance, regulation, provenance, logs for real-time notifications, and timestamped footprints and messages about offline operations.

You can think of the smart contract as being a rules engine, an enforcer of rules, and a guardian of related data and messages. If you want to prove that you bought a Ferrari, you don't upload all your photographs of the car to the blockchain (via smart contract); instead, you store the hash of the title or index of your (off-chain) Ferrari photo album. People can use this on-chain hash to locate and access your collection of Ferrari photos off-chain.

To illustrate the use of off-chain and blockchain-based on-chain data, let's revisit the airline system consortium (ASK) use case from chapter 2 and complete it with a simple web UI, an off-chain data store, and an updated smart contract. The smart contract design in this implementation also illustrates the design guideline for on-chain data definition.

## 6.4    *ASK airline system*

ASK is a decentralized airline consortium creating a marketplace for unused seats on airlines. You were introduced to ASK in chapter 2, with a detailed design description, but the solution was not fully developed because it required you to know more blockchain concepts. Now you are ready to tackle the ASK development task. ASK is not a new idea, but this novel implementation offers an opportunity for newer business models involving the recording capabilities of the blockchain.

ASK illustrates many blockchain concepts, including

- Coexistence of a traditional centralized system and a decentralized blockchain system as parts of a larger system (a concept discussed in chapter 1)
- Off-chain and on-chain data (the topic of this chapter)
- Use of cryptocurrency (tokens) while keeping your fiat currency (say, dollars) for regular operations (covered in chapter 9)
- End-to-end Dapp development using the Truffle IDE (introduced in chapters 4 and 5)

## 6.4.1 ASK concept

If you'd like a refresher on the ASK use case, now would be a good time to flip back to chapter 2. I'll give you more details about it here. At the airport, you see display boards for flights departing from and arriving at that location. No matter what airlines are running them, central display boards consolidate details on all arriving and departing flights. Following the same theme, you can picture one more display board: the ASK display that shows the available seats on flights departing from that airport. Figure 6.11 shows examples of the three displays: arrivals, departures, and available seats (the ASK display). The ASK display is a new display of available seats that is not currently available at the airports. It is a new concept introduced by the ASK application.

**Departures display**

| Departures | | | | | |
| --- | --- | --- | --- | --- | --- |
| Terminal | Flight | Destination | Time | Gate | Status |
| 1 | YV6169 | Washington | 10:30 | 12 | Departed |
| 1 | G76294 | Detroit | 10:28 | 22 | Departed |
| 1 | YX4531 | Philadelphia | 10:42 | 5 | On Time |
| 1 | DL1672 | Atlanta | 11:04 | 25 | On Time |
| 1 | WN2428 | Baltimore | 11:05 | 16 | On Time |

**Arrivals display**

| Arrivals | | | | | |
| --- | --- | --- | --- | --- | --- |
| Terminal | Flight | Destination | Time | Gate | Status |
| 1 | DL1672 | Atlanta | 10:20 | 25 | Landed |
| 1 | WN2296 | Baltimore | 10:30 | 16 | Landed |
| 1 | MQ3352 | Chicago | 10:37 | 6 | On Time |
| 1 | UA680 | Chicago | 10:24 | 10 | Delayed |
| 1 | OO3724 | Detroit | 11:22 | 23 | On Time |

**Available seats**

| ASK display (Available Seats) | | | | | |
| --- | --- | --- | --- | --- | --- |
| FlightID | Airline | FromCity | ToCity | DepTime | SeatsAvail |
| 1 | AirlineA | BUF | NYC | 6:00 AM | 8 |
| 2 | AirlineA | BUF | NYC | 10:00 AM | 6 |
| 3 | AirlineB | BUF | NYC | 6:00 PM | 10 |
| 4 | AirlineC | BUF | NYC | 1:00 AM | 7 |
| 5 | AirlineC | BUF | NYC | 9:00 AM | 8 |

**Figure 6.11  Flight departures, arrivals, and available-seats displays**

If you want to switch to a different flight, you can check the ASK display to see whether a seat that meets your needs is available. If so, you can approach the airline on which you hold your current seat (fromAirline) and ask it to facilitate the change, specifying the airline to which you would like to switch (toAirline). Agents of the airlines process your request by using the ASK UI, assign the seat to you, and message you about the status of your transfer. Payment is settled between the airlines via the smart contract based on previously deposited amounts and any business contracts established between them.

Airlines interested in the ASK model join (register with) the ASK consortium by paying a deposit and applying to become ASK members. ASK member airlines are responsible for updating information about available seats on the ASK display board (off-chain data). ASK is designed for airlines that are not in preexisting partnerships, such as code-sharing alliances. If a customer who holds a seat wants to change to a different seat on a flight run by the same airline or a partner airline, the problem is not a blockchain problem; it can be solved within the airlines' conventional systems and databases.

The ASK display board shown in figure 6.12 has a list of available seats on flights operated by various airlines. The details include flight number, airline name, from city (origin), to city (destination), departure time, and number of seats available. Because the display will show only flights originating from the airport (city) where it is displayed, the origin city is redundant, but that's all right; we'll keep it there to establish the context. You might consider other business operations after you've mastered the concepts of blockchain, including displaying information on flights originating in other cities (airports) and using other request models (such as one-to-many or broadcast instead of one-to-one). These operations could be implemented as a higher-level application using ASK as a blockchain interfacing layer.

Now that you know what information is displayed, let's explore a simple scenario to demonstrate the typical operation of the ASK Dapp. Suppose that a customer who holds a seat on a flight operated by AirlineA finds and wants to change to a seat on a flight operated by AirlineB leaving at 1 p.m. (flightID 5 on the ASK display shown in

| FlightID | Airline | FromCity | ToCity | DepTime | SeatsAvail |
|---|---|---|---|---|---|
| 1 | AirlineA | BUF | NYC | 6.00 AM | 8 |
| 2 | AirlineA | BUF | NYC | 10.00 AM | 6 |
| 3 | AirlineA | BUF | NYC | 6.00 PM | 7 |
| 4 | AirlineB | BUF | NYC | 7.00 AM | 10 |
| 5 | AirlineB | BUF | NYC | 1.00 PM | 4 |
| 6 | AirlineB | BUF | NYC | 5.00 AM | 2 |

**Figure 6.12   ASK available seats display**

figure 6.12). The customer makes a request to AirlineA to change their seat. An agent at AirlineA issues a request (`ASKRequest()`) to AirlineB on the customer's behalf to confirm that the seat is available. An agent at AirlineB examines its system and responds (`ASKResponse()`). Assuming that the response is a success response (the seat is available), AirlineA initiates payment to AirlineB, and the ASK display is updated to show the number of seats now left on the flight with `flightID` 5. Other updates related to the seat vacated by this customer on the original flight also happen offline, but they are not shown here. Either of the airlines involved may message the customer about the change, and all the ensuing operations are carried out offline. Most of the operations are offline except for proof that the request was issued, the transfer took place (Tx receipts), and payment was settled. These actions are captured in the sequence diagram in figure 6.13. (Appendix A shows details on this type of UML diagram.) Follow the operations in the sequence represented by the numbers 1 through 9.

Let's study this sequence diagram. The timeline is from top to bottom; the vertical lines are timelines. The sequence of operations is from top to bottom of the sequence diagram. The operations are numbered in this diagram to follow along with the sequence numbers; this numbering is not part of a standard sequence diagram. In the

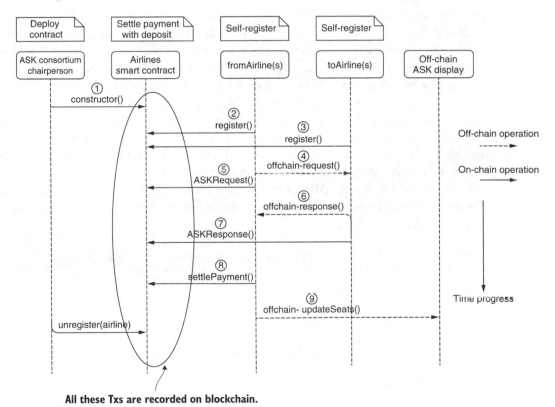

**All these Txs are recorded on blockchain.**

**Figure 6.13   ASK sequence diagram**

top row are notes operations. The second row shows the main users (actors in the use case diagram): the ASK chairperson, the Airlines smart contract (Airlines.sol), the two airlines (`fromAirline` and `toAirline`) involved in the seat change (in this particular scenario), and the off-chain display. The airlines go about their regular business. They send only the information about the seat change to the smart contract. Only transactions related to the seat change are recorded on the blockchain, via the invocation of smart contract functions. All the Txs recorded on the blockchain are shown within the ellipse in figure 6.13. Also, observe the off-chain operations indicated by dotted arrows. These operations include the request and response processing with the airlines' own databases and seat availability notifications to the ASK display board. Take a few minutes to review the sequence of exchanges in figure 6.13 before continuing with your exploration.

> **DESIGN PRINCIPLE 9**: Use a UML sequence diagram to represent the sequence(s) in which functions within a smart contract may (and can) be called. The sequence diagram captures the dynamic operations of a system.

## 6.4.2  Airlines smart contract

The updated Airlines smart contract (Airlines.sol) is shown in listing 6.2. You'll find a copy of this listing in the codebase for this chapter; you can copy it into the Remix IDE to do a bit of exploration. The code illustrates how you can define state variables as an on-chain record representing parameters of operations happening off-chain. You do this by defining a struct data type for recording the state changes effected by the `ASKRequest()` and `ASKResponse()` functions. Observe that the fields in the structs `reqStruc` and `respStruc` match one-to-one the parameters of the functions `ASKRequest()` and `ASKResponse()`, respectively. These data structures facilitate the recording of information about a request and a response and their parameters. These parameters get assigned to smart contract variables, which in turn enables them to be recorded in the state tree. Also note the use of the Solidity `mapping` feature, which allows you to build on-chain data for the status of membership and other operations of the ASK system.

---

**Listing 6.2    Updated Airlines smart contract (Airlines.sol)**

```solidity
pragma solidity >=0.4.22 <=0.6.0;

    contract Airlines  {

    address chairperson;
                                        Data type for request
    struct reqStruc{            ◄──┘    parameters
        uint reqID;
        uint fID;
        uint numSeats;
        uint passengerID;
        address toAirline;
```

```
        }
struct respStruc{                    ←──┐  Data type for response
    uint reqID;                          │  parameters
    bool status;
    address fromAirline;
}
```

```
                    mapping (address=>uint) public escrow;
                    mapping (address=>uint) membership;
On-chain            mapping (address=>reqStruc) reqs;          Mapping account address
data                mapping (address=>respStruc) reps;         to on-chain data
                    mapping (address=>uint) settledReqID;
```

```
//modifier or rules
modifier onlyChairperson {
    require(msg.sender==chairperson);
    _;
}
modifier onlyMember {
    require(membership[msg.sender]==1);
    _;
}
```

```
constructor () public payable  {                Member airline could
                                                be consortium chair
    chairperson=msg.sender;
    membership[msg.sender] = 1; // automatically registered   ←──┐
    escrow[msg.sender] = msg.value;
}
```

```
function register ( ) public payable{

    address AirlineA = msg.sender;
    membership[AirlineA] = 1;
    escrow[AirlineA] = msg.value;
}
```

```
function unregister (address payable AirlineZ) onlyChairperson public {
    membership[AirlineZ]=0;
    //return escrow to leaving airline:other conditions may be verified
    AirlineZ.transfer(escrow[AirlineZ]);
    escrow[AirlineZ] = 0;
}
```

```
function ASKrequest (uint reqID, uint flightID, uint numSeats,
        uint custID, address toAirline) onlyMember public{
    /*if(membership[toAirline]!=1){
        revert();}   */
    require(membership[toAirline] == 1);
    reqs[msg.sender] = reqStruc(reqID, flightID, numSeats,
                    custID, toAirline);               ←──┐

}                       Parameters of ASKRequest() and ASKResponse()
                        are transferred to state on-chain data
```

```
function  ASKresponse (uint reqID, bool success, address fromAirline)
                                  onlyMember public{

    if(membership[fromAirline]!=1){
        revert();
    }

    reps[msg.sender].status=success;
    reps[msg.sender].fromAirline = fromAirline;
    reps[msg.sender].reqID = reqID;
}

function settlePayment  (uint reqID, address payable toAirline,
                    uint numSeats) onlyMember payable public{
    //before calling this, it will update ASK view table
    address fromAirline = msg.sender;

    //this is the consortium account transfer you want to do
    //assume the cost of 1 ETH for each seat
    // computations are in wei

    escrow[toAirline] = escrow[toAirline] +
                    numSeats*1000000000000000000;
    escrow[fromAirline] = escrow[fromAirline] –
                    numSeats*1000000000000000000;

    settledReqID[fromAirline] = reqID;
}

function replenishEscrow() payable public
{
    escrow[msg.sender] = escrow[msg.sender] + msg.value;
}
}
```

**Parameters of ASKRequest() and ASKResponse() are transferred to state on-chain data**

**Request ID is stored in the on-chain state tree as proof of payment**

### 6.4.3   ASK on-chain data

The on-chain data in this ASK Dapp consists of the following:

- The transactions for execution of the functions `constructor()`, `register()`, `unregister()`, `ASKRequest()`, `ASKResponse()`, `settlePayment()`, and `replenishEscrow()`. These transaction details are stored in a tree with the tree root (hash) in the block header, as described in section 6.1.
- The state changes of the variables in the smart contract brought about by the parameters of the Txs. The state values are stored in a tree with the tree root in the block header; the values of tree nodes change from one block to the next, depending on the Txs.

Unlike the blind auction Dapp, the ASK Dapp does not store any explicit return values or event logs as on-chain data because the ASK functions do not return any values and no events are used. The transaction receipts do include the status of function execution (failure or success). Recall from section 6.1 that there is a receipt for every transaction (1:1).

### 6.4.4  ASK off-chain data

Each airline may have many enterprise databases of its own, protected by firewalls. The airlines keep these databases as safe as possible and use them as appropriate for their routine operations. The airlines periodically update a display board showing available seats. The airport or the ASK consortium maintains this display, which is not a centralized database but an integrated view of the seats available on flights operated by the consortium's member airlines. In the Dapp codebase provided, this off-chain data on available seats is stored in a simple JSON file. This file format (instead of a database) is used for simplicity and to preserve this book's focus on the blockchain aspects of Dapp development. If you prefer, you can always create a MySQL or NoSQL database to store the off-chain data. The data schema, along with some sample data, is shown in figure 6.14.

| FlightID | Airline | FromCity | ToCity | DepTime | SeatsAvail |
|----------|---------|----------|--------|---------|------------|
| 1 | AirlineA | BUF | NYC | 6.00 AM | 8 |
| 2 | AirlineA | BUF | NYC | 10.00 AM | 6 |
| 3 | AirlineA | BUF | NYC | 6.00 PM | 7 |
| 4 | AirlineB | BUF | NYC | 7.00 AM | 10 |
| 5 | AirlineB | BUF | NYC | 1.00 PM | 4 |
| 6 | AirlineB | BUF | NYC | 5.00 AM | 2 |

**Figure 6.14  ASK's seat availability off-chain data**

### 6.4.5  ASK Dapp development process

You've already completed significant parts of the end-to-end development of the ASK Dapp. Figure 6.15 provides an overview of the standard development environment, the steps involved, and the tools you've been introduced to that support Dapp development. The steps in the development process shown in figure 6.15 are

1. Analyze the problem and its requirements. The problem definition always comes before the solution.
2. Design the solution, using UML contract diagrams.
3. Develop and test the smart contract, using the Remix IDE.
4. Develop the <Dapp>-contract module, using the Truffle IDE.
5. Deploy the smart contract on the Ganache test chain.
6. Develop the <Dapp>-app module, using Node.js and related software modules.
7. Design the web UI and the web component of the application.
8. Test the Dapp you've developed via the web UI, using a browser with the MetaMask plugin enabled. This step connects the web UI to the contracts deployed on the blockchain (in this case, Ganache).

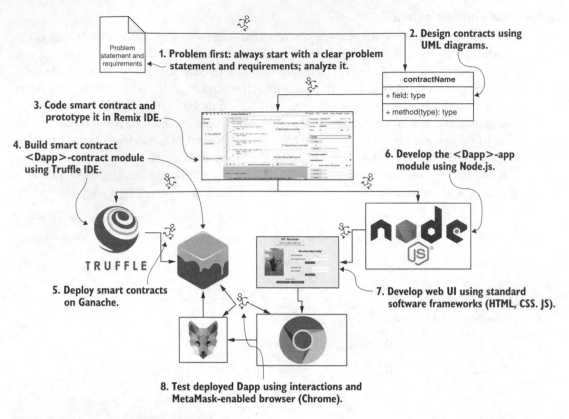

**Figure 6.15   Dapp development environment, steps, and tools**

You can use the development process and tools in figure 6.15 as a roadmap for all your local Dapp development. With this process in mind, let's explore the ASK Dapp (available in the codebase for this chapter so you can download it and follow along). You can start by exploring the Airlines smart contract in the Remix IDE and then move to the Truffle IDE for further deploying the Dapp. Following the standard Dapp directory structure that I've suggested in earlier chapters, the ASK Dapp has two main components: ASK-contract and ASK-app. ASK-contract houses the smart contract in listing 6.2, and ASK-app houses the web part of the Dapp. In a production environment, these two components may be developed by two different teams. A production environment will also require more rigorous and comprehensive automated test scripts, which you'll explore in chapter 10.

### 6.4.6   *ASK web user interface*

A significant part of the ASK-app module is web UI. There are two components: the off-chain data display for the available seats on flights and the interface for airline agent interaction. An important detail you have to recognize is that the ASK system uses the blockchain to record valid Txs for ASK, but all the computations and decisions for the Txs are carried out by off-chain systems, as reflected in the design of web UI. Part of the design of this UI is shown in figure 6.16.

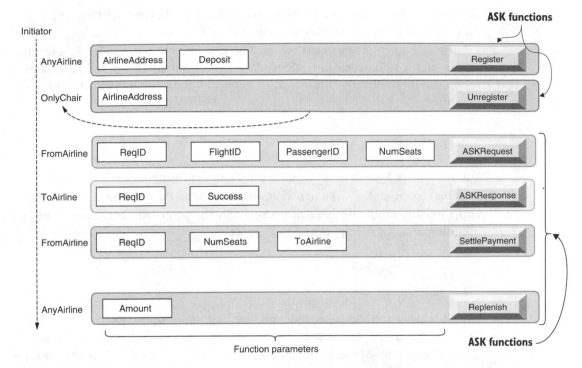

**Figure 6.16   Design of ASK web UI**

Here is a simple technique for designing a web UI for a smart contract. Map the smart contract functions one-to-one with UI buttons. The functions in listing 6.2 (`register()`, `unregister()`, `ASKRequest()`, `ASKResponse()`, `settlePayment()`, and `replenish()` (escrow), all with their parameters) are represented in the UI. This layout of the UI is guided by the Remix IDE's UI for the smart contract. Do make a note of this mapping. You don't have to rethink the UI from scratch, but make use of the UI elements as represented in the Remix IDE's left panel. The request identifier `reqID` in `ASKRequest()`, `ASKResponse()`, and `settlePayment()` ties together the sequence for a single request by a user. Keeping track of this sequence is the responsibility of off-chain code; the blockchain simply records the fact that these `reqID`-related operations happened. An application can query the blockchain recording later for all Txs with a specific `reqID`, for example. You can observe that this UI is closely aligned with the ASK's Remix UI buttons and parameters.

### 6.4.7   *Putting it all together*

With the ASK code base ASKV2-Dapp.zip, you'll use the same process as before. Download, unzip, and get the ASK code ready, and follow along with these steps:

1  *Start the test chain.* Start the Ganache blockchain by clicking the Ganache icon on your development machine and clicking Quickstart.

2  *Compile and deploy the smart contract(s).* The base directory is named ASK-Dapp, and it has two subdirectories: ASK-contract and ASK-app. From the base directory, issue the following commands to deploy all the contracts in the contracts directory:

```
cd ASK-contract
truffle migrate --reset
```

You should see messages confirming the clean deployment of the contracts.

3  *Start the web server (Node.js) and the web component of the Dapp.* Navigate to the ASK-app directory from the base directory, ASK-Dapp; install the required node modules; and run the application's start script:

```
cd ASK-app
npm install
npm start
```

4  You should see the server starting and listening on localhost:3000.

5  *Start a web browser (Chrome) with the MetaMask plugin installed.* Point the browser to localhost:3000. Make sure that MetaMask is linked to the Ganache blockchain server, using your password or 12-word seed phrase.

Now you can interact with the ASK Dapp through the web UI. Take time to study the UI that appears and all its parts.

### 6.4.8   *Interacting with ASK Dapp*

Figure 6.17 shows the display board for available seats and also the addresses of MetaMask Account 1 (the chair), Account 2, and Account 3, which you can use for testing purposes. In a real scenario, the display board will be elsewhere, and the addresses will not be shown in the web UI; this combination of displays is included only for testing purposes. As when you were testing the blind auction Dapp, make sure that you reset the nonce of all three accounts before you begin testing. Now you're ready to test the ASK Dapp.

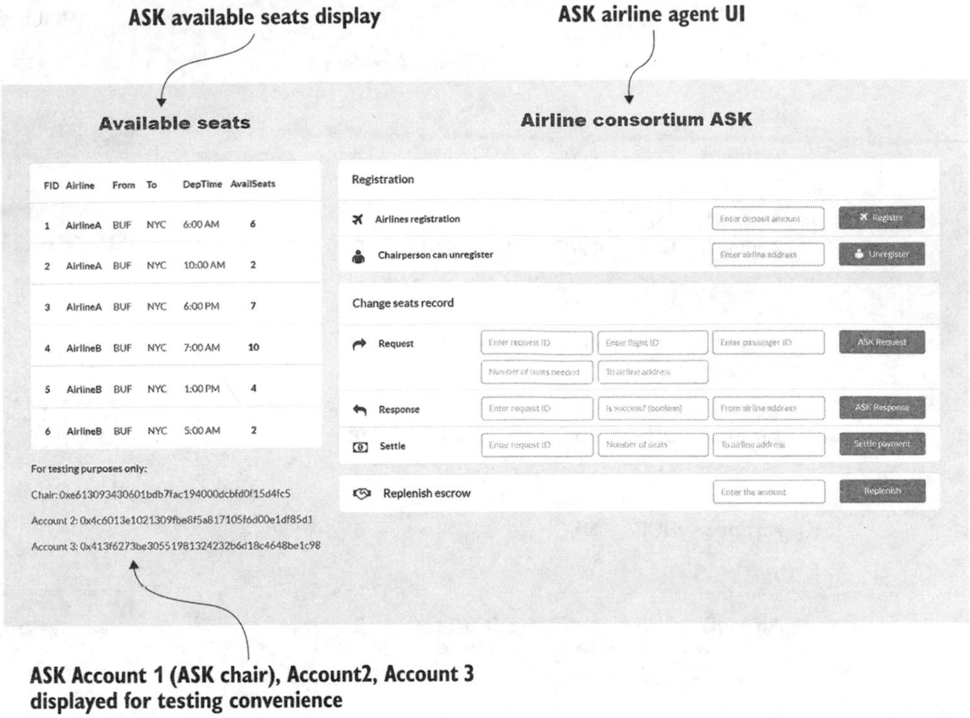

Figure 6.17 Integrated ASK web UI for testing

Figure 6.18 shows just the available seats (the left side of the web UI). For each flight included, it lists the flight number, airline name, origin and destination cities, departure time, and number of seats available. On the right side of figure 6.18 are the functions for

- Recording the evidence that a request (identified by `reqID`) was made
- Sending a response to the requests
- Settling the payment for the request

Valid transactions for the functions `register()`, `unregister()`, and `replenish()` are also recorded on the chain for later analytics.

Here's a simple test sequence to test the Dapp:

1 *Register.* For Account 2, with 50 ether as escrow, click Register. Repeat the same process for Account 3, clicking Confirm in both cases when the MetaMask window pops up. Assume that Account 2 is `fromAirline`, and Account 3 is `toAirline`. Now `fromAirline` and `toAirline` are ASK consortium members.

2 *Send a request.* For Account 2 in MetaMask, fill in these parameter values to request two seats from row 1 of the ASK display table:

```
{reqID = 123, flightID = 1, passengerID = 234, numSeats = 2,
  <toAirline address>}
```

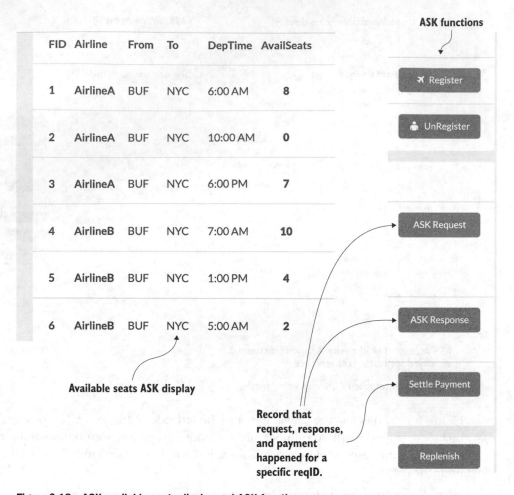

| FID | Airline | From | To | DepTime | AvailSeats |
|-----|---------|------|-----|----------|------------|
| 1 | AirlineA | BUF | NYC | 6:00 AM | 8 |
| 2 | AirlineA | BUF | NYC | 10:00 AM | 0 |
| 3 | AirlineA | BUF | NYC | 6:00 PM | 7 |
| 4 | AirlineB | BUF | NYC | 7:00 AM | 10 |
| 5 | AirlineB | BUF | NYC | 1:00 PM | 4 |
| 6 | AirlineB | BUF | NYC | 5:00 AM | 2 |

ASK functions

✈ Register

👤 UnRegister

ASK Request

ASK Response

Settle Payment

Replenish

Available seats ASK display

Record that request, response, and payment happened for a specific reqID.

**Figure 6.18   ASK available seats display and ASK functions**

For the `toAirline` address, copy the address of Account 3 provided in the left panel of the web UI for your convenience, and click ASK Request.

3  *Send a response.* For Account 3 in MetaMask, fill in these parameter values for the response:

```
{reqID = 123, success = true, <fromAirline address>}
```

For the `fromAirline` address, copy the address of Account 2 provided in the left panel of the web UI for your convenience, and click ASK Response.

4  *Settle payment.* For Account 2, enter {reqId =123, numSeats = 2, <toAirline address>}, and click Settle Payment. You'll find that the payment is settled for two seats, and the table on the left is updated.

5 You'll also notice the ASK Available seats table on the UI getting updated to reflect the seats transferred.

6 You can try to `unregister()` and `replenish()` for either of the two accounts registered. If you try these for an unregistered account, the operations should revert and throw an error because of the modifier `onlyMember` that checks for membership.

7 At this point, you can also examine app.js, which serves as the glue between the web UI and the smart contract. This critical component in the end-to-end design of a Dapp handles the calls from the UI and directs them to the smart contract.

You've completed a simple positive test. You can explore the ASK Dapp further on your own to see how it handles reversions and negative tests.

Finally, you may be wondering about the use of the `ASKRequest()` and `ASKResponse()` operations, which don't do any computations. They merely store the parameters to the smart contract variables, creating on-chain records or the state of what transpired off-chain. This action ensures that the valid transactions and state corresponding to off-chain requests and responses are recorded on the blockchain. You can view these Txs on Etherscan or Ganache. The goal of this chapter is to make sure the data about the valid Txs is recorded and payments are settled automatically.

## 6.5    *Retrospective*

This chapter brought out an important distinction between traditional programming and blockchain programming: you need to design the on-chain data (the data that gets recorded on the blockchain) carefully to avoid overloading the blockchain. You can use the types of on-chain data introduced and discussed in this chapter (receipts and event logs, transaction data, and state data) as guidelines when designing smart contracts. The blind auction Dapp focused only on event-based on-chain data. ASK Dapp illustrated the use of transaction and state-related on-chain data. The state on-chain data records how the variables in a smart contract change over the lifetime of an application. You followed the same development steps for both the blind auction and ASK Dapps, strengthening your understanding of the development process using Truffle. By now, you should be familiar with the `truffle compile` and `truffle migrate` commands and with the use of the npm (Node.js-based) web server to complete your end-to-end Dapp development.

In a traditional database, if there are about 10,000 airline transactions, you'll have an integrated database for 10,000-plus rows of data items. In a smart contract, you'll define one row of data items representing the transaction. When a Dapp executes, one transaction at a time is confirmed and recorded on-chain, along with the state changes and events emitted. One of the records may be in block 234567, another in block 234589, and so on. These records collectively form the distributed immutable ledger of the blockchain. As you can see, blockchain is not your traditional database:

it is a set of records distributed among the blocks of a blockchain along with valid Txs and data from other unrelated applications deployed on it.

In the ASK Dapp example, you may have noticed that the three functions—`ASKRequest()`, `ASKResponse()`, and `settlePayment()`—are not tied together with `if this then that` code or logic inside the smart contract. But these related functions are tied together by a unique identifier: the `reqID`. The airlines' off-chain applications make decisions about calling these functions. ASK member airlines may develop off-chain applications that use the records on the blockchain for provenance, for evaluation of transaction compliance, or for general data analytics purposes.

In blockchain applications, all the overt logic is outside, with the off-chain data and functions. The blockchain is like a covert observer that systematically records relevant information on-chain about activities that happen off-chain.

You may wonder why, then, you didn't write thousands of lines of code and multiple classes for the smart contract code. Even though smart contracts are simple and succinct, a lot of operations are carried out by the blockchain infrastructure behind the scenes. This situation is similar to the famous MapReduce algorithm used in big data analytics that fits within a single page. In that case, all the work is done behind the scenes by the MapReduce infrastructure.

## 6.6    *Best practices*

Here are some best practices, specifically focusing on on-chain and off-chain data:

- Blockchain program is not about translating or porting an application in a traditional programming language (say, Java) into a blockchain programming language such as Solidity. Define in a smart contract only the data needed for on-chain recording—nothing more. In the ASK Dapp, for example, only two data structures are defined for the request data and response data that needs to be recorded.

- Think of a smart contract as being a rules engine. It can serve as a gatekeeper controlling access to specific actions. If a nonmember airline requests an ASK action, the request will be reverted by the smart contract. This feature can be used by an off-chain application to prevent unauthorized users from completing Txs.

- As far as possible, design your smart contracts in such a way that most of the computations are performed off-chain. In the ASK Dapp, for example, the functions `ASKRequest()` and `ASKResponse()` simply record that the respective transactions have happened by transferring the parameter values into state variables. As another example, the decision to call the `settlePayment()` function will be made off-chain, based on the value of `success` in the `ASKResponse()` function.

- You must be aware of the immutable nature of smart contracts (and on-chain data) when you design blockchain-based systems. Think of smart contracts as being long-running programs and provide for repeated execution by using state properly and not using loops.

- Do not define a traditional database in a smart contract. If you do, there will be multiple replicated databases, one copy in each node. Also, do not port a database from a centralized system to a smart contract. Any centralized database has to be off-chain.
- You can design systems with fiat currency payment systems for traditional operations and cryptocurrency payments for the blockchain-based operations. You used ether for the `settlePayment()` function in the ASK Dapp, but the original airline tickets were probably bought with fiat currency such as U.S. dollars or Guatemalan quetzal.

## 6.7 Summary

- In the long line of paradigms in the evolution of programming, from structured to functional to object-oriented to concurrent and parallel programming, blockchain programming is emerging as the next significant component of modern systems.
- The concept of on-chain and off-chain data and operations distinguishes blockchain programming from traditional programming.
- More than transactions are stored on-chain; other data and hashes are stored on-chain as well to support the robustness and usability of the blockchain. These records include the state and state transitions of variables in smart contracts, function return values, events emitted, and items such as logs, all of which are stored in the header of the blockchain to provide provenance for the existence of on-chain data of a specific value.
- Off-chain data sources are application-dependent and are free from the limitations of the blockchain.
- Blockchain enables you to record events emitted by smart contract functions. This feature provides a way other than the function return value to provide notifications from the blockchain layer to upper-level applications.
- Auctions and marketplace models are well suited for blockchain applications.
- End-to-end Dapp design and development roadmap were illustrated by two use cases: blind auction and ASK airline.
- The blind auction Dapp illustrated the use of two types of on-chain data: receipts and event logs.
- The ASK airline Dapp is an example of a blockchain application that includes both on-chain and off-chain data. It shows the beginnings of the use of cryptocurrency in a Dapp. It demonstrates how cryptocurrency payments can coexist with fiat currency payments. It also provides a model of a smart contract purely for recordkeeping (without any complex computations) on the blockchain.

# Web3 and
# a channel Dapp

## This chapter covers

- Using the web3 API to access Ethereum client node functions
- Programming with web3 modules and a web3 provider
- Designing a Dapp with a side channel
- Implementing a micropayment channel for a global cleanup problem
- Connecting off-chain operations with on-chain operations

The focus of this chapter is web3. Using web3, you can pretty much set your Dapp on autopilot. What is web3? The web3 API, called simply *web3*, is a comprehensive package for accessing blockchain functions. Blockchain infrastructure provides services for managing accounts, recording transactions (Txs), and executing smart contracts, all of which you explored in previous chapters. Web3 exposes the functions of the Ethereum blockchain client node; it facilitates the interaction of external applications and the blockchain node, and it facilitates programs to access blockchain services. You used web3 in Dapp application development in chapters 4 and 6, which discussed web3 use at a high level. In chapter 4, you used web3.js in Dapp development as part of the glue code (app.js) between the web application and the smart contract, and you included web3 (the minified version in web3.js.min) in the Dapp.

> **DEFINITION** web3.js is a JavaScript library—commonly referred to as *web3*—that enables applications to access the services offered by the Ethereum blockchain client node.

This chapter demonstrates the role of web3 and strengthens your knowledge of and skills in application development with web3. You'll take steps toward becoming an informed user of web3 API in developing Dapps. This chapter lets you explore the web3 API in-depth, learning web3 concepts and understanding the essential role that it plays in delivering the blockchain services to Dapps. You'll also learn about various functional modules defined in the API. You'll use web3 to develop a versatile channel feature to build a Dapp for cleaning up global recyclable plastics. In this chapter, you'll see how to use a new concept called side channel for a novel application of micropayments. You'll develop an end-to-end solution for a simplified version of a micropayment channel supported by the Ethereum blockchain. Take time to understand web3 concepts, and carefully follow along with the Dapp development described in this chapter.

> **NOTE** I'll use *web3* in this text to refer to the entire library (web3.js). Note that web3 is the class name and web3 is the package name in the web3 JS API codebase in GitHub.

## 7.1 Web3 API

The web3 API provides a standard set of classes with their functions so that all the participants in a decentralized application can use the same syntax and semantics to interact with the blockchain. Otherwise, the interactions may result in inconsistencies among the participants, rendering the blockchain useless. It may be necessary, for example, to ensure that all participants in an application use the same hash function to generate and verify a hash value of data. The web3 API provides standard functions for hashing so that the hash computed for a given data and the hash function used for the computation are the same for all the participant applications, resulting in consistent computations. Hashing functions were discussed in chapter 5.

### 7.1.1 Web3 in Dapp stack

Where does web3 appear in your Dapp stack? Functions supported by web3 can be placed in two categories: those that support the core operations of the blockchain node and those that enable the decentralized application stack on the blockchain. Figure 7.1 illustrates the essential role played by web3 in these two modules, followed by a detailed explanation of each module.

The top part of figure 7.1 shows the *application module,* which has a web server and application code specified in app.js. The bottom part of figure 7.1 is the *blockchain client node module,* which provides the core blockchain services. Let's further analyze the layers of the stack in figure 7.1:

- The top layer of the stack is a web client, but it could be any client—mobile or enterprise—that requires the services of the blockchain.
- In the next layer, the web application's app.js uses the web3.js library to access the blockchain services.
- The layer below is a traditional web server, listening to a port for client requests, and in this case implemented by the Node.js server.
- Web3.js enables app.js application logic to connect to the underlying web3 provider in the blockchain node.

In the stack shown in figure 7.1, the blockchain client node is called *web3 provider* because it hosts (and thus provides) the classes and functions specified in web3. The bottom layer is the actual blockchain functions, including the smart contract execution environment and the ledger recording the blocks of Txs. The Ganache test chain you used in chapters 4 and 6, and an Ethereum node implemented in the Go language (geth node), are examples of a blockchain client node.

In all, figure 7.1 provides an overview of the architecture of a typical Dapp stack. You'll use this stack as a guideline to implement a blockchain feature called a micropayment channel for addressing the global problem of plastics cleanup.

Before you launch into designing the Dapp, let's learn a little bit about web3. If you prefer, you can skip to application design in section 7.2.

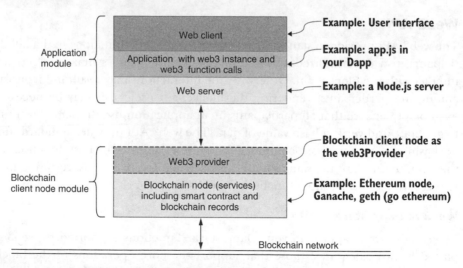

**Figure 7.1   Role of web3 in the blockchain-based Dapp stack**

### 7.1.2 Web3 packages

Web3 API is a large unit with many packages representing various functions. It consists of six packages: `core`, `eth`, `net`, `providers`, `shh`, and `utils` (figure 7.2). You'll use `web3.eth`, `web3.providers`, and `web3.utils` in this chapter:

- The `eth` package and its subpackages enable an application to interact with accounts and smart contracts.
- The `providers` package lets you set a specific web3 provider, such as Ganache.
- The `utils` package provides a standard implementation of common utility functions for their uniform use by the Dapps.

Among the other packages, `web3.core` implements the core protocol for the operation of the blockchain, `web3.net` implements the networking aspects of transaction broadcasting and receiving, and `web3.shh` is for an advanced concept called *whisper protocol* that allows Dapps to communicate with one another.

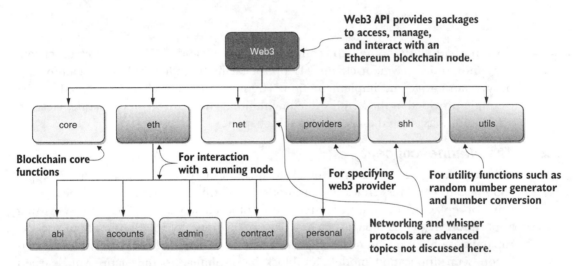

**Figure 7.2  Web3 packages and structure**

The web3 API lets you use the web3 class provided by the web3.js library and all its subclasses. It allows you to communicate with the local node through the RPC port. It also provides access to the `eth` object and its functions via `web3.eth` and network objects, via `web3.net` and its functions. You get the idea.

It is necessary to understand how web3 (of blockchain) works as you learn to develop blockchain applications at various levels. Figure 7.3, an enhanced version of figure 7.1, shows the use of web3 in an application. In the figure, the web3 provider implements the web3 API. The app.js of the application uses this web3 provider's function calls to access and interact with the underlying blockchain client node. The figure also shows the relationship of the client node with the blockchain network. The blockchain network connects many client nodes, such as the one shown in figure 7.3.

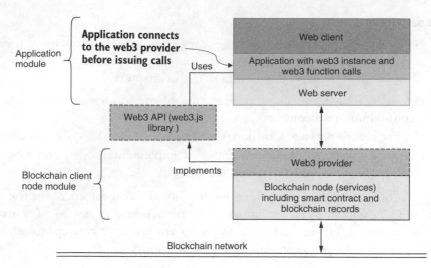

**Figure 7.3   Use of web3 API**

To apply and illustrate the web3 concept, sections 7.2 and 7.3 describe a channel concept and a micropayment channel Dapp for facilitating global plastics cleanup, and provide an end-to-end implementation. The micropayment channel is based on the example provided in the Solidity documentation. The planetary-level plastics cleanup application was created especially for this chapter.

## 7.2   *The channel concept*

You must recognize by now that blockchain is not intended to replace existing applications, but to address issues that are not solvable with traditional approaches. Don't think of replacing your current system with a blockchain system or porting an existing application in one language (such as Java or Python) to Solidity simply to use the capabilities of blockchain technology. You have to be thinking about newer and never-before-seen application models for blockchain. Similar to the Dapps you learned about in chapters 4–6—for voting (ballot), holding an auction (blind auction), and trading in the marketplace (ASK airlines)—the channel concept you'll learn in this chapter is ideally suited for blockchain-based decentralized applications. In section 7.3, you create a micropayment channel that enables new business models and encourages the participation of diverse people in an ecosystem emerging from blockchain technology.

The channel concept is ubiquitous in many domains, from geology to business. *A channel* is a path along which information passes from one point to another. In this chapter, you'll use it for a payment mechanism. This concept is popularly known as the *payment channel*. Many cryptocurrency blockchains (including Bitcoin, Ethereum, and HyperLedger) have implemented the channel concept. The side channel concept is used in Bitcoin as a model for a lightning channel and in Ethereum as a state channel for off-chain transactions among trusted parties. Note that these channels are side channels besides the main cryptocurrency transfer channels. These side channels or side chains have been added to address scalability in blockchain networks, to improve transaction times, and to create micropayment channels.

> **DEFINITION**  A *payment channel* is a means by which payments are transferred from one account to another. A *side channel* is an off-chain instrument enabled by the on-chain blockchain capabilities of smart contracts, hashing functions, cryptographic signatures, and identity management.

## 7.3  *Micropayment channel*

Micropayments are an age-old practice all over the world. Many local mom-and-pop economies depend on micropayments for daily living as well as for sustaining the local economy. These payments typically do not involve conventional financial institutions such as banks. With the advent of the digital age, efforts were focused on digitizing these micropayment methods, but they met limited success. The Bitcoin blockchain changed all that by proving the feasibility of online payments among unknown peers. With that breakthrough, interest in micropayments has been revived, and rightly so.

Here are some basic facts about a micropayment channel:

- It is defined by endpoints identified by the sender and receiver account addresses.
- It facilitates small (micro) and frequent payments between sender(s) and receiver(s).
- Payment values are less than the transaction fees charged on transactions on the main channel. (This characteristic is understandable.)
- The relationship between sender and receiver is temporary, typically terminated after payment is settled and synchronized with the main channel.

Figure 7.4 shows these concepts and the relationship between the on-chain main channel and off-chain side channel between two accounts. Anybody can join and leave the main channel, and any account can transact with any other account. Every transaction on the main channel is recorded on the blockchain. The main channel is permanent, as in Bitcoin's and Ethereum's main chains.

Now look at the side channel in figure 7.4. The micropayment channel is an example of a side channel between selected accounts—in this case, between two accounts—and is temporary. The transactions between the side channel accounts are off-chain and not recorded on the chain until the side channel synchronizes with the main channel. This synchronization happens when one of the participating accounts sends a transaction on the main channel, capturing and summarizing the details of the off-chain transactions. The side channel may be dissolved after synchronization with the main channel. The micropayment channel concept is discussed in the Solidity documentation and in many online publications.

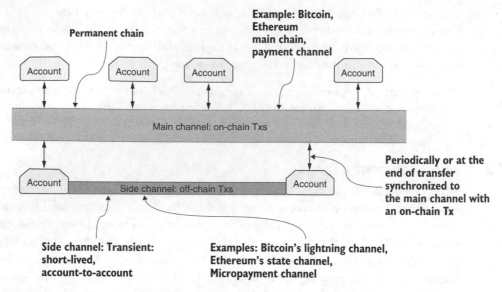

**Figure 7.4   Relationship between the main channel and micropayment channel**

## 7.4   *Micropayment channel use case*

To motivate the micropayment channel, let's consider a real-world problem: recyclable plastics on the earth. No country is immune to this problem, which is affecting ecosystems in the ocean and on land, including forests and rivers. It is simply impossible for any single organization, such as the United Nations, to send people to clean up all the countries in the world. Even if UN-like nongovernmental organizations provide funds, it is cost-effective for locals to do the cleanup. So this problem is a perfect decentralized problem: it has global scope, and participants are decentralized and not necessarily known to one another. Let's examine how blockchain can help solve this problem. Let's use the acronym MPC (Micro Payment Channel) to represent the Dapp.

> **PROBLEM STATEMENT**   Assume that a United Nations-like nongovernmental organization wants to pay individuals certain incentive payments (micropayments) for every bin of recyclable plastics collected from the environment and deposited at a designated location for recycling and proper disposal. You are required to design and develop a decentralized solution to facilitate this process.

Here are some assumptions and further details:

- Some verification mechanism exists to make sure that the bins of plastics collected contain the right amount and correct types of plastics. Otherwise, bins are rejected.
- A human worker or even a robot collects plastics in bins and deposits them at designated locations. Every time the bins collected by a worker are verified, a message is sent to the patron organization. On receiving a message, the patron

organization sends an authorized off-chain micropayment through a channel established between the organization and the worker. Potentially, there may be many micropayments paid to the worker in a single session of plastics collection. In a given session (such as a day), the value of a micropayment is the sum of all the previous micropayments added to the current one.

- Instead of cashing these small payments every time a bin of plastic garbage is collected and incurring fees, the worker waits until the last bin of the day and then receives the payment through one on-chain Tx. By design, this single Tx request is for the value of the last micropayment because it holds the accumulated value.

- After the payment is claimed, the channel is closed. A new channel is created, and the process is repeated for every worker and every session of the worker. This opening and closing of an account is impossible in a traditional banking system but is a normal process in a blockchain system.

Let's design and develop MPC-Dapp to demonstrate how it solves these issues by using an off-chain micropayment channel. This off-chain instrument will be supported by on-chain blockchain services using a smart contract and secure digital signing. And of course, web3 API will be used to access these blockchain services for all these operations. Before you develop a blockchain-based solution, however, don't overlook traditional financial systems, such as banks; assess whether they can solve the MPC problem without involving a blockchain.

### 7.4.1 *Traditional banking solution*

Figure 7.5 shows a possible solution that uses the conventional banking system to pay for the massive, decentralized global plastics cleanup. In this case, the organizer of MPC will deposit the escrow in the bank and somehow (such as through off-chain messaging) let the pre-identified workers know that they can start the cleanup. For this discussion, you can assume that the relationship between the organizer (sender) and a worker is one-to-one. A worker collects garbage in bins (in this case, 5, 1, and 2, as shown in figure 7.5), and keeps sending information about this collection to the organizer. In this scenario, the organizer first issues a check for $5 ($1 per bin), followed by a check for $1, and finally a check for $2.

The worker gives the bank the checks to cash in. The bank verifies the signature on the checks and pays the worker from the escrow deposited by the organizer. The worker can stop working at any time. The process is like working for a ridesharing service; workers can work when they want to and cash in when they want to. The cycle continues, with many decentralized workers connecting and establishing a channel with the organizer to get paid for the global cleanup effort.

Note that this solution uses the traditional banking system to create a new payment model: small payments for workers who may not have accounts at a bank. This model is a hypothetical attempt to overfit a new feature into traditional infrastructure. Conceptually, this idea seems possible, but there are significant issues with the traditional

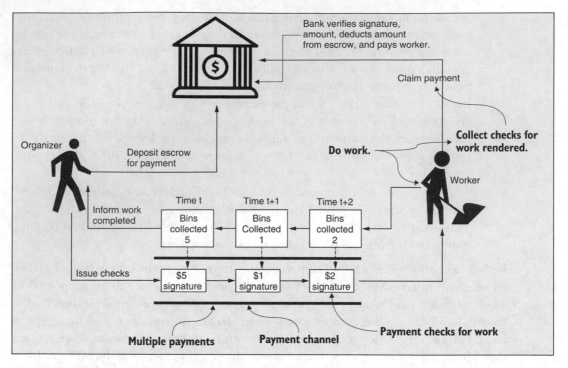

**Figure 7.5   Traditional approach of bank check payment for work**

approach compared with the blockchain solution, as shown in table 7.1. The table highlights issues such as account creation and small payments; it examines where the traditional system falls short and how the blockchain solution elegantly addresses these issues.

**Table 7.1   Traditional banks vs. blockchain payment channels**

| Traditional banking system | Blockchain payment channel |
| --- | --- |
| *Account creation*—For millions of people, it is impossible to open an account in the traditional banking system due to a lack of credentials, such as a job or a home address. | Blockchain is built on this very concept of account-based identity and peer-to-peer interaction between unknown participants. It can facilitate quick account (digital identity) creation. |
| *Small payments*—Payment amounts involved may be too small to warrant account creation. | Blockchain by design naturally supports online digital micropayments. |
| *Check-cashing fees*—Payment in regular checks for every collected bin of plastics may generate numerous checks, and check-cashing fees may be higher than the payments. | The blockchain approach uses a cumulative check-payment approach to address cashing of online digital checks, which helps minimize fees. |
| *Check verification process*—Signing checks and signature verification in a traditional system can be cumbersome for a large number of checks. | Blockchain uses hashing and cryptographic functions for automatic digital signature verification at scale. |

**Table 7.1**  Traditional banks vs. blockchain payment channels *(continued)*

| Traditional banking system | Blockchain payment channel |
|---|---|
| *Account permanency*—When an account is opened, it is permanent and not amenable to a casual open–close model, which is suitable for decentralized users. | Blockchain users can join and leave as they wish, and the open–close channel is naturally supported; thus, short-lived channels are a norm. |
| *Cost-effectiveness*—It is not cost-effective for a casual decentralized user to create an account for a small payment. | Blockchain naturally supports small payments and casual users. |
| *Agility*—A traditional bank account by design is long-running and permanent, and takes considerable time (days) to create. | Blockchain-based payment channels can be opened and closed quickly, and are transient to suit new application models such as MPC. |

Let's compare the two approaches. Figure 7.6 shows a modified version of figure 7.5, but the solution depicted is that of a blockchain-based micropayment. The differences between the blockchain version and the traditional system are highlighted in figure 7.6. Take a few minutes to review the figures carefully, noting the differences in the blockchain application for MPC.

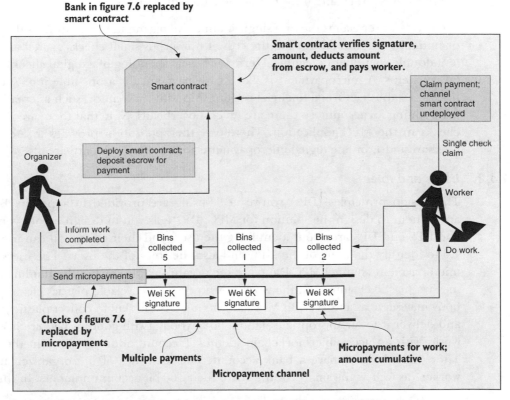

**Figure 7.6**  Traditional vs. blockchain-based system with differences highlighted

Here are the important differences between traditional and blockchain solutions: a smart contract replaces the bank, and digital micropayments replace the payment checks. Note the operations of the blockchain-based MPC shown in figure 7.6:

- Organizer opens a channel. A smart contract is deployed and initialized with the accounts of the two participants: the organizer and the worker. The organizer deposits an escrow for payments. A channel is created for every worker.
- Micropayments replace checks.
- The organizer pays for micropayments in wei (for example, 1,000 wei for one bin), sending signed messages off-chain.
- The micropayments sent are monotonically increasing in value, the latest one holding the cumulative payment until that point.
- A worker claims payment by sending the most recent message that the organizer sent to collect payment and then closes the channel by destructing (via a self-destruct function) the smart contract.

As you can see, the blockchain solution is ideally suited to addressing the issues discussed in table 7.1.

> **NOTE**  If the bins collected are 3, 1, and 2, for example, the micropayments are for 3, 4 (3+1), and 6 (3+1+2)—the cumulative values.

After the worker claims the one single cumulative payment, the contract is destructed or undeployed, thus addressing the cost of numerous small checks as well as fraudulent double spending (a technical term for repeat spending of a digital check) of digital payments. A micropayment is like a cash payment for a one-time job. You don't have to establish a formal financial relationship with the vendor, such as creating and maintaining an account, so there are no cost overheads. Note that there are no paper checks in the MPC application. Therefore, the application provides a safe, secure mechanism for online digital micropayments to decentralized participants.

### 7.4.2  *Users and roles*

The design principles (DPs) you've been using are provided in appendix B. Let's apply them to design the solution for MPC. DP1 tells you to design before you code, and DP2 and DP3 are about identifying the users and their roles. You can use figure 7.6 to identify the users of the MPC and also the roles of the users. The users of the micropayment channel MPC-Dapp are the organizers who secure the funding for the massive plastic cleanup and the workers who do the recyclable plastics cleanup. Anybody may serve as a worker. In MPC, all you need is the skill to collect plastic garbage and deliver it to an appropriate station. So anybody (with good or bad credit) in the world with an accessible blockchain identity (account address) can join the effort. They don't have to have a bank account. The identities of the organizer and the worker (as well as the smart contract) are their 160-bit account numbers. In this case, these account numbers are the Ethereum blockchain accounts that can be created in a few minutes.

A high school student in Mombasa, Kenya, could generate an identity for themselves, access the MPC web page or app, and initiate opening a microchannel between themselves and an organizer. As they walk every day to school, they collect recyclable plastic garbage, deposit it at a verification station, and get a 0.001 ETH micropayment message from the MPC organizer. On the way back home, they do the same. They collect two bins because they have more time. They get a micropayment of 0.002 ETH after depositing it at a station near their home. After a month or so, their last micropayment is 0.09 ETH. They are happy that they can spend the payment on a movie weekend, and they claim it (0.09 ETH) by sending a message (Tx) to the MPC smart contract. The worker enjoys this little extra fund, and some plastic garbage has been removed from the streets of Mombasa. When the payment is settled, the channel is closed. The worker may choose to open another channel and continue with the effort, or they may not. Their friends and neighbors may join in the effort. Thus, the blockchain-based solution is loosely coupled but agile (with quick, efficient setup and dissolution). That is the beauty of this paradigm.

### 7.4.3   *On-chain and off-chain operations*

From the discussions, comparisons, and the scenario in the preceding sections, it is evident that the interaction pattern in MPC is significantly different from that of typical web applications, in which the interaction often follows a request-response pattern. You can even say that the micropayment channel is a new paradigm that is well-suited to blockchain technology. In this new paradigm, there are off-chain and on-chain operations, like the on-chain and off-chain data you learned in chapter 6, which leads to the next design principle.

> **DESIGN PRINCIPLE 10**   An important design decision in blockchain applications is to determine which data and operations are to be coded on-chain and which data and operations are to be implemented off-chain.

To better understand on-chain and off-chain operations, let's analyze the MPC problem once more. As shown in figure 7.7, the sequence of operations provides an overview of the micropayment channel for global massive plastics cleanup. The details of the operations are as follows:

1   *Micropayment channel opened.* A single-use micropayment channel between sender (organizer) and receiver (worker) is created by deploying a smart contract.
2   *Plastics collected.* In off-line (and off-chain) operations, people or robots (workers) collect plastics garbage in bins.
3   *Collections verified.* Off-chain verification is done by appropriate automatic instrumentation, with sender-organizer being informed of how many bins were collected and by whom (using worker identities).

4   *Micropayments paid.* Organizer sends off-chain signed micropayment messages to the worker for bins verified in step 3.

5   *Payment claimed.* Using a single on-chain transaction executed on the smart contract, the worker is paid from escrow deposited by the organizer.

6   *Channel closed.* After the payment, the channel is closed by the destruction of the smart contract.

This list guides the design of the smart contract and web user parts of the MPC-Dapp. Operations 1, 5, and 6, for deploying the MPC and the payment claim, are on-chain and will guide the design of the smart contract next. Operations 2, 3, and 4 are off-chain; only operation 4 is within the scope of the MPC application implementation in this book. Identify the operations in figure 7.7, and make sure that you understand them before moving on to the design.

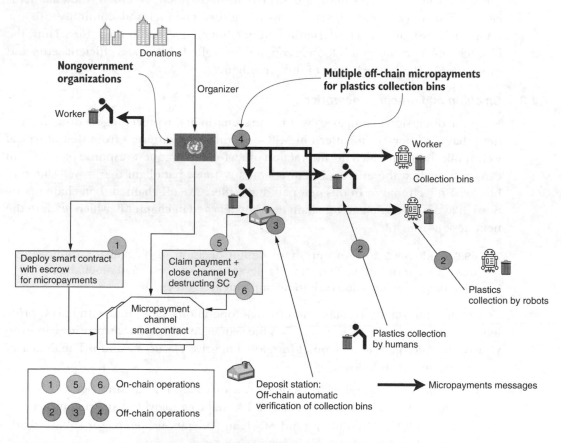

**Figure 7.7    Concept of micropayment channel (MPC) for the decentralized global cleaning**

### 7.4.4 MPC smart contract (MPC-contract)

Recall the application pattern that you followed in earlier chapters. You'll use the same structure for the MPC-Dapp, as shown here:

```
MPC-Dapp
|
|--MPC-contract
|
|--MPC-app
```

For the MPC-contract, the smart contract you'll use is a simplified version of the code discussed in the Solidity documentation. The contract diagram will help you better understand the code. Figure 7.8 shows the contract diagram for MPC (applying DP 4).

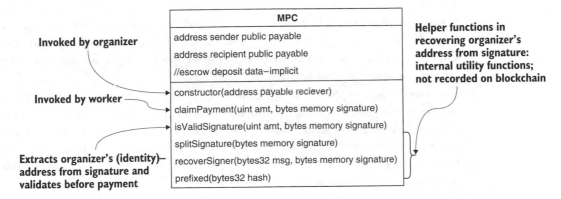

**Figure 7.8   Contract diagram for MPC**

The contract has two public functions, including the constructor. These functions code the two on-chain operations (1 and 5) identified in the analysis in figure 7.7:

- The constructor allows the organizer to deploy the smart contract.
- The claimPayment() function is invoked by the worker when they want to claim a micropayment.

The claimPayment() function is where all the data sent by the claimant is validated. Many items may be validated, but in this case, the only one validated is the signature of the sender. In this case, isValidSignature() is called to check the cryptographic signature. This function in turn works with three more functions—recoverSigner(), splitSignature(), and prefixed()—along with the built-in function ecrecover() to obtain the signer info/data from the signature hash sent by the worker/claimant. This multifunction process is necessary to ensure the robustness of the automatic verification system and the blockchain network, which participants can join and leave as they wish. Moreover, when you are replacing a physical bank with a digital smart contract, you need all these cryptographic functions to replace the measures that traditional systems use to thwart fraud and prevent misuse. Also, you can use this code snippet for recovering the signer in any of your future Dapp development.

Here is the smart contract code that implements all the functions specified in the contract diagram:

- The link or microchannel between the organizer and worker is established by the organizer calling the constructor to deploy the smart contract.
- The worker's address is sent as the parameter `recipient` in the constructor. The organizer is the `msg.sender` of the call that deploys the contract.
- Note that the `claimPayment()` method has various validation checks at the entry of the function body. These validation checks are specified with the `require` clause. If the condition stated within the `require` clause fails, the function call is reverted, and failure is recorded in the receipt tree. If it fails, there is no record of this Tx on the blockchain's distributed ledger technology (DLT).
- A smart contract can hold a balance of ether implicitly because every valid address in Ethereum can have an account balance. You can send and receive value (ether) from a smart contract address. MPC uses this unique property of smart contracts. Imagine a piece of computer code having an identity (account address) and an account balance!
- The conditions explicitly verified include a valid signature, valid recipient (worker), and sufficient balance in the escrow. If verification of these conditions is successful, the claim amount is transferred, and the smart contract and the micropayment channel are closed via the self-destruct statement. Imagine a bank getting imploded after every single channel is closed! This is impossible for a bank but possible with a smart contract.

Review this new paradigm by examining the smart contract code in the next listing.

### Listing 7.1   MPC.sol

```
contract MPC{
    address payable public sender;
    address payable public recipient;
    constructor (address payable reciever) public payable
    {
        sender = msg.sender;        Addresses of the organizer and worker:
        recipient = receiver;       endpoints of micropayment channel
    }

    function isValidSignature(uint256 amount, bytes memory signedMessage)
        internal view returns (bool)
    {
        bytes32 message = prefixed(keccak256(abi.encodePacked(this,
                                                     amount)));
        return recoverSigner(message, signedMessage) == sender;   ←
                            Address of organizer in the signedMessage validated
    }
    function claimPayment(uint256 amount, bytes memory signedMessage)
                                        public{
```

claimPayment pays worker if conditions are met

```
                    require(msg.sender == recipient,'Not a recipient');
                    require(isValidSignature(amount, signedMessage),'Signature
                                                               Unmatch');
  Smart             require(address(this).balance > amount,'Insufficient Funds');  ◁──┐
contract self-      recipient.transfer(amount);
destructs after     selfdestruct(sender);              Balance is a predefined attribute
sending the    ┌─▷                                         of an account address.
 balance to    }
  organizer
               function splitSignature(bytes memory sig) internal pure        ◁────┐
                   returns (uint8 v, bytes32 r, bytes32 s)
               {
                   require(sig.length == 65,'Signature length');
                   assembly{
                       r := mload(add(sig, 32))
                       s := mload(add(sig, 64))
                       v := byte(0, mload(add(sig, 96)))        Functions for
                   }                                          recovery of signer
                   return (v, r, s);                          from claim message
               }

               function recoverSigner(bytes32 message, bytes memory sig)   ◁────
                   internal pure returns (address)
               {
                   (uint8 v, bytes32 r, bytes32 s) = splitSignature(sig);
                   return ecrecover(message, v, r, s);
               }

               function prefixed(bytes32 hash) internal pure returns (bytes32){  ◁────
                   return keccak256(abi.encodePacked("\x19Ethereum Signed
                                                      Message:\n32", hash));
               }
           }
       }
```

The smart contract has taken care of the on-chain operations of opening a channel (1), paying the claim (5), and then closing the channel (6). There is significant work left for the off-chain part, the most important of which is signing the micropayment when the worker completes verification of bins of collected garbage. The signing of the micropayment message is the responsibility of the off-chain part or the MPC-app module of the Dapp.

### WHY DESTRUCT THE SMART CONTRACT?

Consider on-chain operation 6 in figure 7.7 and the corresponding self-destruct(sender) code in the claimPayment() function. Do you wonder why the smart contract is destructed after the payment is transferred? Imagine somebody collecting recyclable bottles and depositing them in a machine for a few cents. The person need not establish a bank account for this purpose; neither do they have to remember or keep track of the machine after cashing the collection. Similarly, in the decentralized channel, you do not want the worker to incur more overhead than the payment they may collect. Also, they should not be cashing the same micropayment repeatedly (double-spending, in Bitcoin terminology). These issues are precipitated by the fact that online participants in MPC are temporary and are typically unknown to the organization. That's why the smart contract is a transient channel between the organizer and a worker. Also, the cost of deploying and undeploying the MPC contract is significantly less than the typical micropayments to the workers.

These ideas about temporary channel are new concepts that you may not have seen in your traditional programming, but you may want to remember them when designing blockchain programs with smart contracts.

### 7.4.5  *MPC application development (MPC-app)*

Let's develop `MPC-app`, the off-chain part of the Dapp where the user interface is typically located. Recall from chapter 4 the design pattern or structure for the MPC-Dapp:

- A web application hosted on a Node.js server
- A web stack with a user interface
- app.js implementing the application's glue code with web3 calls for interfacing with the blockchain services

Among the off-chain operations—plastics collection, verification of bins at a station that informs the organizer, and digital signing of micropayments by the organizer (2, 3, and 4 in figure 7.8)—the only concern for the developer of MPC-Dapp is the digital signing of the micropayments. The organizer digitally signs the micropayments for later verification during the claim process.

Let's examine the digital signing operation, which is a crucial feature of the MPC-Dapp and highly useful in blockchain-based digital networks of unknown participants.

#### DIGITAL SIGNING

What is digital signing? Consider a typical bank check, shown in figure 7.9. It has the amount, bank details, sender details, receiver details, check number, and signature of the sender (a unique signature authorizing the payment). The same figure shows a digital payment message of a payment channel with details mapped one-to-one with the traditional bank check.

Observe that bank details are replaced by the smart contract address and the check number by the unique nonce of the sender account. The micropayment message of the MPC could have all these data elements or a subset of them. The date on the traditional check is replaced by the timestamp of the transaction in the blockchain. The timestamp of a transaction is created at the time of recording, not at the time of creation of the message! You should be aware of these significant differences between bank checks and cryptopayment message. It is possible to pack more elements into a micropayment message to add to the robustness. You'll use the minimum required data so as not to overload the blockchain.

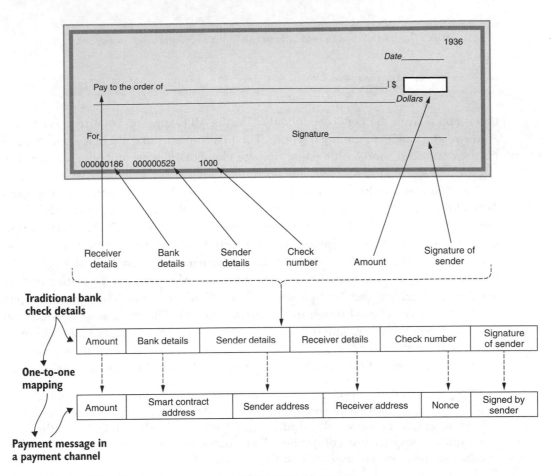

Figure 7.9   Traditional bank check mapped to a micropayment message

Before the message is signed, it is hashed to a fixed size. (Chapter 5 discusses hashing in detail and provides examples.) Regardless of the number of items packed in a message or the size of the message, the message is hashed to a unique 256-bit value. The digital signing operation encrypts this hash value with the private key of the sender. MetaMask can help in securely signing the hash value.

> **DEFINITION**   *Digital signing* of a message involves hashing elements of the message into a fixed-size unique value and then encrypting it with the private key of the sender account.

Let's examine the code in the MPC-app that does this hashing and signing. For the micropayment message in the MPC-Dapp, you'll consider only the amount and the smart contract address. The following code snippets from app.js do the magic—hash the message, and sign it:

```
constructPaymentMessage:function(contractAddress, weiamount) {
    return App.web3.utils.soliditySha3(contractAddress, weiamount)
  }
...
web3.personal.sign(message, web3.eth.defaultAccount, function(err,
                                                signedMessage)
```

Open app.js from the codebase for MPC (in the MPC-app/src/js/ directory) in any editor-reader, such as Sublime or Atom. The first snippet shown here is a `construct-PaymentMessage()` for hashing the message elements; the second snippet does the signing and is from the `signMessage ()` function.

You can observe the use of web3 to access the blockchain functions in the web3 API. The `web3.utils` package is used to call the hash function `SoliditySha3` (*Sha* means *secure hash*), and the `web3.personal` package is used to call the function sign that encrypts the hash computed with the private key of the account. Review the parameters of the sign function. The first parameter is the hashed message to be signed, the second parameter is the account number whose private key is used in signing the message, and the third parameter is a callback function. The signed message or an error is returned through this callback function. This code snippet is general enough. Open the src/js/app.js from the MPC-app directory, and examine the functions `constructPaymentMessage()` and `signMessage()`. You can reuse these functions and patterns in other Ethereum-based applications that need secure digital signing.

> **NOTE** In the UI, the app.js, and the smart contract, the signed message in the MPC plays the role of a personal signature on a bank check. In the latter case, a bank employee personally verifies the signature. In the MPC-Dapp, the signed message is the composite of attributes derived from the contract address, the payment amount, and the account address.

In response to the `sign()` function call, MetaMask facilitates signing the message without exposing the private key of the sender account. The sample MetaMask window that requests confirmation of the signing (appropriately titled Signature Request) is shown in figure 7.10. The figure shows the hashed message, the account number of the signer, and the message requesting the sign. You have to click the Sign button to confirm and go ahead with signing the micropayment. Also, you have the option of canceling the request by clicking the Cancel button.

> **NOTE** MetaMask will require you to connect to the web application before interaction because privacy mode on MetaMask is enabled by default.

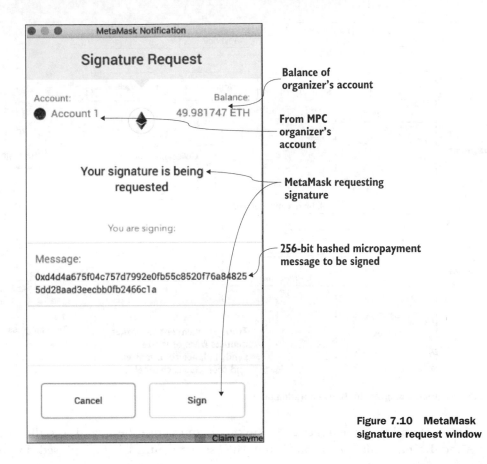

**Balance of organizer's account**

**From MPC organizer's account**

**MetaMask requesting signature**

**256-bit hashed micropayment message to be signed**

**Figure 7.10   MetaMask signature request window**

### 7.4.6   *MPC sequence diagram*

The UML sequence diagram (appendix A) is usually used during the design stage, as specified in design principle 9 (DP 9). You can use it to study other interactions. In this section, let's use a sequence diagram to recap the interactions among the various entities in the MPC-Dapp. Figure 7.11 shows the sequence diagram with four interacting entities: the organizer, the smart contract, the worker, and the verifier.

Follow the diagram from top to bottom along the timeline. The organizer account deploys the MPC smart contract with the two addresses that are participants in the micropayment channel: the address of the sender-organizer and the address of the receiver-worker. This action opens the channel for off-line micropayments. The worker collects the plastics garbage in bins and delivers it to a verifier. The verifier could be an automatic machine that validates the contents of the bins and sends the data about the bins collected to the organizer. Every time this data arrives, the organizer sends an equivalent micropayment (off-chain data) for the work performed to the worker. This cycle is repeated until the worker decides to call it a day. They send the `claimPayment()` request to the MPC contract with the amount (in the latest

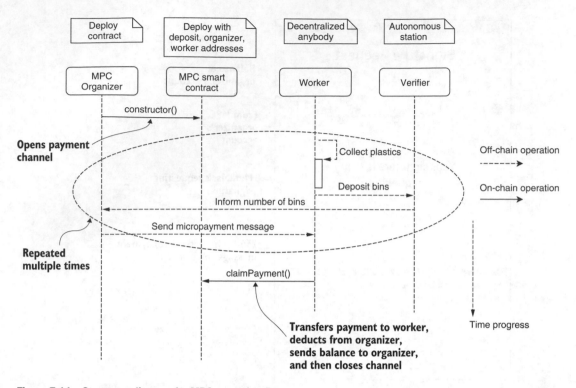

**Figure 7.11   Sequence diagram for MPC operation flow**

message) and the signed message. The smart contract verifies it and pays the worker. After the payment is confirmed, the MPC smart contract is undeployed, by which action the channel is closed.

### 7.4.7   *Demonstration of MPC execution*

Now it is time to demonstrate the workings of MPC. The web interface is a single-page UI, with many extra details that will not be revealed during actual field deployment of the MPC-Dapp. These details are provided to facilitate comprehension of the MPC interaction. The interface displays a running account balance of the sender, receiver, and the smart contract address, for example, as well as the micropayment messages. These extras usually are not presented to the user, but they are displayed here for demo purposes.

Download MPC-Dapp.zip from the codebase for this chapter, and unzip the file to extract the code. Then compile and deploy in Truffle as described in the following sections.

#### SET UP THE MPC-DAPP

1   *Start the test chain.* Start the Ganache blockchain by clicking the Ganache icon and then clicking Quickstart. The Ganache test chain services are enabled on localhost:7545 port and linked to the web UI by MetaMask. (You can also start Ganache from the command-line interface with `ganache-cli` options.)

**2**  *Compile and deploy smart contract(s).* The base directory is named MPC-Dapp, and it has two distinct parts: MPC-contract and MPC-app. From the base directory MPC-Dapp, enter the following commands:

```
cd MPC-contract
  (rm -r build/ for subsequent builds)
truffle migrate --reset
```

These commands deploy all the contracts in the *contracts* directory. You should see messages for the clean deployment of the contracts. Note the smart contract address. You'll also see messages for two smart contracts deployed: Migrations.sol and MPC.sol. Remove the build directory using `rm -r build/` before subsequent builds using `truffle migrate` command.

**3**  *Start the web server (Node.js) and the web component of the Dapp.* Migrate to the MPC-app directory from the base directory for MPC-Dapp:

```
cd MPC-app
npm install
npm start
```

You should see a message indicating that the server is starting and listening on localhost:3000.

**4**  *Start a web (Chrome) browser with the MetaMask plugin installed.* Start a browser at localhost:3000. Using your MetaMask password, make sure that MetaMask is linked to the Ganache blockchain server. You may have to reconnect using 12 seed words of the Ganache test chain. Click MetaMask, and make sure that MetaMask is on Ganache. Go to account 1, and log out. By clicking `Import account by using seed phrase`, copy the seed words from the top of the Ganache GUI, and use them to link MetaMask to the local Ganache test chain.

Now you can interact with the MPC-Dapp web interface, which appears as shown in figure 7.12.

In figure 7.12, the screen is both color-coded and numbered (1 through 5) for the off-chain and on-chain operations discussed in section 7.4.3. Note that the organizer or sender UI is on top of the worker UI on a single web page. The timeline is shown with significant events indicated by a dot. The UI presents several extra details for demo purposes. Note points 1 through 5 in the interface. Point 1 is the indication of the deployment of the MPC smart contract with the addresses of the organizer and the worker initialized. Point 2 represents the worker collecting recyclable plastics in bins and getting them verified. Point 3 is the organizer (Account 1 in MetaMask for this demo) sending micropayments in response to the collection. Note that the worker-receiver address-account number is prepopulated (for this demo). Point 4 is the area where the micropayments will be displayed (again for demo purposes). Point 5 is the claim interaction with the MPC smart contract by the worker (Account 2 in MetaMask

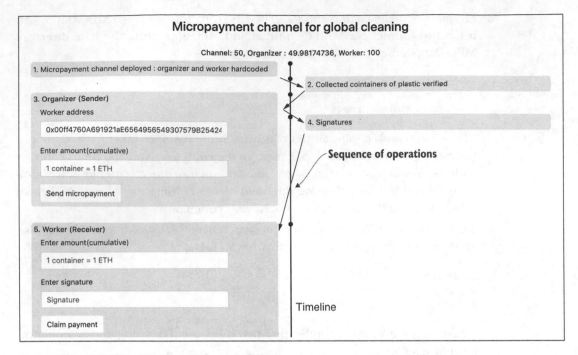

**Figure 7.12   Web UI for MPC-Dapp before interaction**

for this demo). Also, note the balances of the three accounts: the smart contract, the organizer, and the worker. The values are updated as you progress through the demo.

**INTERACT WITH MPC-DAPP**

Here are the steps to follow to simulate a complete micropayment channel interaction. You can follow along with these commands when you complete the deployment of the smart contract and the Node.js server per instructions given in section 7.4.7:

1  In MetaMask, reset Account 1 and Account 2 for initializing the nonce to the starting point. You reset the nonce of accounts by clicking the Account icon and then selecting Settings > Advanced Settings > Reset Account. You reload the UI web page when switching between organizer and worker roles.

2  In Account 1 on MetaMask, on the organizer UI, enter 1 for the container (bins), and click the Send Micropayment button. MetaMask pops up and asks you to sign the micropayment. After you click Sign in MetaMask, a micropayment shows up in the right panel with the value, 1, and the signed message.

3  Repeat step 2 for monotonically increasing values, using first 3  and then 7 for the value, meaning that seven bins were collected, as shown in figure 7.13.

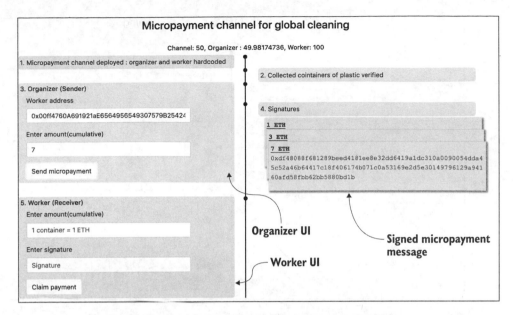

**Figure 7.13  MPC web interface after three micropayments of 1, 3, and 7 ETH**

**4**  Now let's assume that the worker wants to claim payment. Make sure you are in Account 2, which is the worker account in MetaMask. Enter the highest micropayment value (7, in this case) in the Worker UI, copy the signed micropayment message, paste it for validation, and then click the *Claim Payment* button. These actions invoke the MPC contract. If the data entered is correct, the worker will be paid from the smart contract. If the transaction is completed successfully, the balance of the escrow deposit after payment to the worker is returned to the organizer, and the MPC smart contract is closed. Notice that the balances at the top of the UI will change accordingly (Channel = 0; Organizer = 92.98…; Worker = 106.99…), as shown in figure 7.14.

**5**  If the claim payment is successful, a green notification message appears in the bottom of the UI, as shown in figure 7.14. If the payment is not successful, a red notification message appears.

  Both organizer and worker accounts started with a balance of 100 ether and ended up with 92.98 and 106.99, with some fractional ether spent for gas points for transaction execution on the blockchain.

**6**  After claiming payment and closing the channel, the smart contract does not exist, so any operation invocation will result in an error in MetaMask, as shown in figure 7.15.

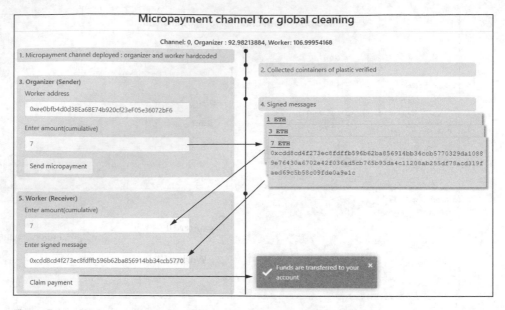

Figure 7.14   **MPC sequence of operations and successful claim payment**

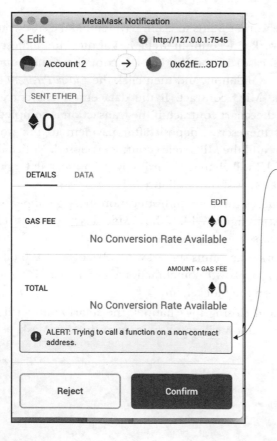

**After closing channel, smart contract does not exist; if you access it then, you'll get this error**

Figure 7.15   **Error message when the smart contract is accessed after channel closure**

### 7.4.8 Accessing the web3 provider

One of the major goals of this chapter is to introduce web3 as an API for accessing blockchain node services. You looked at most of these services in section 7.4.5. So where are the other web3 calls in the MPC-code? They are in the app.js of the MPC-app. In fact, web3 is the means by which the MPC-app web application accesses the MPC-contract and the blockchain services. The core component of MPC-app is app.js, which acts as the bridge between the UI and the blockchain node services, including the smart contract. You already saw in section 7.4.5 how web3 is used for micropayment message formation through a hashing function available in the web3.utils package.

This function is for hashing the micropayment details:

```
web3.utils.soliditySha3(contractAddress,weiamount)
```

Another function specified in the personal package of web3 is for signing a message:

```
web3.personal.sign(message,web3.eth.defaultAccount,function(err,
                                    signedMessage)
```

Access to the smart contract deployed on the blockchain, MPC on Ganache, is provided by

```
web3.eth.Contract(data.abi, contractAddress, ..)
```

Internal computations related to cryptocurrency are in the wei denomination of ether, so when a conversion is required, web3.utils is called:

```
web3.utils.toWei(amount,'ether')
```

A function for accessing the balance of accounts on the chain (in this case, the Ganache test chain) is frequently used in the app.js code:

```
web3.eth.getBalance(accounts[1])
```

Web3 appears in the app.js code in more than 30 locations and is called during its execution many more times. Thus, knowledge of web3.js is essential for Dapp design and development.

Listing 7.2 shows the app.js code. There are five types of calls to web3 packages in this app.js:

- For initializing the web3 object with the web3 provider—in this case, the Ganache local test chain at http://127.0.0.1:7545
- For initializing the web3 contract object with the smart contract application binary interface (abi) and contract address
- For accessing account and balance details to display in the UI to support user interaction

- For application-specific (in this case, MPC-specific) hashing and signing of messages
- For utility functions that convert wei to ether

---

**Listing 7.2   app.js**

```
App = {
    web3: null,
    contracts: {},
     url:'http://127.0.0.1:7545',              ◁──   Data for initializing
     network_id:5777,                                 application App
    …
    init: function() {
      return App.initWeb3();
    },

    initWeb3: function() {
        …
        App.web3 = new Web3(App.url);        ◁──   Web3 initialized with Ganache,
      }                                              the web3 provider here
      return App.initContract();
    },

    initContract: function() {
        …
        App.contracts.Payment = new App.web3.eth.Contract(data.abi,
                    data.networks[App.network_id].address, {});   ◁──   Connect to
        })                                                               the smart
    …      },                                                            contract ABI
                                                                         and address.

    populateAddress : function(){
        ..
        new Web3(App.url).eth.getAccounts((err, accounts) => {   ◁──   Get accounts
    …      },                                                          created in
                                                                       the web3
    handleSignedMessage:function(receiver,amount){                     provider
    …                                                                  Ganache.
      var weiamount=App.web3.utils.toWei(amount, 'ether');
        …
      },

    constructPaymentMessage:function(contractAddress, weiamount) {
      return App.web3.utils.soliditySha3(contractAddress,weiamount)   ◁──
      },
                                                                  web3.utils used to
                                                                  hash the message
    signMessage:function (message,amount) {
        web3.personal.sign(message, web3.eth.defaultAccount, function(err,
                            signedMessage)          ◁──
    {                                                    web3.personal
    …      },                                            to sign it

handleTransfer:function(amount,signedMessage){
```

```
if(App.web3.utils.isHexStrict(signedMessage)){
var weiamount=App.web3.utils.toWei(amount,'ether')
var amount=App.web3.utils.toHex(weiamount)
...}
```

**web3.utils used to convert the payment to wei**

app.js in MPC-Dapp demonstrates the use of a variety of the web3 packages, from web3.eth to web3.utils. Observe the structural flow of the various functions in listing 7.2. Next, let's examine how you can use this information in your development of a Dapp.

#### CODING THE DAPP APPLICATION

Take the time to study the entire app.js code, because you'll have to code a specific one (app.js) for every Dapp. You can use listing 7.2 as the basis for coding app.js in future Dapp development. When you want to code an app.js for a Dapp, armed with the knowledge of web3 in this chapter, you can use the following guidelines:

- Define data for initialization.
- Instantiate the web3 object, and initialize it with a web3 provider. In this chapter, the web3 provider is Ganache; in future chapters, it will be other Ethereum client nodes.
- Link the contract, using its ABI (.json file) and the address at which it is deployed.
- Code the access to the smart contract functions and interaction with the (web) UI.
- Add any supporting functions to facilitate Dapp testing and demonstration. In listing 7.2, populateAddress() is such a function, displaying the account addresses and their balances in the UI.

You've completed your exploration of the new Dapp introduced in this chapter, MPC, and the side channel concept.

### 7.4.9 Extensions of MPC

Unlike the digital democracy (Ballot in chapter 4), marketplace (ASK in chapter 6), and online auction (blind auction in chapter 6) models, the micropayment channel model you learned in this chapter cannot be solved by traditional methods. I am sure you are wondering whether the smart contract for MPC can be kept open instead of self-destructing after a single claim. The smart contract for MPC can be extended to handle other conditions and situations, such as

- Time duration-based channels
- Worker not claiming the payment within a certain time
- Extending the channel instead of closing it
- Premature closure of the channel by the organizer
- Inclusion of other items, such as nonce, in the message of the micropayment
- Bidirectional payments
- One-to-many channels
- Other application-dependent criteria

### 7.4.10  *The relevance of the micropayment channel*

When you have a large payment to transfer, you can still go through the regular financial system. Recently, JP Morgan Chase used the Quorum blockchain (http://mng.bz/6AZD) to transfer a significant amount of value between its clients. This transaction was an on-chain transaction. You may argue, of course, that you can use regular on-chain transactions for commerce, payments, and purchases involving the transfer of cryptocurrencies such as Bitcoin and Ethereum. But the difficulty with current financial systems is in the transfer of micro values that are not significant to the businesses but are valuable to the participant customers. This issue is addressed by off-chain channels, which provide a convenient means for transferring smaller fractional denominations (micropayments) combined with periodic or one-time synchronization with the main channel. You used that pattern to solve the use case of global recyclable plastics cleaning in sections 7.4.4 and 7.4.5.

### 7.4.11  *Other web3 packages of interest*

Web3 is indeed a powerful package, as you can see from the discussions, and as demonstrated in listing 7.2. Let's study a few more of the web3 subpackages.

In general, web3.eth lets an external application interact with a running Ethereum node. Among its subclasses, `web3.eth.personal` deals with the creation and management of accounts within a node, and also manages private keys in a key store, which why it is called a personal API. `web3.eth.personal.newAccount()`, for example, creates a new account within a node. You may have noticed that in the MPC-app, I used a `web3.personal.sign()` instead of `web3.eth.personal.sign()`. The latter requires a password for more security, and a user has the option to use the extra security of a password when signing from a common device.

`web3.eth.debug` helps with debugging at block level. `debug.dumpBlock(16)`, for example, displays the block header details of block number 16. Thus, the debug object of web3 enables you to peek into the blockchain, study it, and debug any issues with the application by looking at the data recorded in the block.

`web3.eth.miner` allows you to control the node's mining operation and set various block mining-specific settings. It's quite simple to understand with an example. `miner.start()` starts the mining operation; `miner.stop()` stops mining. You can also use `miner.start(6)`, in which six parallel threads are assigned to the mining operation. By the way, *mining* is the process of selection a new block for the chain.

You can explore many more packages based on the problem you are trying to solve. You can always install web3 (`require("web3")`) in your Node.js environment, connect to the web3 provider in the Ganache test chain, and test the web3 commands from the command line to learn how they operate before coding them into your application.

## 7.5 Retrospective

You got firsthand experience with digital signing in this chapter. Even though this feature was initiated in the application part (MPC-app) of the Dap, it used the blockchain services for hashing and signing the message. Web3 accessed the hashing and signing functions of the web3 provider in the Ganache node to accomplish these tasks (hashing and signing). It is very important to note that you cannot use any hashing method you wish and sign with anything you like. You are in a common blockchain network; everyone has to speak the same language and follow methods offered by the blockchain services. That's what you did. You used the web3-provided SHA3 function for hashing and used the private key of the account for signing with the help of web3 and MetaMask.

The smart contract for the micropayment channel was quite simple, with a constructor and two public functions to validate the signature and to pay the claim. The other functions in the smart contract accessed the underlying blockchain functions to get you the signer of the micropayment message. Once again, you must use the standard functions to accomplish the tasks in a smart contract. Smart contracts run in a sandbox (EVM in Ethereum) controlled by the blockchain infrastructure so that all the participants have consistent outcomes when a smart contract function executes.

The web3 API is an interface to the underlying blockchain services. Even for simple conversion from ether to wei and hexadecimal numbers to display numbers, you use the web3 (utils) library function because the operations have to be consistent among all participants.

You don't write thousands of lines of code or use composition and inheritance of other pieces of code in the smart contract. The blockchain infrastructure provides many services that are invoked with appropriate calls from the application.

Finally, did you realize that all the entities—such as the organizer, smart contract, worker, and verifier—can be autonomous machines and software programs, automatically cleaning up the earth and collecting cryptopayments for the work? (What? No humans in the loop?)

## 7.6 Best practices

Here are some best practices for payment channels:

- Examine traditional solutions before resorting to blockchain solutions. The conventional banking system may work fine for many of your daily needs, such as bill-paying for your credit card expenses. Where a traditional solution exists, use it instead of overfitting a blockchain solution.
- Analyze a problem and the feasibility of a blockchain solution with real-world scenarios before you start designing a Dapp.
- There are off-chain and on-chain operations in the blockchain ecosystem. Keep the off-chain operations where they are, and link them to on-chain operations, using appropriate methods.

- Use web3 library functions for any computations that are performed on the blockchain node: the web3 provider. Be aware that the computations performed on a blockchain node are in 256 bits, and your regular web application may be running on a standard 64-bit server. A conversion may be needed. Use the functions in the `web3.utils` package for that purpose, not your converters.
- The side channel concept is useful for addressing the scalability issue and for lowering Tx times on the main channel.
- In general, you can remove the unwanted smart contracts deployed if you call the `selfdestruct()` command inside a function. This feature is used in the micropayment channel in the MPC example for closing the channel. Cleanup is needed not only for plastics but also for smart contracts when their use is over. Cleanup is necessary to prevent overloading the blockchain network.

## 7.7    *Summary*

- The micropayment channel concept is uniquely suited to services offered by a blockchain.
- Digital signing of a message involves packing it to a standard size, hashing it, and encrypting it with the private key of the sender.
- A smart contract, though immutable when it's deployed, can be removed with the `selfdestruct()` command.
- Web3 API exposes the services of the blockchain to the application layer.
- The concept of on-chain and off-chain operations complement the on-chain and off-chain data covered in chapter 6.
- A smart contract can be a long-running permanent program as well as a fixed-life program destroyed after a short-time use.
- The channel and side channel combination is a versatile instrument for solving planetary-level decentralized applications involving unknown peers.

# Going public with Infura

**This chapter covers**

- Exploring Ethereum nodes and network infrastructure
- Understanding services offered by infrastructure provider Infura
- Defining a roadmap for deploying a Dapp on a public network
- Deploying Dapps on Infura nodes and the Ropsten network
- Working with multiple decentralized participants

Blockchain is fundamentally a public infrastructure, like a highway or a road. Up to this point, you've been using the Ganache test chain (Ganache on localhost:7545) to deploy your applications, which is like learning to drive in a parking lot or proto-typing an experiment in a lab. Now let's move to the public roads to practice the Dapp development skills you've learned. To drive on the public roads, you don't build the roads yourself; you use the existing infrastructure. Similarly, to deploy on a public blockchain, you'll need public infrastructure support, similar to cloud services. I'll introduce Infura (https://infura.io), a cloudlike service for hosting blockchain nodes. Infura also provides a gateway to public networks such as Ropsten.

In this chapter, you'll take a significant step toward expanding the blockchain ecosystem and enhancing the development skills you have acquired so far: graduating from hosting Dapps on a local test chain to a public chain. This step is indispensable to enable decentralized participants to access and interact with your Dapp. You'll learn about working with Infura by deploying the familiar blind auction and micropayment channel Dapps. For both deployments, Infura will provide scalable infrastructure for hosting the nodes, and Ropsten will serve as the public network. The focus will be on simulating multiple roles of participants in a decentralized network.

NOTE   You must complete chapter 7 to get the most out of this chapter.

## 8.1    *Nodes and networks*

When we consider applications such as email and messaging, most of us see only the user interface of the client (the email client, for example). Behind most applications are servers—application servers that manage the emails, store them, format, and filter them, and so on. Similarly, the nodes are servers for blockchain services, as you learned in chapter 6. The nodes manage blockchain-related operations. A network connects nodes. The operations on the network of nodes (chapter 1) are controlled by a protocol or a set of rules. Figure 8.1 is replicated here from chapter 1 to refresh the network-of-nodes concept.

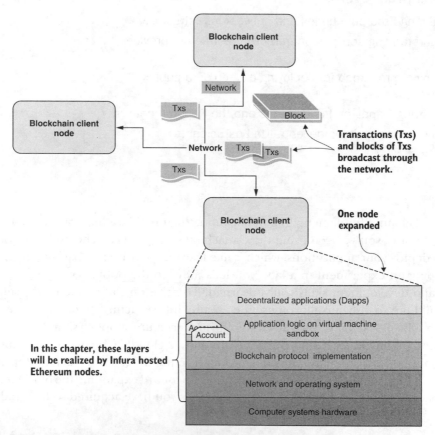

**Figure 8.1   A network of Ethereum nodes (adapted from figure 1.6)**

In earlier chapters, you worked with nodes implemented by the simulated JavaScript environment of the Remix IDE and the local test node in Ganache. These local test environments are fine for prototyping purposes. But how do you graduate from test node in Ganache to a production node in Ethereum? This move requires standing up the Ethereum nodes, securing them as specified in the Ethereum protocol, and managing the accounts and the requirements of the protocol. It typically is not the responsibility of an individual developer to set up and manage blockchain nodes. Consider this: Do you run an email server yourself to interact with your email client? No. Your IT department does that for you. That is precisely the role played by Infura: *it is a secure, production-ready, scalable infrastructure to support your blockchain nodes* in place of your prototype local environment. It provides the nodes and API to access Ethereum networks. Let's learn to use the nodes and networks offered by Infura.

## 8.2 Infura blockchain infrastructure

Figure 8.2 provides an overview of the various services offered by Infura in support of the expanding ecosystem of blockchain-based Dapps. In the bottom-left corner is the familiar Ganache that you used as a test node for the Dapps in earlier chapters—your blockchain development on training wheels. You can take the training wheels off with

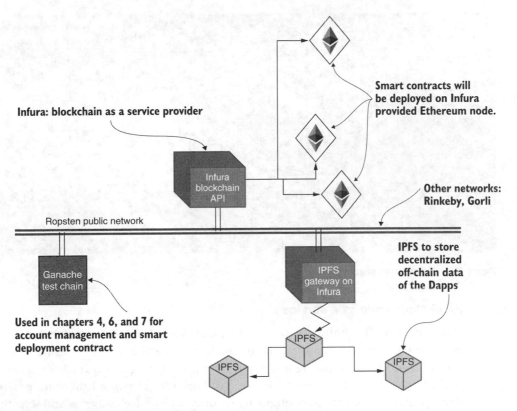

**Figure 8.2 Expanding blockchain ecosystem: Infura, Ropsten, and IPFS**

Infura. Most of figure 8.2 is about services offered by the Infura infrastructure, the primary function of which is to provision Ethereum blockchain nodes. It also makes available the endpoints and the API to connect to the nodes. A public network connects these nodes. You'll use the Ropsten network, as shown in figure 8.1. Infura also provides other services, such as a gateway to connect to IPFS (Interplanetary File System) that can serve as the decentralized store of some of the off-chain data. In this chapter, you'll focus on the endpoint for the Ethereum network and developing with the API to access it.

## 8.3    Going public with Infura

Infura is an infrastructure service for Ethereum Geth client nodes. (Geth is the acronym for the Go-language-based Ethereum node.) There are two offerings of Infura: one that is free but with a limited number of projects, and Infura+, a paid service that offers more projects and resources, as well as technical support for deployments. You'll use only the free version of Infura in this book.

Figure 8.3 shows the Infura opening page, displaying the services offered for Ethereum blockchain node, IPFS for off-chain decentralized storage, and web3 provider. Sign up for the free version of Infura to follow along with the exploration of its features.

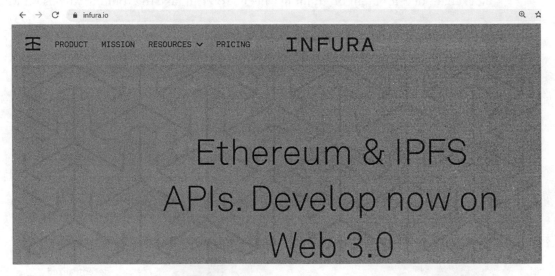

**Figure 8.3   Infura home page**

### 8.3.1    Blockchain node as a service

Infura is a cloudlike infrastructure that enables the Ethereum node as a service. It also facilitates linking with many public networks, such as the mainnet (using real ether), Ropsten, and Rinkeby (using test ether); and provides a gateway for IPFS, a decentralized file system. It offers an easy-to-use dashboard for creating Ethereum projects for deploying smart contracts, configuring security settings for projects, and selecting the public network to connect to.

Figure 8.4 shows Infura's dashboard for creating projects. After you sign up on Infura, you should be able to log in and open the dashboard by clicking Dashboard and then clicking the Ethereum symbol in the left panel. You are allowed up to three projects (in the free version), and you can name them appropriately. In the dashboard, click Create New Project.

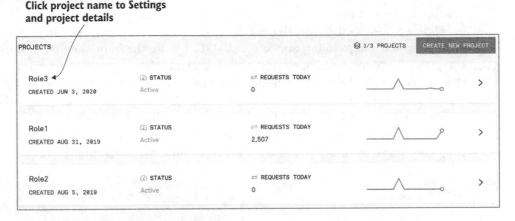

**Figure 8.4   Infura dashboard for project creation**

The creation of a project involves naming the project and optionally configuring its security setting with a password. The project names and node configurations can be viewed and edited after the project is created. In figure 8.4, I named the nodes or the projects Role1, Role2, and Role3 to stand for the generic roles of the Dapps I may deploy on them. You can think of each project as being equivalent to a Ganache node, but a production version capable of driving a reasonable decentralized network of participants. Even though I named the projects Role1, Role2, and Role3 to be agnostic of any particular application, each project can host multiple smart contracts. You can deploy many Dapps in a single project of Infura, depending on the expected load. But this assignment of role names in different projects is for convenience of interaction and testing, load balancing, and avoiding co-tenancy and separation of concerns of Dapps. The blind auction smart contract of chapter 6 could be deployed on project Role1, for example, and the MPC (micropayment channel of chapter 7) smart contract could be deployed on the Role2 project of the Infura infrastructure. Infura also adds useful features such as monitoring the health status and the load metrics (such as the number of incoming requests) on the project nodes.

   When you have familiarized yourself with the new infrastructure of Infura, you're ready to modify some familiar smart contracts and prepare them for deployment on Infura Ethereum nodes and the Ropsten network.

**NOTE**   The Infura interface keeps changing as Ethereum technology evolves. Be aware of the differences when you develop with Infura.

## 8.4    *End-to-end process for public deployment*

To deploy a smart contract on Infura and a public network such as Ropsten, you need a few items, shown in figure 8.5. This roadmap begins from account generation with a private-public key pair and ends with decentralized end-user interaction. In earlier chapters, the accounts were precreated and made available through a test chain such as Ganache. In this chapter, however, you are going to start from the beginning: generating the private key.

Figure 8.5 shows the steps that will be described in detail in this chapter, using two of the familiar Dapps: blind auction and MPC. I'll use the blind auction to introduce the public deployment process and a second Dapp MPC to repeat and reinforce the steps learned with the blind auction Dapp. The figure illustrates the process of deploying a Dapp on Infura-provisioned Ethereum blockchain nodes that are networked via the Ropsten test network. Although it's possible to deploy the smart contracts of the two Dapps (blind auction and MPC) on a single Infura project, I've chosen to use two projects offered by Infura to illustrate the separation of unrelated projects.

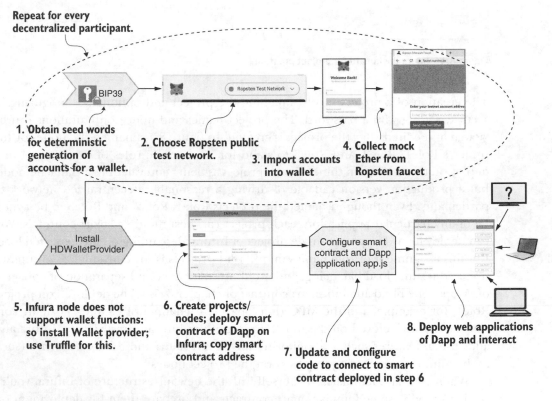

Figure 8.5    Steps in deploying a Dapp on Infura

### 8.4.1    *Account generation and management*

Ganache provided you an initial set of accounts with a balance of 100 test ether for each. You used the 12 seed words to import these accounts into your MetaMask. When you move from the test environment to development, you don't have the Ganache test chain, so you have to self-manage the account addresses yourself. Step 1 of figure 8.5 describes the details. To begin, you need to generate a seed phrase to serve as a mnemonic for accounts. You'll use the BIP39 (Bitcoin Improvement Protocol 39) method (figure 8.6); a tool for generating it is available at https://iancoleman.io/bip39.

> **NOTE**   Mnemonic is a method of remembering facts and items—a memory hook. Here is a common mnemonic for the order of planets: *my very educated mother just served us nachos* (Mars, Venus, Earth, Mercury, Jupiter, Saturn, Uranus, and Neptune). In the case of a blockchain account, the mnemonic maps to the numerical seed from which a deterministic set of account numbers is generated. *Deterministic* means that the same account sequence is restored every time you use this mnemonic.

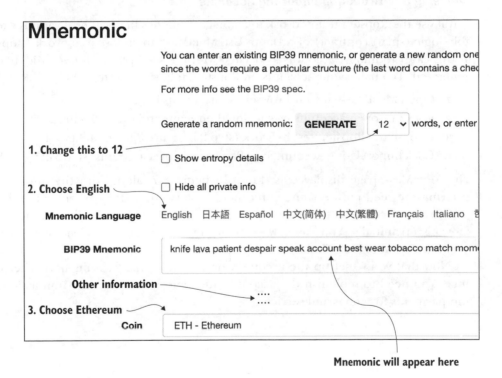

**Figure 8.6   BIP39 Mnemonic generation interface**

Open the BIP39 tool, and do the following:

1   Choose the value 12 from the drop-down Generate a Random Mnemonic box for the number of words in the mnemonic representing the private key.
2   Click English as the language of choice.
3   In the Coin box, select ETH.
4   In response to these selections, a mnemonic of 12 words appears in the mnemonic box, representing a unique private-public key pair.
5   Copy the mnemonic or seed phrase into a file for use in later steps.

You can use this mnemonic to generate a deterministic set of accounts for a wallet every time you restore it. Why should you use a mnemonic rather than actual accounts? A mnemonic is easier to remember and less error-prone during transcription.

> **PRO TIP**    It's a best practice to keep the mnemonics safe, secure, and private. After you obtain the mnemonic, keep it safe in a password-protected file.

### 8.4.2   *Choosing a network and importing accounts*

You'll use the Ropsten test network to connect the nodes that will host various executable logic (smart contract) of a Dapp. Use MetaMask to choose a network (Ropsten, in this case) to import accounts associated with the seed phrase mnemonic that you generated. To enable your accounts on Ropsten, follow these steps:

1   Open MetaMask in your browser by clicking its icon.
2   Lock any open accounts by clicking their icons and then clicking Lock.
3   Choose the Ropsten test network (step 2 in figure 8.5) in MetaMask.
4   Click Import Using Account Seed Phrase to recover accounts (step 3 in figure 8.5).

The MetaMask page displayed is shown in figure 8.7, along with the interface for entering the seed phrase (mnemonic) and a password. After you enter the data, it restores (or reconnects to) accounts in the MetaMask interface, with only account 1 showing up initially. You can always create more accounts by clicking the Create Account option in MetaMask.

Now that you've set up the accounts, observe that the accounts have a zero balance. You need to replenish the account with some (test) ether for transaction fees and payments for goods and services.

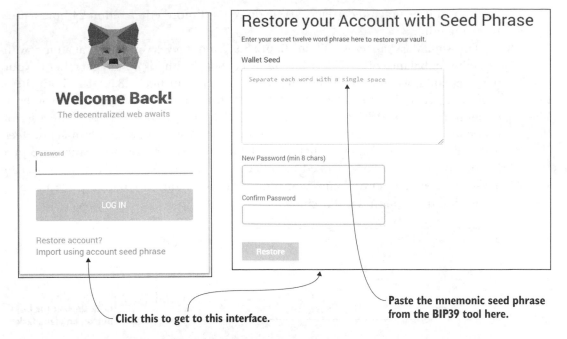

Figure 8.7   Restore account in MetaMask by using the seed phrase

### 8.4.3   Collecting ether from faucets

To operate on any public network, you need ether. Ganache provided you 100 ETH for each account, but now you need to collect the test ether from a faucet—a means by which you can request and obtain test ether for your development. Many test ether faucets are available, but I recommend two of them: the MetaMask faucet (https://faucet.metamask.io) and the Ropsten faucet (https://faucet.ropsten.be). Figure 8.8 shows the Ropsten faucet, which has a limit of 1 ETH per account in 24

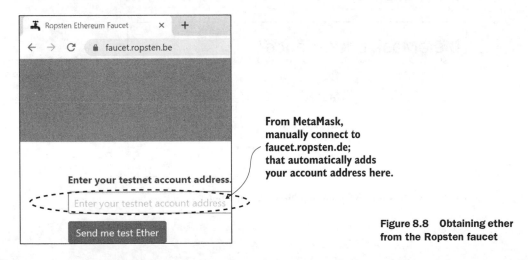

**From MetaMask, manually connect to faucet.ropsten.de; that automatically adds your account address here.**

Figure 8.8   Obtaining ether from the Ropsten faucet

hours. You'll be graylisted (rejected) if you request more ether within 24 hours after receiving ether.

The MetaMask faucet is built-in (figure 8.9), and it gives you 1 ETH at a time, with a maximum balance of 5 ETH per account. Try both methods now to get ether to your newly created account(s). (Collecting ether is step 4 in figure 8.5.) Use both these ether faucets, and keep collecting ether for your accounts every day so that you have enough to run the MPC, blind auction, and other Dapps. Also, you can write a script that collects ether for your accounts automatically! You can pay the transaction fees with 1 ETH, but the Dapps in such a blind auction may require more ether—up to 5 for demo purposes. So you need to collect more ether. As a workaround, you can always work with lower denominations (wei, dai, and so on) of ether for price and payments, but that option is not exciting.

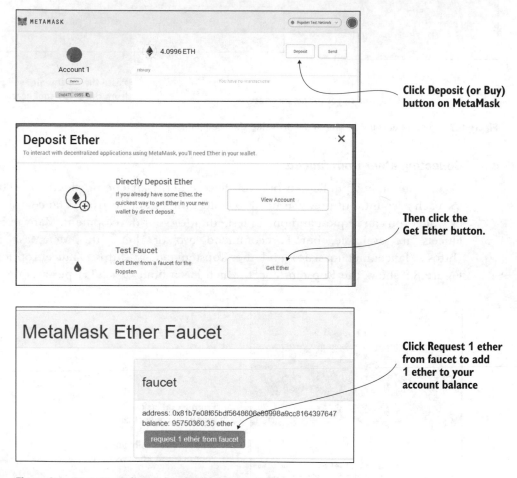

Figure 8.9    MetaMask faucet for obtaining test ether

### 8.4.4 Creating blockchain nodes on Infura

It is time to provision blockchain nodes on Infura. If you have not already done so (section 8.3), you can sign in and create new projects with appropriate names. You can always edit any of the attributes of a project, as well as delete and re-create a project during the development phase. The blockchain nodes work on any of these public networks: mainnet (real Ethereum public) and the Kovan, Ropsten, Rinkeby, and Gorli test nets. Here are the steps to obtain the Infura-Ropsten endpoint address:

- Click the word Dashboard in the top-left corner of the Infura home page.
- Click the Ethereum symbol in the left panel.
- Click the name of the project you created (Role1, for example) and then click Settings. You'll see the screen shown in figure 8.10.
- Choose Ropsten as the network endpoint from the drop-down list of endpoints, and copy the endpoint address that appears. Even though the Ropsten test network is selected for your experimentation, it is simple to switch to other networks by choosing the network name from the endpoints drop-down list.

The endpoint address shown in figure 8.10 is required for configuring your smart contract and the Dapp configurations so that they deploy and interact on the Infura nodes and Ropsten network. In Figure 8.10, the endpoints are hidden so that you don't inadvertently use the nodes I created. You should protect the endpoints that you use in your development.

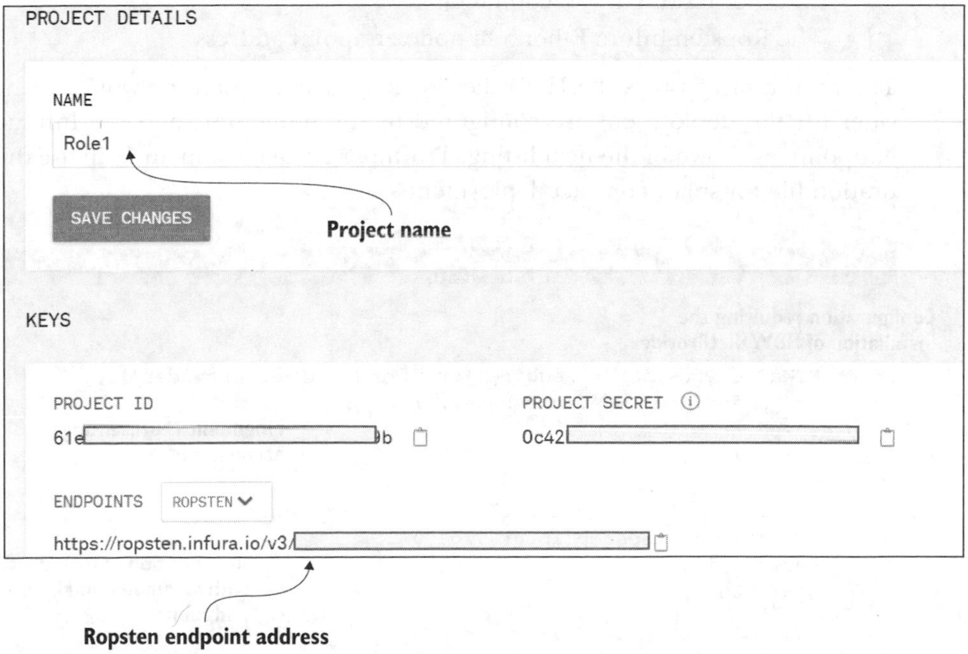

**Figure 8.10   Infura node and network endpoint details**

### 8.4.5   *Installing HDWalletProvider*

An Infura node manages the blockchain gateway and infrastructure services. But for security and privacy reasons, it does not support functions such as transaction signing and managing accounts, so you need a software module for a wallet manager. The Truffle suite includes a web3 provider called HDWalletProvider (http://mng.bz/oRar) that includes wallet management. To install the HDWalletProvider module, you'll use the npm installer. Add a line of code to truffle-config.js in the contract directory to install this module. This file is already included in the code we've provided:

```
const HDWalletProvider = require('truffle-hdwallet-provider');
```

You have other parameters to configure before you deploy the smart contract and web application.

### 8.4.6   *Configuring and deploying the smart contract*

Smart contracts require a node, network, account addresses, and ether balance for successful deployment. You configure these elements by adding to the truffle-config.js that you used for the configuration to the Ganache local chain. You need to configure these items for the smart contract deployment:

- The HDWalletProvider installation specified by `require('truffle-hdwallet-provider')`
- The mnemonic representing the deployer's account addresses for deployment and withdrawing transaction fees
- The Ropsten-Infura Ethereum node endpoint address

The npm utility installs the HDWalletProvider. The Ropsten network and node provider for the deployment are configured by the mnemonic and the Infura-Ropsten endpoint, as shown in the next listing. Truffle's `migrate` command will use this configuration file for smart contract deployment.

> **Listing 8.1   truffle-config.js**

**Configuration requiring the installation of HDWalletProvider**

```
const HDWalletProvider = require('truffle-hdwallet-provider');
mnemonic='  add your mnemonic here,,';          ⟵    Mnemonic representing
module.exports = {                                    account address
  networks: {
    ropsten: {
      provider: () => new HDWalletProvider(mnemonic,
      ➥ 'https://ropsten.infura.io/v3/…'),      ⟵    Instantiation of HDWalletProvider
      network_id: 3,                                  with mnemonic and Infura-Ropsten
      gas: 5000000,                                   endpoint
      …
    }
  },…
```

You can deploy the smart contract by using the `truffle migrate` command with Ropsten as the network option (two dashes before `network`):

```
truffle migrate --network ropsten
```

This command does the following things:

- Compiles the smart contract
- Generates the application binary interface (ABI) code of the smart contract as a JSON file in the build directory
- Generates the address of the smart contract
- Deploys the smart contract on the Ropsten network specified in the truffle-config.js file

As the next step, you'll configure and deploy the web application to access the smart contract and interact with it.

### 8.4.7 Configuring and deploying the web application

To configure the web application, you'll need these items:

- *The network where the smart contract is deployed*—This network is identified by its name or number, such as mainnet identifier ID 1, ganache 5777, Ropsten is 3, and so on. The MetaMask wallet lets you select the network you'd like to connect, as shown in figure 8.11.
- *A smart contract address*—Within the network, select the smart contract address to access.
- *The ABI*—The ABI, an interface that applications use to invoke or call a smart contract's functions, is generated as a JSON file during the compilation of the smart contract and is available in the build directory.

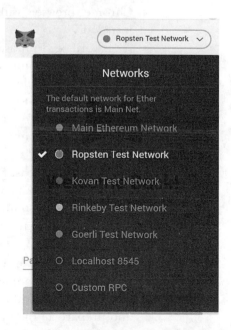

The last two items are configured in the app.js (src/js/app.js of the web application part of the Dapp). When app.js is configured with these details, the web application can be deployed with npm commands. Upon successful deployment of the smart contract and web applications, you can interact with the Dapp through web interfaces.

So far, I've provided an overview of the steps involved in the public deployment of a Dapp. Let's put the methodology into action.

**Figure 8.11   Ethereum network choices for MetaMask wallet**

In the next sections, I'll demonstrate the steps in the public deployment on Infura nodes and Ropsten network by using a familiar blind auction Dapp (section 8.5) and reinforce it by using the MPC-Dapp (section 8.6).

## 8.5    *Deploying BlindAuction-Dapp on Infura*

The blind auction problem and a basic solution are covered in earlier chapters, so you should be familiar with that Dapp by now. If not, review chapters 5 through 7. There are three significant steps: setting up the environment, configuring and deploying the beneficiary, and configuring and deploying bidders. This pattern is the same one that you'll follow in the development of other Dapps:

- Set up the environment.
- Configure and deploy different roles (beneficiary and bidder).
- Interact with the various web interfaces.

### 8.5.1    *Setting up the blind auction environment*

Let's apply all the steps in the roadmap detailed in figure 8.5. Here are some prerequisites before launching the demonstration. These steps should be familiar to you from chapters 4–7 and the detailed discussions in section 8.4:

- Blind auction with codebase for two roles: beneficiary and bidder. Download it from the chapter's code files: BlindAuction-Dapp-Infura.zip. Extract it or unzip it to extract all the files.
- Chrome browser with the latest MetaMask plugin (https://metamask.io) installed.
- A 12-word seed phrase mnemonic generated by the BIP39 tool for each role. You'll have one mnemonic for each beneficiary, bidder1, and bidder2; save these roles in a file called BAEnv.txt (listing 8.2) for quick reference for the project parameters or automatic access for configuration later.
- Account address for each role. Restore or import the mnemonic for three roles into MetaMask (one by one), and copy the account1 address for each role into BAEnv.txt.
- A balance of at least 5 ETH in each of the accounts collected with a Ropsten and/or MetaMask faucet. You can also receive ether in one account and send them to other accounts.
- An Infura project to host the smart contract deployed by the beneficiary.
- Ropsten network endpoint addresses for the project, saved in BAEnv.txt. (See section 8.4.4 for Ropsten endpoint on Infura.)
- Gather all these configurations in a BAEnv.txt file that contains the details given in listing 8.2. Download the template BAEnv.txt from this chapter's codebase, and prepare all the data required, as discussed in this section. All the missing data in the file should be filled with your setup details before you start the exploration of the blind auction Dapp.

**NOTE**   The parameters in the environment can be set up in the .env file and accessed as a variable of the .env instance. That will introduce a layer of obscurity that is common in a production environment. For testing purposes, you'll use this ready reference in the xyzEnv.txt file that contains all the configurations details, such as the mnemonic and Infura endpoints. This file also contains argument values for interacting with the application.

**Listing 8.2   BlindAuction configuration parameters (BAEnv.txt)**

```
BIP39 mnemonic generation tool:
     https://iancoleman.io/bip39/#english

Beneficiary details:
     1. Mnemonic or seed phrase from BIP39 tool:

     2. Account address Account1 on Metamask:

     3. Infura project name: Role1

     4. Infura endpoint address for Ropsten:
     https://ropsten.infura.io/v3/......

Bidder1 Details:
     1. Mnemonic or seed phrase from BIP39 tool:

     2. Account address Account1 on MetaMask:

Bidder2 details:
     1. Mnemonic or seed phrase from BIP39 tool:

     2. Account address Account1 on MetaMask:

BlindAuction contract address on deployment of smart contract from
➥ Beneficiary:
...

Keccak hash values for 1, 2 and 3: for bids
1
0xeef3620c18bdc1beca6224de9c623311d384a20fc9e6e958d393e16b74214ebe
2
0x54e5698906dca642811eb2f3a357ebfdc587856bb3208f7bca6a502cadd7157a
3
0x74bbb8fdcb48d6f82df6e9067fd9633fff4cab1103f0d5cb8b4de7214cbdcea1
```

> This address is available on the deployment of the smart contract.

> Used in the calculation of hash for the bids

### 8.5.2   *Decentralized participants*

In the blind auction problem, the beneficiary and bidders are distinct participants with their own laptops or machines to configure and deploy the Dapp. But you're going to simulate all three roles on a single laptop by

- Switching the account in MetaMask every time you interact from a different role: beneficiary, bidder1, or bidder2.

- (Optional) Using different listening ports for the web server of the beneficiary and bidders—3000, 3010, 3020 for quick identification of the various roles when interacting. If you prefer, you can change the server port number in the index.js file along with the message that is displayed.

After you download the blind auction code and expand it, you'll see a graphical layout of the directory structure (figure 8.12). The figure shows the different roles that you identified early in your design process. The directory structure of the beneficiary has both the usual components, auction-contract and auction-app, and the bidders have only the auction-app web component.

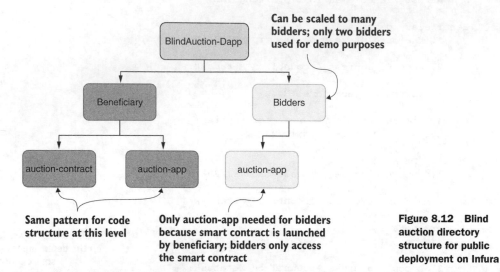

Figure 8.12   Blind auction directory structure for public deployment on Infura

Note the home directories of the beneficiary contract, beneficiary app, and the bidders' app in figure 8.12. You'll have to navigate to these directories for the corresponding deployments. Next, configure the code with the parameters of your Ethereum blockchain network and node setup in the code. Follow these instructions carefully, being sure not to skip any steps.

### 8.5.3   *Configure and deploy the beneficiary account*

You'll begin by deploying the smart contract from the beneficiary account. This step requires the installation of the HDwalletProvider module with the npm command:

```
cd Beneficiary/auction-contract
npm install
```

These commands install the HDWalletProvider module. You'll see a series of messages ending with some warning and zero vulnerabilities. Sometimes, depending on your version of Truffle and npm, you may get some low warnings. That's okay.

Next, in the auction-contract directory, locate and edit the file truffle-config.js as shown in listing 8.3, and enter two details: the mnemonic of the beneficiary and the Ropsten-Infura endpoint that you saved in BAEnv.txt. Note that the mnemonic is within single quotes and that the Ropsten-Infura endpoint string is appended to https://, also within quotes. Save the truffle-config.js file.

---

**Listing 8.3   truffle-config.js**

```
const HDWalletProvider = require('truffle-hdwallet-provider');
beneficiary=' ';                   ←
module.exports = {                        Add the beneficiary mnemonic
  networks: {                             inside the single quotes.
    ropsten: {
      provider: () => new HDWalletProvider(beneficiary, 'https:// '),  ←
      network_id: 3,
      gas: 5000000,                       Add the Infura-Ropsten endpoint.
      skipDryRun: false    ←
    }                            Dry run simulates deployment of
  },                             contracts before real deployment

  compilers: {
    solc: {
      version: "0.5.8"
    }
  }
};
```

After saving this configuration, deploy the smart contract by running the following Truffle command from a terminal window of the beneficiary-contract directory:

```
truffle migrate --network Ropsten
```

The step will take more time than local deployment, and you will see messages on the page indicating the progress of the simulated dry run of deployment. When the deployment completes, you'll see the actual deployment of the blind auction smart contract on the Infura-Ropsten public network. As with any public infrastructure, this process will take time, depending on the traffic on the network. Be patient, and try the command again if it times out. I have experienced it timing out as well as failing due to network traffic.

This step will also create the BlindAuction.json ABI file in the build directory. Web (and other external) applications use the ABI for accessing the smart contract functions.

Part of the output from my deployment of the contract is shown in figure 8.13. In the output, locate the smart contract address displayed; copy and store it in BAEnv.txt for use later in the configuration of bidder web applications. Also, study the other items that are output, such as account balance and final cost. Note that the application src/js/app.js directly accesses the smart contract JSON (BlindAuction.json) file that was created during the smart contract deployment process.

```
> Saving migration to chain.
> Saving artifacts
--------------------------------------
> Total cost:          0.00522786 ETH


2_deploy_contracts.js
======================

   Deploying 'BlindAuction'
   -------------------------
   > transaction hash:    0x1b26dc6d12503edab3b8909b09e77b2165d70507a27e98d7b33acf3568b9ea0c
   > Blocks: 0            Seconds: 8
   > contract address:    0xF32FBacBADd156B98A0D188Bb9564948c996dD77
   > block number:        6302276
   > block timestamp:     1567286655
   > account:             0x02812c612a84ACbc6EF82878d8645112964843A9
   > balance:             8.617107969
   > gas used:            1031064
   > gas price:           20 gwei
   > value sent:          0 ETH
   > total cost:          0.02062128 ETH        Address of deployed smart contract


   > Saving migration to chain.
   > Saving artifacts
   --------------------------------------
   > Total cost:          0.02062128 ETH


Summary
=======
> Total deployments:   2
> Final cost:          0.02584914 ETH

binas-MBP:auction-contract bina$ cd ..
```

**Figure 8.13   Output from contract deployment**

When the contract is successfully deployed, navigate to the web application (auction-app of the Beneficiary branch of figure 8.12). Update the Infura endpoint as URL in the app.js, and save it. Install the required node modules, and start the web server (Node.js server). The commands are shown here:

```
cd Beneficiary/auction-app
npm install
npm start
```

That step will start the beneficiary application with listening port 3000, and you'll see the message `Auction Dapp listening on port 3000!`

Now use MetaMask to connect to the Ropsten network, where the BlindAuction smart contract has been deployed. You can open a Chrome browser on localhost:3000 and reload. You'll see the beneficiary interface. Click the MetaMask plugin; import and restore the account by using the Import Account Using Seed Phrase command at the bottom of MetaMask and by copying the mnemonic of the beneficiary from BAEnv.txt and a password to operate the beneficiary wallet. Now you are all set with the beneficiary.

Next, you'll configure the two bidders, each with their parameters. They are simulating and representing two unknown peer participants: bidders in the blind auction Dapp.

### 8.5.4 *Configure and deploy bidders*

Configuring the bidders involves updating the web application app.js of each bidder. I'll deploy two bidders for demonstration purposes. In reality, all bidders will have the same code but will be configured with parameters from their environment file at BAEnv.txt that you created by filling out listing 8.2.

From the base directory of the Dapp, navigate to Bidders/auction-app/src/js, and edit the app.js file with any code editor of your choice. Update the smart contract address as follows. The parameters are filled with values you saved earlier in BAEnv.txt for bidder1. Save the file app.js:

```
App = {
    web3Provider: null,
    contracts: {},
    names: new Array(),
    …
    chairPerson:null,
    currentAccount:null,
    address:'…',
… // smart contract ABI is already embedded in the app.js provided
```

Save the app.js in the src/js directory, navigate back to the base directory of auction-app (`cd ../..`), install all the required modules, and start the web server (Node.js server). Update index.js file's port number to 3010:

```
npm install
npm start
```

That step will start the bidder1 application with listening port 3010, and you'll see the message `Auction Dapp listening on port 3010!`

Now you can open a Chrome browser on localhost:3010 and reload. You will see the web interface of bidder1. Click MetaMask; import and restore the account by using the Import Account Using Seed Phrase command at the bottom of MetaMask and by copying the mnemonic of the bidder1 from BAEnv.txt and a password to operate the bidder1 wallet. Now you are all set with bidder1.

Repeat the same steps to configure and deploy bidder2 in a different terminal window. Configure bidder2's index.js so that the port number is 3020, as shown in the following code:

```
var express = require('express');
var app = express();
app.use(express.static('src'));
app.listen(3020, function () {
  console.log('Bidder 2: Blind Auction listening on port 3020!');
});
```

Now that all the participants are up and running, you can start the interaction.

### 8.5.5    *Interact with deployed blind auction Dapp*

Before you begin the interaction of the bidders with blind auction Dapp, make sure that MetaMask has restored the wallet in the respective participant and is ready to transact. Also make sure that all the participant accounts have a balance of at least 4 ETH. You must be cognizant that you are role-playing for at least three participants: the beneficiary, bidder1, and bidder2:

- *Beneficiary*—Web app for the beneficiary is bound to localhost:3000, and the account address for Ropsten network is restored by its mnemonic.
- *Bidder1*—Web app for the bidder1 is bound to localhost:3010, and the account address for Ropsten network restored by its mnemonic.
- *Bidder2*—Web app for the bidder2 is bound to localhost:3020, and the account address for Ropsten network is restored by its mnemonic.

Unfortunately, every time you switch between participants, you'll have to restore the MetaMask wallet corresponding to that participant. You can avoid this switching if you have different machines, one for each test participant.

Figure 8.14 shows the interaction test plan with the time flow from top to bottom.

You saw this interaction sequence in the local version of the blind auction Dapp in chapters 5 and 6. This figure shows the same interaction sequence in a public environment. Every transaction takes significantly more time than the local version because you are contending with network traffic and remote nodes on Infura and a public network in Ropsten. Note that the interactions in figure 8.14 are numbered in the order of execution:

- Actions 1, 4, 7, and 10 are by the beneficiary; they advance the phases of the auction and finally close it.
- Action 2, by bidder1, happens in the `Bidding` phase. Input the Keccak hash with an obscured one-time password from BAEnv.txt for a bid of 2 ETH and a deposit of 3 ETH.
- Action 3, by bidder2, happens in the `Bidding` phase. Input the Keccak hash with an obscured one-time password from BaEnv.txt for a bid of 1 ether and a deposit of 3 ETH.
- Auction 5, by bidder1, happens in the `Reveal` phase. Reveal the bid of 2 ETH and the one-time password 0x426526.
- Auction 6, by bidder2, happens in the `Reveal` phase. Reveal the bid of 1 ETH and the one-time password 0x426526.
- Action 8 can be by anybody who wants to find out about the winner after the auction ends.
- Action 9 is a withdrawal of deposit by any loser whose deposit has not been returned.

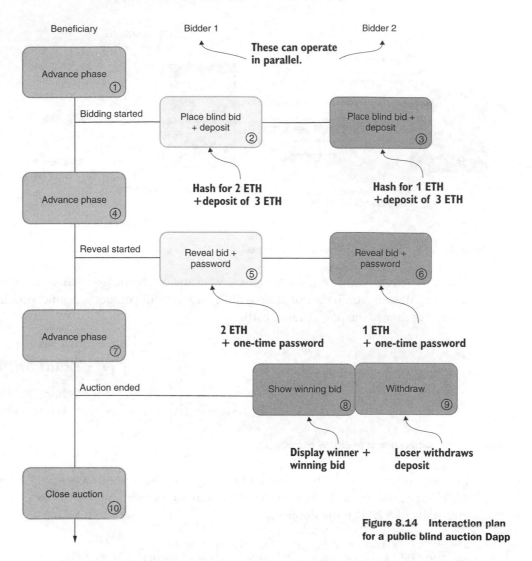

Figure 8.14    Interaction plan
for a public blind auction Dapp

**TIP** You can use figure 8.14 as a guideline for the order of interactions, which are also color-coded for different participants. If you can get two friends from anywhere in the world to operate on the two bidder interfaces, they can interact in parallel. In this case, there's no need for the MetaMask switching that happens in a single-machine simulation of interaction.

The network sequences the transactions as they arrive, and they may even have the same timestamp if they get packed in the same block. The beneficiary page and one of the bidder pages are shown side by side in figure 8.15, with buttons for various interactions such as Advance Phase and Bid. Take a few minutes to review the interfaces and familiarize yourself with the buttons. Now you are ready to run the sequence of the operations in the order specified in figure 8.14 and the list of actions preceding it.

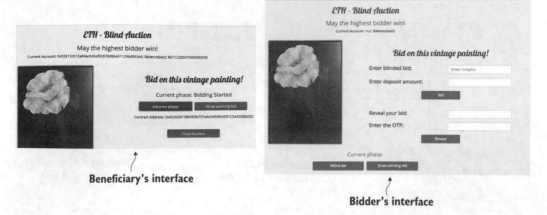

Figure 8.15   **Beneficiary's and bidders' interfaces**

The interaction begins with the beneficiary advancing the phase to Bidding. Wait for the MetaMask to confirm your transaction; also wait till you get a notification in the top-left corner of the page (figure 8.16).

Figure 8.16   **Notification of Bidding phase**

Let the bidders place the blind bid and the deposit. The hashed values for 1 ETH and 2 ETH are provided in BAEnv.txt, repeated here for convenience. The second parameter value of 3 ETH is the deposit:

```
Bidder 1: (a bid of 2 ETH and deposit of 3 ETH)
0x54e5698906dca642811eb2f3a357ebfdc587856bb3208f7bca6a502cadd7157a
3
Bidder 2: (a bid of 1 ETH and deposit of 3 ETH)
0xeef3620c18bdc1beca6224de9c623311d384a20fc9e6e958d393e16b74214ebe
3
```

After the bidders—two of them, in this case—place their blinded bids from their machines, the beneficiary advances to the reveal phase by clicking the Advance Phase button in the interface. Wait for the reveal notification to show up in the left corner. Then the bidders reveal their bids along with the one-time password used in obscuring or hashing the bids earlier in the Bidding phase. The one-time password I used is 0x426526 (that is zero X, indicating that the number that follows is in hexadecimal encoding):

```
Bidder 1:
2
0x426526
Bidder 2:
1
0x426526
```

After that, the beneficiary advances the phase to end the auction by clicking the Advance Phase button. By the design of this experiment, you know that bidder1 won the bid. Bidder2 can verify this by clicking the Show Winning Bid button, which shows the winner's address and bid in wei in the bottom-left corner of the page. Then bidder2 can click the Withdraw button to withdraw the deposit. The balance of the winner's deposit is returned after the winner is decided.

When these interactions are complete, you can verify the balance in all three accounts and make sure that they are the original balance minus the execution cost. I am not giving absolute numbers because these may vary with the account balances at the time you begin testing. The beneficiary can close the auction. Also, you can try other operations, such as Bidding, Reveal, or Advance Phase; they should error out because the contract has been closed. The nodes on Infura, the Ropsten network, and your three account addresses still exist even after the application has been closed. You may reuse these resources in the next exploration of MPC-Dapp in which you can reinforce the concepts of public deployment that you learned in this blind auction example. Let's follow the same steps to deploy and test MPC.

## 8.6 Deploying MPC-Dapp on Infura

Let's now apply the steps in the roadmap of figure 8.5 to the micropayment channel problem. The MPC is about a smart contract and an off-chain channel for digital micropayment incentives for massive plastics cleanup. There are two main roles: the organizer, who deposits an escrow in a smart contract for payments, and any participant (worker) who cleans up plastics in bins and collects micropayments for the bins collected. The MPC problem and a solution for it deployed on a local chain are covered in chapter 7. This exploration of MPC reinforces the steps for preparing, configuring, and deploying a Dapp on Infura-provided nodes with a public network such as Ropsten.

### 8.6.1 Setting up the MPC environment

Review the prerequisites before launching into the MPC demonstration; these prerequisites correspond to steps 1 through 8 of figure 8.5 and set up the public blockchain nodes on Infura and Ropsten to deploy the Dapp for public interaction. You can reuse the mnemonic, accounts (with their balances), and Infura nodes you created for the blind auction application. This exploration requires these items:

- MPC with codebase for two roles: organizer and worker. Download it from the chapter's code files: MPC-Dapp-Infura.zip. Extract it or unzip it to extract all the files.

- Chrome browser with the latest MetaMask plugin (https://metamask.io) installed.
- A 12-word seed phrase mnemonic generated by the BIP39 tool for each role. You'll have one mnemonic each for organizer and worker; save them in MPCEnv.txt (listing 8.4) for quick reference for the project parameters or automatic access to configuration later.
- Account address for each role: restore or import the mnemonic for two roles into MetaMask (one by one), and copy the account1 address for each role into MPCEnv.txt.
- A balance of at least 5 ETH in each of the accounts collected with a Ropsten and/or MetaMask faucet.
- An Infura project. Reuse the project you created on Infura with a Ropsten endpoint address. See section 8.4.4 for details on Ropsten endpoint on Infura node.
- When you complete the prerequisites, you should have an MPCEnv.txt file that contains the details given in listing 8.4. Download MPCEnv.txt from this chapter's codebase, and fill in all the data required for your demo. All the blank data except the smart contract address should be filled in before you start the demo of the MPC-Dapp. Make sure that the .env file is secured and password-protected.

---

**Listing 8.4    MPC configuration parameters (MPCEnv.txt)**

```
Organizer details:
    1. Mnemonic or seed phrase for organizer:

    2. Account address Account1 on MetaMask:

    3. Infura project name: Role2

Infura end point address for Ropsten: https://ropsten.infura.io/v3/
    ...


Worker Details:
    1. Mnemonic or seed phrase from BIP39 tool:

    2. Account address Account1 on MetaMask:

MPC smart contract address obtained during deployment:
    ...
```

This demo is simulated on a single machine by switching the account in MetaMask every time you interact from a different role: organizer and worker. I have also used different listening ports for the web server of organizer and worker—3000, 3010 for quick identification of the different roles: organizer and worker when interacting.

After you download the MPC code and extract it, you will see the directory structure, as shown in figure 8.17. The directory structure is expanded to include the different roles that you identified early in your design process. The directory structure of the organizer has both the usual components, MPC-contract and MPC-app, and the worker has only the app component, MPC-app. Configure the code with the parameters of the Ropsten network and Infura node setup in the code. Note that you are following the same steps you used in deploying the blind auction Dapp. Follow these instructions carefully, and don't miss any steps.

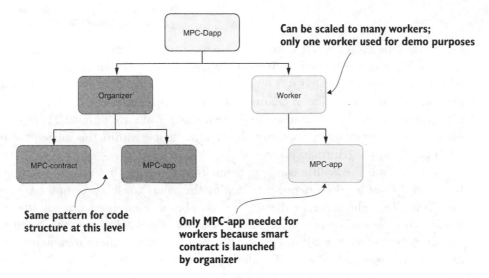

**Figure 8.17   Directory structure of MPC for public deployment on Infura**

### 8.6.2   *Configure and deploy the organizer*

You'll follow the same steps as in the blind auction deployment, but with certain MPC-specific configurations, such as providing the worker's address as a parameter for the smart contract deployment and channel escrow deposit by the organizer. You'll need a Infura Ropsten endpoint for deploying the MPC smart contract. You'll also need two sets of Ropsten accounts, and ports on your local machine, one set representing the organizer (sender of micropayment) and the second one representing the worker-receiver. You'll use these items to configure the MPC-contract directory:

- Worker (receiver) address in the migrations/2_deploy_contracts.js (listing 8.5)
- Setup escrow deposit or channel balance in migrations/2_deploy-contracts.js (listing 8.5)
- HDWalletProvider address with Infura endpoint and account mnemonic of the organizer in truffle-config.js (listing 8.6)

**Listing 8.5    2_deploy_contracts.js**

```
var MPC = artifacts.require("MPC");

module.exports = function(deployer,networks,accounts) {
  …
  if(networks=='ropsten'){
    var receiver='0xd47fEd9f17622d64e154C3af70eE18C4920Bc9B5';
    var balance=1000000000000000000;
    deployer.deploy(MPC,receiver,{value:balance});
  }
};
```

Change the worker's account address from MPCEnv.txt.

Channel balance or escrow deposit
IETH = 1000000000000000000

The parameters you set in 2_deploy_contracts.js, the receiver or worker's address, and the channel balance or escrow deposit are passed on to the smart contract when the constructor deploys it. That sets up the channel and the value the channel holds for micropayments. This value of channel balance is displayed in the web interface along with the balances of the organizer and the worker. You have only 1 ETH available for work, so the micropayments cumulatively have to be within this amount. Save the updated 2_deploy_contracts.js file.

Now update the truffle-config.js to include the organizer's mnemonic and the Infura endpoint for the organizer to deploy the smart contract. Listing 8.6 shows the file. This file is the same as the one for the blind auction except for the variable names. You can get the parameters from the cheat sheet MPVEnv.txt that you created earlier. Now you see the advantage of collecting the environment parameters and having them ready to use. Save truffle-config.js after the update.

**Listing 8.6    truffle-config.js**

```
organizer=' ';          ← Add the organizer's mnemonic.
module.exports = {
  networks: {
    ropsten: {                          Add the Infura-Ropsten endpoint.
      provider: () => new HDWalletProvider(organizer, 'https:// '),  ←
      network_id: 3,
      gas: 5000000,
      skipDryRun: false    ← The dry run simulates deployment
    }                        of contracts for any issues.
  },
  …
};
```

Navigate to the base directory MPC-Dapp, and run the following commands to install the required modules and to compile and migrate the smart contract on the public Ropsten network. The second command will take some time to complete because you are deploying on the Infura infrastructure and public Ropsten test network:

```
npm install
truffle migrate --network ropsten
```

You will get messages about the successful completion if everything goes well. Sometimes, if traffic is too high, the deployment command may time out; be aware of this possibility. Then repeat the `truffle migrate` command until the deployment of the smart contract is successful.

Now navigate to MPC-app of the organizer directory. Start the web server (Node.js server). That step will start the organizer application with listening port 3000:

```
npm install
npm start
```

You'll see the message `MPC Dapp listening on port 3000!` Now you can open a Chrome browser on localhost:3000 and reload. You will see the organizer's interface. Click MetaMask; then import and restore the account by using the Import Account Using Seed Phrase command at the bottom of MetaMask by copying the mnemonic of the beneficiary from the file MPCEnv.txt and a password to operate the beneficiary wallet. You'll see the familiar web interface of the organizer, shown in figure 8.18. Note the smart contract address shown in the top-left corner, enabling configuring of the workers. You can copy this address into the MPCEnv.txt file to configure the worker application. You can also see the balances of the accounts in my deployment. Yours may be different.

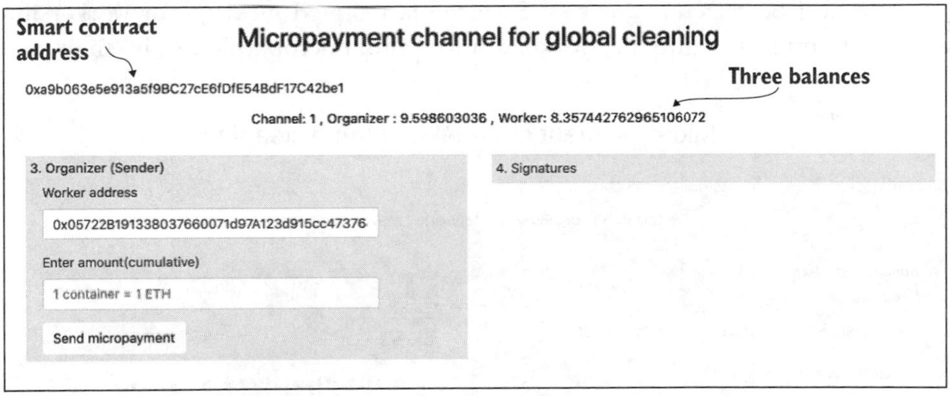

**Figure 8.18  Organizer's interface**

Now you are all set with deploying the organizer. The interaction details for the entire MPC-Dapp are shown in figure 8.19. In this figure, you can observe that organizer and worker interaction are sequential. In other words, the organizer keeps sending the micropayments off-chain as the bins come in, and after all the signed micropayments off-chain are issued, the worker claims one accumulated payment.

Let's assume that worker has completed 0.1, 0.1, and 0.1 bins' worth of plastics, resulting in cumulative micropayments of 0.1, 0.2, and 0.3. Enter the micropayments in the organizer's interface one by one. These steps are all the interaction you'll have

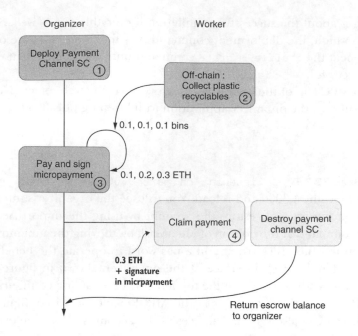

Figure 8.19   Interaction plan for the organizer and a worker

with the organizer, and the resulting page will be as shown in figure 8.20. The numbers will be different for you. Save the last signed message for worker interaction. Next, you'll configure the worker or receiver of micropayments with their parameters.

Figure 8.20   Three cumulative micropayments: 0.1, 0.2, and 0.3 ETH

### 8.6.3   *Configure and deploy the worker*

Configuring the worker and deploying involves working with the Worker path of the MPC-Dapp that only has the MPC-app component. Recall the directory structure in figure 8.17. Update src/js/app.js of MPC-app of the Worker directory with two parameters—the address of the smart contract and the ABI of the smart contract (included in app.js):

```
App = {
  web3: null,
  contracts: {},
  address:'0xb86709182892a6e28dedfF3cB591DAF9dCFfcF24',  ◁──┐  MPC smart contract
  network_id:3,                                                  address from MPCEnv.txt

  ...
```

Save the app.js, navigate to the MPC-app directory of the worker, and run the following commands. By now, you should be familiar with the routine:

```
npm install
npm start
```

After a successful deployment of the worker application, you can open a Chrome browser on localhost:3010 with the MetaMask wallet. Make sure to restore the worker account on MetaMask with the seed phrase mnemonic of the worker. You'll see the familiar page shown in figure 8.21. Enter 0.3, the cumulative micropayment, and the signed message you saved from the interaction with the organizer. Click Claim payment, and when you confirm in MetaMask, you see that a transaction is pending. After the transaction is confirmed, you see the notification about the transfer of the amount to the worker account. After that, the smart contract channel is closed. Figure 8.21 shows that the Worker's balance field is empty because the smart contract is no longer available to answer the balance query.

## Micropayment channel for global cleaning

0x72B6EED2B0034aA7732382Fce8EbF273923

Channel: 0 , Organizer : , Worker:

5. Worker (Receiver)

Enter amount(cumulative)

```
0.3
```

Enter signature

```
0x7a68f7ba5357d92f876e6ee93008557687fddb9{
```

Claim payment

✓ Funds are transferred to your ✕ account

**Figure 8.21  Worker interaction with single cumulative micropayment**

That completes the demonstration of the MPC-Dapp. I have not elaborated on the outcomes of MPC because they were discussed in detail in chapter 7. The goal of this chapter was to learn the steps of deploying on the public chain and an Ethereum node infrastructure provided by Infura. We did that for two different types of interactions: hashed and blinded inputs and decoding, using a one-time password (blind auction Dapp) and micropayment and off-chain side channel (MPC-Dapp).

## 8.7     Retrospective

Deploying on public infrastructure is a multifaceted process, but a review of the road-map shows that it is about setting up blockchain nodes and configuring the system. These steps in the roadmap are necessary to move from testing with a local blockchain to a public chain, where you are operating among thousands of other participants unknown to you.

Dapp deployment (truffle migrate command) and confirmation of transactions took a longer time than local deployments. This delay is understandable because you are among many peer participants and their transactions. You got to experience firsthand users' concern about transaction confirmation times on real blockchain networks.

You may think that creating Ethereum blockchain nodes on infrastructure such as Infura is once again going back to a centralized system. But this setup is experimental; in a real production, environment participants will host the projects on nodes that may reside on their premises or in their cloud environment.

The economics of managing the ether or cryptocurrency balances for the applications is a mostly unexplored area. You may wonder why you need this cryptocurrency for the deployment of Dapps and interaction with Dapps. All your previous development did not need these accounts and balances! Remember that you are in a decentralized realm with unknown peers, especially in a public network. The cryptocurrency or ether is the cost of trust and security in a decentralized system, thwarting the misuse of open resources.

## 8.8     Best practices

Blockchain is inherently public. Consider the blockchain to be a part of the solution for decentralized public use cases. Think of newer application domains and roles, users, and demographics that have not been touched by the current applications.

Similar to how you used Ganache, set up a permanent three-project, three-roles environment on Infura, and reuse the setup for your development and learning. Reuse the same accounts for replenishing the ether from the faucets. Ether faucets can give you only a limited amount per day or an amount decided by the balance in your account. Keep collecting ether every day, the way you get an allowance or per-diem pay. You can always buy any amount of real ether to transact on the Ethereum mainnet, so why waste real ether on test development?

Keep the mnemonics generated safe and secure. Don't give out the mnemonics. Also, keep the same account addresses during testing and development—at least three and one more as a bank for ether. Keep reusing the same accounts for the various roles during Dapp development. This kind of reuse is convenient for learning purposes.

## 8.9    *Summary*

- The public infrastructure of Infura that provisions Ethereum blockchain nodes as a service enables public deployment of your Dapps.

- A roadmap in this chapter provides steps for deploying a Dapp on a public infrastructure. These steps include obtaining parameters for environment setup, configuring the various components with parameters, deploying the smart contract, performing package-based management of the web server, and creating an interaction plan for testing the Dapp.

- Two Dapps—blind auction and MPC—illustrate how to configure Dapps for public deployment.

- When you operate on a public network, you need the cryptocurrency allowed in that network. That is a cost of trust.

- MetaMask wallet helps with account management. As in real life, you switch accounts for different purposes.

# Part 3

# A roadmap and the road ahead

Part 3 focuses on the expanding Ethereum ecosystem, covering tokenization of assets, standards, test-driven development; a roadmap that captures the concepts, tools, and techniques introduced in parts 1 and 2; and the opportunities that lie ahead. The concepts of fungible and non-fungible tokens and standards are presented with a real estate token development. You'll learn to develop JavaScript-based test scripts. I show an intuitive approach to write JS tests and run them by using Truffle test frameworks and commands. I discuss a roadmap and provide a blockchain-based solution to address inefficiency in a certificate program I manage at my institution. I conclude by reviewing many open issues in blockchain technology that the community is actively engaged in solving. Perhaps you can contribute too. You should be looking for opportunities to use blockchain's trust and integrity features to solve problems.

Chapter 9 focuses on two areas of high interest in the blockchain field: tokens and coins. You'll learn to code a non-fungible token application (RES4-Dapp) as an ERC721 standard token. Chapter 10 is about writing test scripts. Automating testing is explained by using `it()`, `describe()`, and `beforeEach()` primitives with three sample scripts to test Counter.sol, Ballot.sol, and BlindAuction.sol. In chapter 11, I provide a roadmap to help you navigate your Dapp developments. I also illustrate the use of the roadmap with an application from my domain of interest: educational credentialing (DCC-Dapp). Chapter 12 provides an overview of the road ahead for blockchain by discussing issues and solutions unique to blockchain applications.

# Tokenization of assets

9

**This chapter covers**

- Developing smart contracts for tokenization of assets
- Reviewing the Ethereum improvement proposal process and standards
- Understanding fungible and non-fungible tokens
- Exploring ERC standard tokens ERC20 and ERC721 for fungible and non-fungible assets
- Designing and developing of ERC721-compliant real estate token

A smart contract can tokenize any asset, tangible (real, financial) or intangible (brand, performance). *Tokenize* means representing the asset with a digital unit that can be transferred, traded, exchanged, regulated, and managed like fiat currency or cryptocurrency. Examples of assets are computing artifacts, files, and photos on digital media, real estate, collectibles, stocks, and even intangible concepts such as security and performance. The asset can be virtual, physical, or imaginary! Crypto-Kitties is an example of the successful tokenization of an imaginary pet family launched on the Ethereum blockchain. You can buy, trade, and breed CryptoKitties as digital pets. You can view many other working tokens on Etherscan. Beyond the

227

hype of digital pets, tokenization has the potential to be a disruptive, visible aspect of blockchain innovation.

Tokenization of assets further helps with the following:

- Standard management of asset behavior with smart contract features
- Streamlined recording and sharing of information about assets via blockchain distributed ledger technology (DLT)
- Traceability of goods and services, such as in supply chains
- Faster confirmation of business transactions such as the sale of real estate (a few hours instead of a few months)
- The ongoing digital transformation in many businesses
- Commoditization and monetization of assets
- Development of new instruments for online trading of assets
- Development of innovative application models

Overall, tokenization is expected to boost the broader applicability of blockchain technology.

In chapters 6–8, the focus was on end-to-end decentralized application development. In this chapter, you'll explore the broader impact of blockchain technology with the introduction of the token concept. You'll learn about standards built around tokens and about *fungible* and *non-fungible* tokens. A new smart contract, the RES4 token, demonstrates the token concept for transforming real estate assets into crypto-assets. You'll design and develop a RES4 Dapp, which illustrates how to take advantage of the blockchain features of trust, immutable recording, and intermediation for efficient transactions of real estate assets.

Tokens need to comply with standards to facilitate seamless interaction among different token applications. This situation is similar to the way that different fiat currencies behave in financial markets and exchanges. Ethereum provides these standards through its protocol improvements initiated by the Ethereum Improvement Proposal (EIP) process. The RES4 is not just another smart contract; it will be designed as an Ethereum standard token to show you how to develop a token that is compliant with Ethereum standards.

## 9.1   *Ethereum standards*

Any time a technology grows exponentially in many directions, with deep and broad impact on all walks of life, from politics to pet shops, we need to pay attention to bringing some order to the situation. This expectation is not unusual. Take a look back at when operating systems became a big deal. Portable Operating System Interface (POSIX) standards were introduced for interoperability among operating systems. The Internet Engineering Task Force (IETF) was established for defining internet standards through requests for comments (RFCs). Commercial flights can land in any compliant airport in any country because of aviation standards—those of the International Organization for Standardization (ISO). Standards bring order, safety, regularization, and clarity to any field. They are especially imperative for a nascent and high-interest technology such as blockchain. Let's explore a little bit of token history. During the years since the advent of Bitcoin and smart contracts, many standalone coins and tokens emerged. This expansion gave rise to many issues and questions about a token such as

- What does it represent?
- What is the value of this token, and how do you assess the value?
- What can you do with it?
- Is it an investment or utility token?
- Can you exchange it for another type of token or for any fiat currency?
- Is it fungible or non-fungible?
- Is it limited in number?

These are concerns not only for you and me but also for the U.S. Securities and Exchange Commission (SEC) and regulatory agencies that are trying to regulate the cryptocurrency industry to protect investors from fraudulent products and investments. The Ethereum community continually addresses these issues through a process that includes development, discussion, and introduction of standards. It has developed a method to improve the protocol that underlies its blockchain and provides standards for advancing application development.

### 9.1.1   *Ethereum improvement proposal*

Let's examine how standards evolve in Ethereum. A standard is developed under the EIP (https://eips.ethereum.org/EIPS/eip-1) to promote improvements in the Ethereum ecosystem. The EIP is a means to manage the protocol specification, improvements, updates, client APIs, and contract standards. EIP handles issues in different categories, including

- Core or core Ethereum protocol
- Network or network level improvement
- Interface or interfaces such as ABI, RPC
- Ethereum request for comments (ERC) or application-level conventions and standards

### 9.1.2   *ERC20 token standard*

As an immediate response to introduction of Ethereum, numerous cryptocurrency tokens emerged to represent various services and businesses. The ERC20 standard interface was introduced so that Ethereum-based cryptocurrency tokens follow a standard and are compatible. The ERC20 standard specifies a set of rules that allows the tokens to interact with one another, exchange with one another, and transact on the Ethereum network.

The OpenZeppelin organization (https://openzeppelin.com) is an active community that supports Ethereum protocol. Its improvements and token standards are discussed at https://docs.openzeppelin.com/contracts/3.x/api/token/erc20#IERC20. Here is a partial definition of the ERC20 interface:

```
contract ERC20 {
        function totalSupply() public view returns (uint256);
        function balanceOf(address tokenOwner) public view returns (uint256
                                      balance);
        function allowance(address tokenOwner, address spender) public view
                          returns (uint256 remaining);
        function transfer(address to, uint256 tokens) public returns
                                                    (bool success);
        function approve(address spender, uint256 tokens) public returns
                                                    (bool success);
        function transferFrom(address from, address to, uint256 tokens)
                                        public returns (bool success);
        //events
        event Transfer(address indexed from, address indexed to,
                                        uint256 tokens);
        event Approval(address indexed tokenOwner, address indexed spender,
                                        uint256 tokens);
    }
```

The ERC20 definition also includes the token `name`, token `symbol`, and an attribute (`decimal`) that specifies how to represent a fractional of a token—the scale factor. To create and deploy a token for an asset or utility compliant with the ERC20 standard, you'll implement a smart contract with the functions required by the ERC interface:

```
contract  MyToken is ERC20 {

// implement the functions required by ERC20 interface standard
// other functions…
}
```

Hundreds of ERC20-compliant tokens have been deployed, and you can see them on Etherscan. These tokens piggyback on the Ethereum network and can operate with the same address as your Ethereum node. More important, theoretically, an ERC20 token can be exchanged for any other ERC20 token on crypto exchanges. This notion opens a whole new world for Dapps!

Here is a view of ERC20 token Txs on the regular Etherscan (https://etherscan.io/tokens), shown in figure 9.1. It shows two different ERC20 tokens transferred from one account to another. You can also locate many such transfers by exploring a token tracker for ERC20 tokens. The link here for the Tx is shown in figure 9.1. It shows the history of the Tx (http://mng.bz/nzYg). Click it and view the record of the Tx to understand the details of a token Tx.

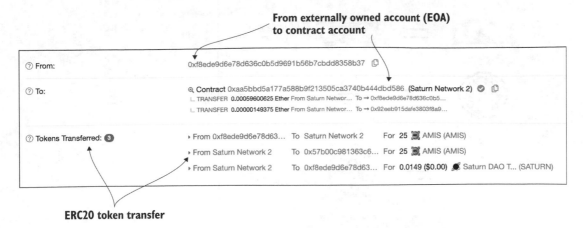

From externally owned account (EOA)
to contract account

ERC20 token transfer

**Figure 9.1   Transaction with ERC20 token transfers**

> **NOTE**  At the time of this writing, ERC20 is being replaced by ERC777, an improved version fungible token standard.

### 9.1.3  *Fungible and non-fungible tokens*

An ERC20 token is like currency, letting users buy certain utility or services by spending the tokens. There is an ERC20 token for paying for energy consumption in the Grid+ application, for example. One ERC20-compliant token of a kind (such as the REP token of Augur) is exchangeable with a token of the same kind, which means that it is a *fungible* token (FT).

A dollar bill can be exchanged with another dollar bill, so it is fungible. When a token represents an asset or a pet, like a real-world puppy, and it grows into a super dog that wins a world competition, this token value would appreciate enormously. Pokémon cards are another example. How about baseball cards and real estate? In these cases and many more practical examples, a given token value may appreciate or depreciate depending on many factors. This type of token is known as a *non-fungible* token (NFT). In this case, tokens are of the same kind, but they are not equal in value and so are not exchangeable for equal value.

> **DEFINITION**  A fungible token (FT) is identical to every other token in value for the same class of tokens. One FT is equally exchangeable with any other within the given class.

> **DEFINITION**  A non-fungible token (NFT) is a unique token within given token class. An NFT is not equal to any other NFT within the given class.

Figure 9.2 further illustrates the concepts of fungible and non-fungible.

As in figure 9.2, every ordinary dollar bill has the same value as every other dollar bill. This equation applies to 1 ETH and 1 Bitcoin, which are said to be fungible items. One item is replaceable by any other item of the same kind. But one pet dog is not the same as any other pet dog in the world. The pet dog Milli is not the same as the pet dog Riley!

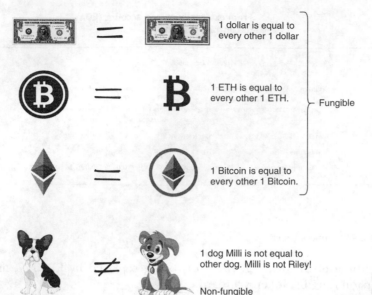

1 dollar is equal to
every other 1 dollar

1 ETH is equal to
every other 1 ETH.

1 Bitcoin is equal to
every other 1 Bitcoin.

} Fungible

1 dog Milli is not equal to
other dog. Milli is not Riley!

Non-fungible

**Figure 9.2    Fungible vs.
non-fungible assets**

In the highly popular Cryptokitties (https://www.cryptokitties.co) Dapp, a token (symbol CK) is used to represent a kitty, and the rules for its creation, life cycle, breeding, and so on are written into the immutable Ethereum blockchain and the smart contracts supported by it. At predetermined times, a certain number of new tokens are released and auctioned off to raise new funds. Assets—kitties, in this case—also appreciate or depreciate (value) based on demand and individual characteristics. Every asset is unique; one asset is not the same as the other. The kitties are not interchangeable. So these tokens are also *non-fungible*.

The Ethereum community designed a fungible and non-fungible token and a standard for each type. ERC20 is the fungible token, and thousands of exchangeable ERC20-compliant cryptocurrencies were deployed. ERC721 is the standard for a non-fungible token, and Cryptokitties, where it originated, made it famous.

Fun aside, you'll have to consider the ERC721 token model seriously. ERC721 applies to a broad range of non-fungible assets. It can represent a lot of use cases, from stocks and real estate to collectible art. Consider a ERC721 token to be a model for timeshare and rental properties—maybe even a piece of land on Mars. The possibilities are endless.

In section 9.2, you'll explore an ERC721-compliant token representing real estate assets.

## 9.2    *RES4: Non-fungible real estate token*

Property ownership—including land ownership, housing, and real estate—has been a tricky problem everywhere on earth since the dawn of history. Many wars and feuds are about land assets. Let's consider real estate to be a non-fungible asset and then design and develop a token Dapp for it. It is worthwhile to note that even though real estate is the asset of focus in this exploration, the token we design stands for numerous other assets in many businesses, as well as in socioeconomic, cultural, and art applications.

We'll begin with a problem statement and then apply the design principles (appendix B) to design and develop the application. This real estate token will be called RES4 (real estate for all).

> **PROBLEM STATEMENT**   Design and develop a real estate token decentralized application representing new real estate developments in a town. The town supervisor can add a piece of real estate as an asset (RES4 token) and at the same time assign it to an owner. This task is accomplished by the process of the creation of the RES4 token. (Assume that the funds for asset ownership are transferred by other means that are not within the scope of this problem.) The owner of the token can add value to the token by building on it, as well as approve a sale to a buyer, and an approved buyer can buy the asset. The real estate asset may also appreciate or depreciate as determined by a town's assessor. For simplicity, assume that the town supervisor and the assessor have the same identity, and that they represent the town and perform operations on behalf of the town.

RES4 is a simplified version of the real-world real estate business. You can improve this basic design after you complete development of the RES4 smart contract and Dapp.

### 9.2.1    *Use case diagram*

To get to the smart contract design, you begin with design principle 2: designing the use case diagram. Figure 9.3 shows the actors for the RES4 token as follows:

- Town supervisor (developer or creator of the asset)
- Owner of the asset
- Builder of the asset (adds value to asset)
- Buyer of asset
- Assessor of the value of the asset

Now let's depict these elements in a use case diagram to begin solving the RES4 token Dapp problem. You can observe the four roles: town supervisor, assessor, owner, and buyer. Essential operations are represented as use cases: add an asset, build, approve buyer, buy and transfer, and assess the property.

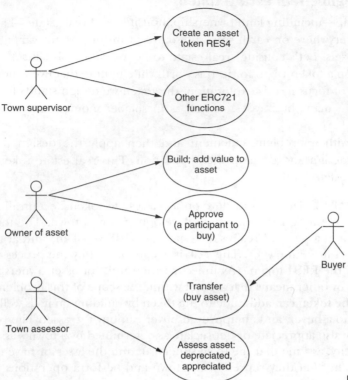

**Figure 9.3  Use case diagram for RES4 asset token Dapp**

### 9.2.2    *Contract diagram*

The contract diagram expands on the guideline provided by the use case diagram and adds more elements of design: data structures, modifiers, events, and functions (function headers). The contract diagram has only three elements: data, events, and functions. The access rules are specified inside the functions with `require` statements (`require (condition);`), not at the header of the functions. The RES4 follows the ERC721 standard that defines a set of function headers.

Figure 9.4 shows the contract diagram for RES4. Besides the data and the events, the RES4 functions in the contract diagram follow the use case diagram. These functions are `addAsset()`, `build()`, `approve()`, and `transfer()`. The functions `appreciate()` and `depreciate()` are for supporting the operations of the assessor role. These operations allow town officials to increase or decrease the current value of an asset. The events specified in the contract diagram are required by the ERC721 standard.

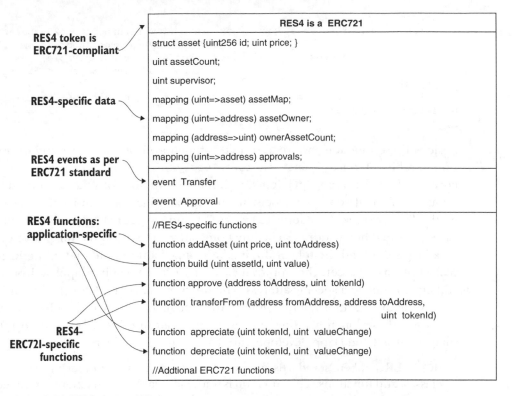

**Figure 9.4   RES4 contract diagram**

### 9.2.3   *RES4 ERC721-compliant token*

Do you wonder how ERC721 is defined? A smart contract implements the specifications of the ERC721, so it is ERC721.sol, written in Solidity. In this section, let's look at the details of ERC721 token and at how to make RES4, an ERC721-compliant token.

**ERC721 TOKEN STANDARD**

Every ERC721 token is unique. One of the requirements of the ERC721 standard is the limited supply of tokens. The limited number of tokens is not an issue with real estate assets; only a limited number of assets is possible if you consider all the real estate assets in an entire town or country, or the whole world. The standard is an interface that specifies functions (headers) that are required to be implemented. For a token to be ERC721-compliant, it has to implement the required functions of the ERC721 interface standard. The design of the ERC721 interface piggybacked on the ERC20 definition. The ERC721 standard is also evolving as I write this chapter. A new function called safeTransferFrom() has been added to the ERC721 interface, for example. Here are the functions of the ERC721 interface that are used in the development of RES4:

```
interface ERC721 {
function balanceOf(address _owner) external view returns (uint256 balance);
function ownerOf(uint256 _tokenId) external view returns (address owner);
function approve(address _to, uint256 _tokenId) external payable;
function transferFrom(address _from, address _to, uint256 _tokenId) external
➥ payable;
function safeTransferFrom(address _from, address _to, uint256 _tokenId)
➥ external payable;
…}
```

Besides these functions, we've also used a function from another standard ERC721-Enumerable interface: `function totalSupply() public view returns (uint256 total)`. The `totalSupply()` function limits the number of tokens. The number of items are limited for many assets, including paintings, art, and habitable land on earth. The next two functions, `balanceOf()` and `ownerOf()`, gives details on tokens (assets) owned by an address. The function `approve()` is required for ERC721 to allow an address to spend the token. But it is very important to note that in the RES4, with real estate as an asset, the approval has a different meaning: approval of an asset (token) for sale to a specific address. The functions `transferFrom()` and `safeTransferFrom()` are variations of functions to transfer an asset from one address to another.

Given these functions, how do you incorporate the ERC721 standard into your smart contract and Dapp development? That's what you'll learn next.

> **NOTE**  ERC token standards are in flux, changing in numbering, support classes, and functions. This situation is understandable for an emerging subject such as tokenization. Some tokens are implemented as only partially compatible with the standards. Be aware of these aspects when you develop a token.

### RES4 SMART CONTRACT

Using the use case diagram (figure 9.3) and the contract diagram (figure 9.4) as guidelines, develop the smart contract for RES4. Figure 9.5 shows the block diagram of the Dapp. Observe a new element: the ERC721 token interface. The RES4 smart contract will use the inheritance of traditional object-oriented design for involving ERC721, as shown in figure 9.5. You'll have to add ERC721 as another smart contract (ERC721.sol) in the contracts directory. It also needs other support contracts. These contracts are located in `helper_contracts` directory to separate them from the main RES4 contract. The ERC721 interface is incorporated into the code by the following additions to the smart contract. Follow these steps to inherit the features of one smart contract into another:

1   Import the ERC721 standard interface at the beginning of the smart contract code for RES4:

```
import "./helper_contracts/ERC721.sol";
```

The ERC721 smart contract is imported from a `helper_contracts` directory that also has other contracts used by ERC721.sol. Open the contracts directory, and browse the helper contracts. You'll find many support contracts.

2   This relationship between RES4 and ERC721 is also shown in figure 9.5. RES4 smart contract is an ERC721 token; this is how you specify inheritance in smart contracts:

```
contract RES4 is ERC721
```

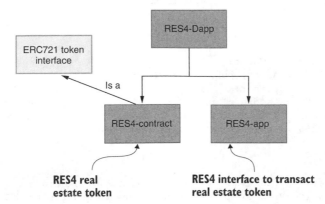

**Figure 9.5   RES4 Dapp with ERC721-compliant smart contract**

## 9.2.4   *RES4 Dapp*

Figure 9.5 shows the overall structure of the Dapp with the contract and app parts. Listing 9.1 shows the RES4 contract. The ERC721 interface is imported from the Ethereum EIP site (http://mng.bz/v9oJ). For convenience, we've downloaded and added this ERC721 smart contract and other related standard smart contracts to the RES4-contract/contracts in a directory called `helper_contracts`.

### DEVELOPMENT OF RES4 SMART CONTRACT

The data defined is mostly for managing the various attributes of the tokens. The functions are developed in four major categories, as delineated by comments in listing 9.1:

- Mapping for various attributes
- Functions, events, and data for ERC721 compliance
- Application-specific (RES4-specific) functions
- Internal functions to support these and other utility functions
- You'll have to implement all the functions for ERC721 compliance, but your Dapp may not need or use all of them. That's why you see two sections in listing 9.1: one for the ERC721 functions required for the RES4 Dapp and one at the bottom that has ERC721 functions used by the RES4 token Dapp but implemented for compliance. You can find the complete smart contract in the codebase of this chapter.

**Listing 9.1    RES4 smart contract (RES4.sol)**

```solidity
pragma soldity >=0.4.22 <=0.6.0;
import "./helper_contracts/ERC721.sol";

contract RES4 is ERC721 {          ⤺  RES4 is an
    struct Asset{                     ERC72l token.
        uint256 assetId;
        uint256 price;
    }

    uint256 public assetsCount;
    mapping(uint256 => Asset) public assetMap;
    address public supervisor;                              Hash tables
    mapping (uint256 => address) private assetOwner;        for managing
    mapping (address => uint256) private ownedAssetsCount;  tokens
    mapping (uint256 => address) public assetApprovals;


//Events
    event Transfer(address from, address to, uint256 tokenId);
    event Approval(address owner, address approved, uint256 tokenId);
                                             Events indexed and
                                             recorded on blocks
    constructor()public {
        supervisor = msg.sender; }
                                   ERC72l functions
// ERC721 functions      ⤺         used by RES4

    function balanceOf() public view returns (uint256) {… }

    function ownerOf(uint256 assetId) public view returns (address) {… }

    function transferFrom(address payable from, uint256 assetId)…{ …}

    function approve(address to,uint256 assetId) public { …}

    function getApproved(uint256 assetId) … returns (address) { …}

                                              RES4 Dapp-specific
// Additional functions added for RES4 token  ⤺  functions

    function addAsset(uint256 price,address to) public{ … }

    function clearApproval(uint256 assetId,address approved) public {…}

    function build(uint256 assetId,uint256 value) public payable { …}

    function appreciate(uint256 assetId,uint256 value) public{ …}

    function depreciate(uint256 assetId,uint256 value) public{ … }

    function getAssetsSize() public view returns(uint){…      }

// Functions used internally   ⤺ - Internal functions

    function mint(address to, uint256 assetId) internal { …}
```

```
function exists(uint256 assetId) internal view returns (bool) { … }

function isApprovedOrOwner(address spender, uint256 assetId) {…}
```
`// Other ERC721 functions for compliance }`

Follow the model provided by this ERC721-compliant smart contract, and use it as a guideline for implementing any other NFT Dapp. You can reuse the ERC721-based code and add to your application-specific code to this base code.

**TRANSFERFROM FUNCTION**

The signature of the `transferFrom()` function implemented in RES4.sol is slightly different from the one defined in ERC721. It has two parameters—`from address` and `asset id`—instead of the three parameters of the same function of ERC721. In the RES4 case, the third parameter is implied and can be obtained from the `msg.sender`. Instead of a centralized authority or a designated person requesting the transfer, the approved person, or the account buying the asset, requests the transfer. In my opinion, this deviation is justifiable, as it (RES4 version of `transferFrom()`) implements a decentralized peer-to-peer transfer, with the blockchain acting as an intermediary.

### 9.2.5 *Interaction with RES4 Dapp*

The next step is developing the app part of the RES4 in the RES4-app module, which exposes its functions in a web UI. Download RES4-Dapp.zip, unzip it, and review the structure. You'll deploy it on the local Ganache test chain, where ten accounts with balances are readily available. Following the structure in figure 9.5, locate the various parts of the Dapp. Then run the following steps to explore the workings of the RES4 token:

1 Start the Ganache test chain by clicking Quickstart. Copy the mnemonics at the top of the Ganache GUI. Link MetaMask to Ganache, using the mnemonics copied from the Ganache interface.

2 Assume that the town supervisor and assessor represent the identity of the town and represented by the address of Account1.

3 Deploy the RES4 token from the RES4-contract directory. Navigate to RES4-contract, and issue the Truffle command to deploy the smart contracts. By default, the first account on Ganache will be the deployer and town supervisor:

```
truffle migrate --reset
```

4 Deploy the web application from the RES4-app directory:

```
npm install
npm start
```

You can view the RES4 web interface (figure 9.6) when you access it by using localhost:3000.

5 Move to the MetaMask wallet and link it to the Ganache test chain, using the mnemonics on the Ganache interface.

In MetaMask, reset the accounts for resetting nonce on Account1 through Account4. Click the Account1 icon, and select Settings > Advanced > Reset Account. Repeat this step for Account2, Account 3, and Account4.

6 The web UI in figure 9.6 shows five operations. Before initiating every operation, refresh the browser:
   – *Add an asset*—by the town supervisor, the deployer of the RES4 token
   – *Assess*— by the town supervisor, the deployer of the RES4 token
   – *Build*—by the owner of the property
   – *Approve*—by the owner of the property
   – *Buy*—by the approved buyer

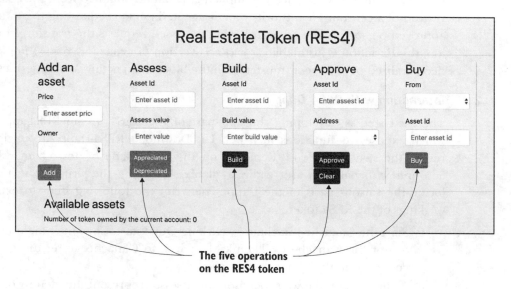

**Figure 9.6  RES4 interface**

7 Add a few assets (by town supervisor). Asset numbers are allocated automatically starting at 0. In a production application, the asset IDs will be 256 bits.

From Account1 (town supervisor's) in MetaMask, add an asset of value 20, choose Account2 as owner, click Add, and confirm.

From Account1 in MetaMask, add an asset of value 30, choose Account3 as owner, click Add, and confirm.

You see the assets added at the bottom of the UI, as shown in figure 9.7.

Assets #0 and #1 are added to the UI, and the owners are Account2 and Account3 respectively. The values of these assets are 20 and 30 as specified when they were allocated (created) by the town supervisor (Account1).

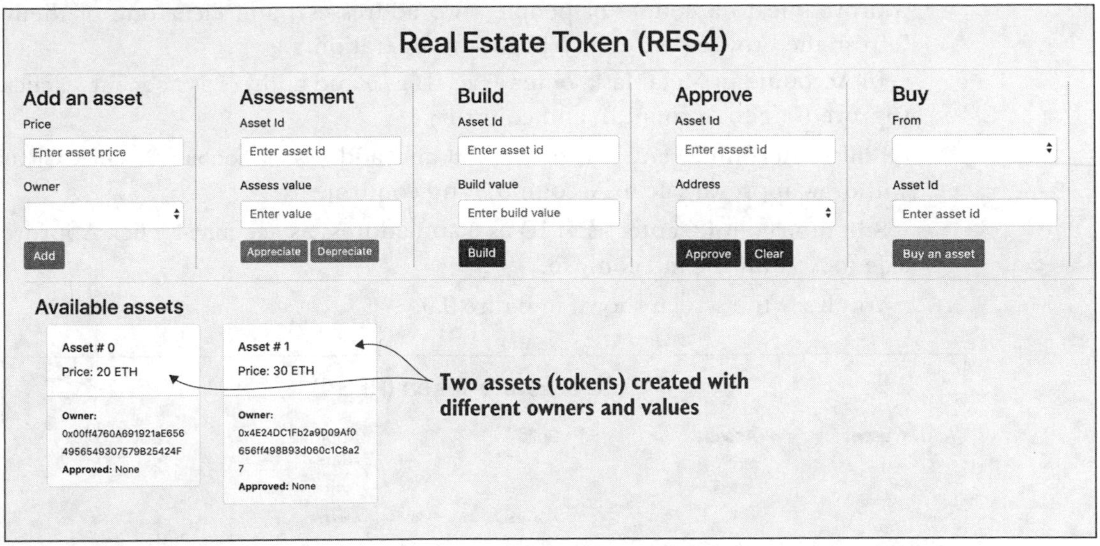

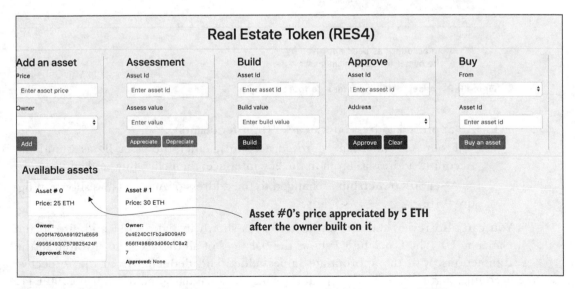

**Figure 9.7 RES4 interface after addition of two assets #0, #1, values 20 and 30 for two different owners**

8 Build on the asset (by owner) increases the value of the asset. Reload (refresh) the browser, and move to Account2 in MetaMask. In the Build interface, enter the asset ID as 0 and the build value as 5, click Build, and confirm

You see that the value of asset #0 has increased to 25, as shown in figure 9.8.

**Figure 9.8 RES4 interface with asset #0 after building and increasing its value by 5 ETH**

9  Approve sale to a couple of people (two addresses), and clear one of them. Refresh the browser before you begin this operation.

In Account2 in MetaMask, enter asset ID as 0 and address as `Account3`, click Approve (sale to Account3), and confirm.

Still in Account2, enter asset ID as 0 and address as `Account3`, click Clear (withdraw approval sale to Account3), and confirm.

Still in Account2, enter asset ID as 0 and address as `Account4`, click Approve (sale to Account4), and confirm.

You'll see the screen shown in figure 9.9.

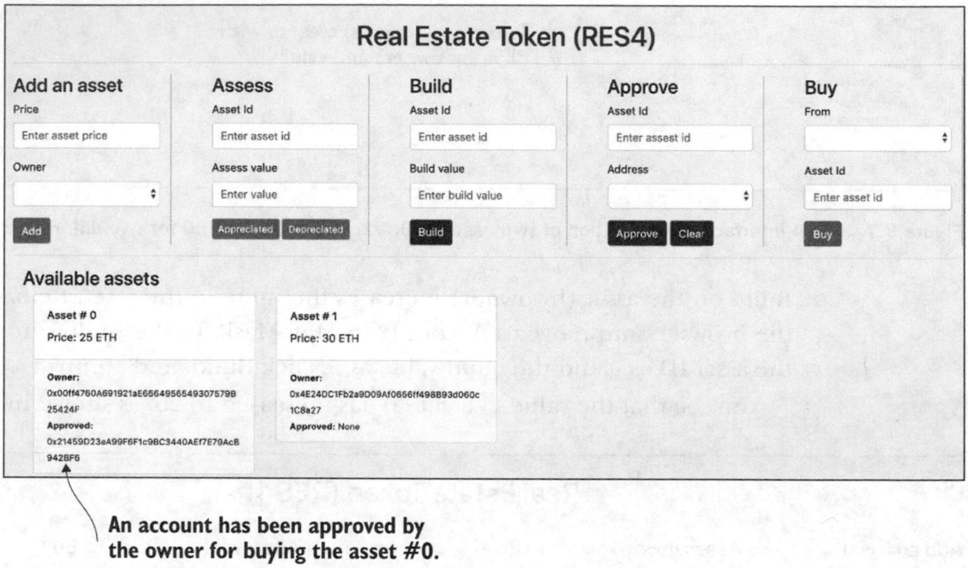

Figure 9.9   Asset#0 approved for sale to Account 4

10  An approved address buys an asset (transfer occurs).

From Account4 (an approved account), enter the asset ID as 0 and the Account2 address as From in the `Buy` interface; then click Buy, and confirm.

Asset #0's ownership is changed to the address of Account4, as shown in figure 9.10.

You can also review the account balances, as shown in figure 9.11 and also in the Ganache UI. The Ganache UI shows the balances of all the accounts involved in the transactions, with the appropriate values added and deducted from the respective accounts. Figure 9.11 shows Account4, whose balance has gone down from 100 ETH to 73 ETH after buying the asset #0 and paying for the Txs. As shown in the middle of figure 9.11, Account2's balance is about 118—an increase from the initial balance of 100 ETH because it incurred fees for selling asset #0 and the transaction fees. On the

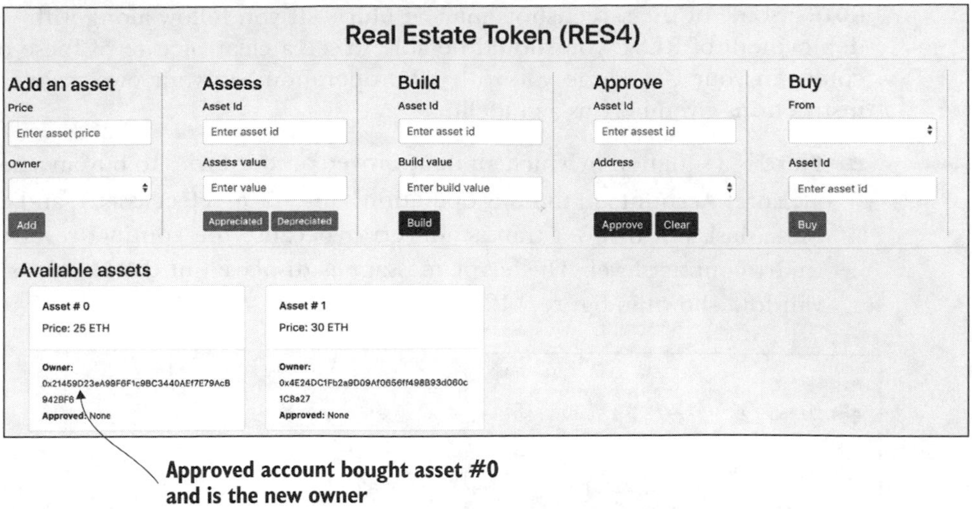

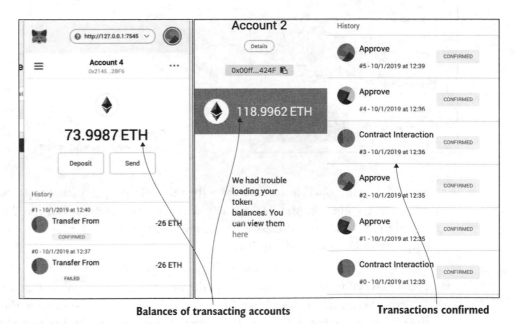

**Figure 9.10  Asset #0 transferred to Account4**

right side of figure 9.11 are logs of some of the transactions discussed earlier, displayed in MetaMask's history of transactions. The balances you observe may be slightly different for you, depending on other transactions that you may have tried. Don't hesitate to explore beyond the instructions given in these steps.

**Figure 9.11  Account balances for Account4 and Account2, and a trace of operations**

**NOTE**   Some of the screenshots may be blurry. If you follow along with your deployment of RES4, you should be able to see a clear picture of these outcomes in your UI. I urge you to try the operations on your own, using the instructions given here as a guideline.

11   Here is a situation in which an unapproved account tries to buy an asset.

Enter Account3 in the Buy operation's interface, select asset 1, and click Buy. MetaMask will throw a transaction error because the contract reverted at the smart contract level. This error message is displayed in the MetaMask pop-up window, shown in figure 9.12.

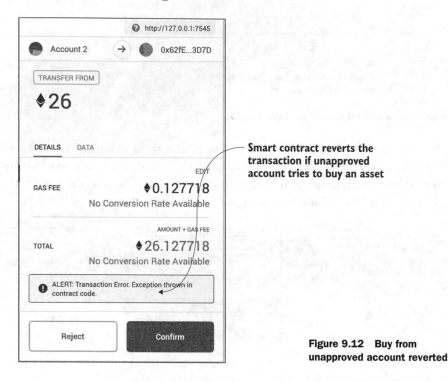

Smart contract reverts the transaction if unapproved account tries to buy an asset

**Figure 9.12   Buy from unapproved account reverted**

12   From Assess interface, assessor assesses the value of a property (that appreciated).

From Account1 in MetaMask (the town supervisor and assessor use the identity of the town), enter the asset ID as 1 and the appreciated value as 5, click the Appreciated button, and confirm.

You should see the value of asset ID 1 increased by 5 ETH.

13   From Assess interface, assessor assesses the value of a property (that depreciated).

From Account1 on MetaMask (the town supervisor and assessor use the identity of the town), enter the asset ID as 0 and the depreciated value as 5, click the Depreciated button, and confirm.

You should see the value of asset ID 0 decreased by 5 ETH.

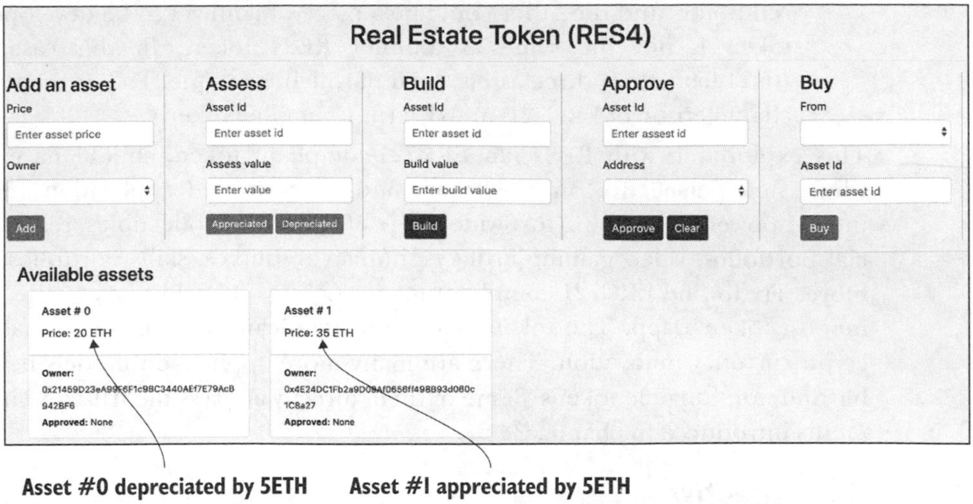

**Asset #0 depreciated by 5ETH     Asset #1 appreciated by 5ETH**

**Figure 9.13   Asset #0 depreciated by 5 ETH, Asset #1 appreciated by 5 ETH**

The asset values after the assessment are shown in figure 9.13.

**14** Add two more assets to Account4 of the same value from Account1 in MetaMask.

From Account1 (town supervisor's) in MetaMask, add an asset of value 10, choose Account4 as owner, click Add, and confirm.

From Account1 in MetaMask, add an asset of value 10, choose Account4 as owner, click Add, and confirm.

You see the newly added assets in the UI, as shown in figure 9.14. Even though the assets are of equal value, they are not the same. One could be a little

**Account #4 owns assets #0, #2, and #3.**

**Figure 9.14   Account4 has three different assets (#0,#2,#3): ERC721 tokens**

red house, and the other could be a piece of land yet to be developed. A RES4 token is not the same as another RES4 token. In this case, Account4 (0x21459...) has three assets, each of which is unique. That is the fundamental characteristic of ERC721, an NFT (non-fungible token).

This exploration with RES4, an ERC721-compliant token, should have revealed a whole new perspective on blockchain and decentralized applications. The NFT is indeed powerful, applying to a wide range of fields: art, collectibles, real estate, financial portfolios, video gaming artifacts, human resources, skills portfolios, and many more. Try to find ERC721-compliant token use in your field of expertise, and implement a token Dapp. The token Dapp is a significant advancement enabled by the cryptocurrency innovation. There are many more application models beyond fungible and non-fungible tokens. Some of them directly address the trust and integrity elements introduced in chapter 3.

## 9.3    *Retrospective*

The RES4 ERC721-compliant token implemented in this chapter is a proof of concept for NFT. The RES4 designed and developed here is a minimal implementation. By including a domain expert, you can further build RES4 into a full-fledged real estate token. This design could include rules for governance and local laws, and other such limitations.

The concept of NFT assets has a broad impact on numerous application domains. The models and standards developed based on this concept can enable a whole range of applications, from managing stored value assets to the human resources skills portfolio. It has the potential to bring art collectors, fund managers, and online gamers into the blockchain world, building a rich and diverse ecosystem for blockchain applications.

Consider this: FT can be transferred in any denomination. That is, you can transfer 0.5 ERC20 tokens or even 0.000005 tokens. This characteristic is true of any FT. For most NFT, a partial token transfer is practically impossible and infeasible. Can you transfer 0.5 kitties physically? On the other hand, for NFT, such as a house, you can have partial ownership. Still, one property (house) is not exchangeable with any other house one to one. All these aspects open many exciting opportunities for the ERC721 standard.

ERC20 and ERC721 tokens have opened a new world of opportunities and application models for blockchain technology. These tokens also represent the beginning of many more innovative standards and improvements to enrich the Ethereum ecosystem. As I write this chapter, ERC20 has been updated to ERC777, an improved version. ERC721 is augmented with ERC165, which checks whether the ERC721 token is indeed compliant with the standard.

Other application models are as exciting as the token Dapp. One of them is a decentralized autonomous organization, in which decisions for action items are made autonomously based on facts input and recorded on the blockchain. The decision made, as well as the explanation (reasons) for decisions, can be tracked by examining the distributed ledger that recorded the transactions and relevant state information.

ERC token standards are being proposed for identity, governance, and security. These tokens and EIPs of Ethereum are sure to enable new application models, transform the Dapp ecosystem into mainstream application framework, and propel Dapps as natural systems.

The token application model enhanced by standards has opened enormous opportunities to monetize services and utilities from the energy marketplace (Grid+) to decentralized prediction markets (Augur). Ultimately, broader adoption and monetization possibilities are important for the sustainability of a technology. Blockchain is no exception.

## 9.4    Best practices

- Various application models have emerged from the initial cryptocurrency innovation in Bitcoin. Review the different existing application models and standards before designing and developing a Dapp. Existing application models and standards may guide and simplify your design.
- Standards have been developed to streamline tokens and their features and to enable exchangeability and interoperability. Wherever possible, actively research the existing standards, and make sure that your smart contract design is compliant with the standards.
- Determine whether public, permissioned, or private membership is appropriate for your Dapp. This important design consideration will determine which blockchain you'll use. Ethereum and Bitcoin are relevant as public Dapps, for example, whereas the Hyperledger framework is by design permissioned and appropriate for private deployments. For the RES4 token, you need a public blockchain network to offer equal opportunity for anybody to buy and sell real estate.

## 9.5    Summary

- Blockchain can not only enable cryptocurrency transfer between unknown decentralized participants, but also empower decentralized participants in applications for robust and transparent asset transfers.
- The EIP manages continuous improvement to the protocol as well as the application models through its standards.
- Two types of token models are fungible (FT) and non-fungible tokens (NFT).
- The FT and NFT token are defined by Ethereum standards ERC20 and ERC721.
- An NFT token model is suitable for assets such as real estate and collectibles.
- RES4-Dapp for management of real estate assets is an example of an end-to-end development NFT model.
- NFT token Dapp methodology includes implementing a standards-compliant smart contract using inheritance feature and an openly available ERC721 interface and other related artifacts for token management.

- The non-fungible token is a disruptive application model covering diverse domains, from collectible assets to financial portfolios.
- This chapter takes a significant step toward advancing blockchain applications from cryptocurrencies to cryptoassets.

# Testing smart contracts

This chapter introduces you to a systematic approach for writing test scripts for the smart contracts of your Dapps. Testing is an essential step in any system development process: hardware or software. It is all the more critical for decentralized blockchain applications with unknown peer participants. In chapters 2–9, you tested the integrated Dapp consisting of the smart contract (Dapp-contract) and the app (Dapp-app) by interacting with the web UI. Although this approach is acceptable for testing the functionality of Dapp, systematic testing of a smart contract is required to ensure the robustness of the core logic of a decentralized application. This testing involves exercising every function and every modifier of a smart contract. For this exhaustive and extensive testing, covering all the possible execution paths, inputting the test commands and parameters manually is cumbersome. Then how do you do it? You do it by writing a script that automatically runs through test commands and verifies that the results match the expected behavior specified in the script. For this type of testing, you'll write a script file of all the tests and automate the testing process.

In this chapter, you'll learn about this test automation process for smart contracts. Writing test scripts requires specific knowledge of primitives such as `beforeEach`, `it`, and `describe`, as well and how and when to use them. This chapter illustrates the development of test scripts with three different but familiar smart contracts: counter, ballot, and blind auction. Thus, you are gradually moving from a simple test script to a more complex one. You'll also learn about using the Truffle suite of tools for running the test scripts and verifying that the tests pass (or fail) as you are developing and deploying the smart contracts.

## 10.1  *Importance of testing smart contracts*

Those of us who grew with the emergence of integrated chips and system on a chip know the importance of testing. Testing is an essential phase of hardware development. Once a microchip is mass-produced, it is impossible to go back and fix bugs. The design is hardcoded. How about smart contracts, the core logic of our Dapps? Smart contracts are like hardware chips—immutable code. Once deployed, they are final and cannot be updated (unless special provisions or escape hatches are built in). More recently, several million-dollar heists in a DAO hack and other wallet issues were due to bugs in smart contract code. So smart contracts must be tested thoroughly before deployment for production use.

### 10.1.1  *Types of testing*

Software testing takes many forms, depending on the granularity of tests and time of test execution during the development phases:

- *Unit testing*—Testing of individpual components such as a single function
- *Integration testing*—Testing of the operation flow of the integrated system
- *System-level test-driven development*—Testing done to verify the integrity of the system developed by different members of the team as functions are added and checked into repositories

In previous chapters, for testing the Dapps, you used an ad hoc plan that exercised the operations of a Dapp by invoking them from the web UI. In this chapter, you focus on unit testing that involves exhaustive testing of the smart contract functions and modifiers. These tests are code scripts that simulate the execution of functions of the smart contract being tested. With the support of the Truffle test framework, the passing and failing of a test can be visually verified by check (✔) and X marks.

### 10.1.2 *Language choice for test programs*

Usually, testers or test programs are written in the same language as the main application to be tested. In this case, you can write the tester itself as a smart contract in the Solidity language. The Pet Shop example provided with the Truffle documentation illustrates tests written in Solidity (https://www.trufflesuite.com/tutorials/pet-shop). But many smart contracts, such as Ballot, use the address data type for the chairperson and the voters. This causes a problem when another smart contract is used as a tester. So we will use the alternative language supported by Truffle—JavaScript (JS)—for writing our tests. Truffle supports both languages and has tools to support JS-based testers, as well as JS test frameworks such as Mocha and Chai. These tools provide commands that are specially designed to write clean, expressive test code. You'll explore testing with the three Dapps developed in chapters 2–5. Choosing these familiar Dapps helps you focus on the testing aspects. In the following sections, you'll use

- The familiar smart contracts Counter.sol, Ballot.sol, and BlindAuction.sol
- Test commands (it, describe) of the Mocha test framework
- The Truffle assertion framework in Chai (assert)
- Test commands with reverting conditions within a smart contract

## 10.2  *Testing counter smart contract*

The counter smart contract discussed in earlier chapters is a simple one, with functions to initialize, increment, decrement, and get (value). Let's require that this counter be allowed to hold only positive values, including 0. To make this counter contract robust, let's add modifiers that enforce rules for incrementing and decrementing so that the positive value of the counter can be maintained. The resulting smart contract for the counter is shown in the next listing. The requirement that the value has to be positive is enforced by the modifiers added to the base code of the counter smart contract.

---

**Listing 10.1   Counter.sol**

```
contract Counter {
    int value;    //positive value counter

  constructor() public{
    value = 0;
  }
  modifier checkIfLessThanValue(int n) {        ◁─┐  Modifiers for
    require (n <= value, 'Counter cannot become negative');   maintaining
    _;                                                        positive value for
  }                                                           the counter
  modifier checkIfNegative(int n) {             ◁─┘
    require (n > 0, 'Value must be greater than zero');
    _;
  }
```

```
function get() view public returns (int){
  return value;
}

function initialize (int n) checkIfNegative(n) public {
  value = n;
}

function increment (int n) public checkIfNegative(n) {
  value = value + n;
}

function decrement (int n) public checkIfNegative(n)
    checkIfLessThanValue(n) {
  value = value - n;
}
}
```

**Functions of the counter contract that use the modifiers**

I'll begin discussing the test script with the counter smart contract. This discussion is followed by two more test scripts: one for the ballot smart contract and another for the blind auction. For the counter, both the smart contract and the corresponding test scripts are provided (listings 10.1 and 10.2). For the next two smart contracts, I'll discuss only the test scripts, because you've already seen the workings of the ballot and blind auction.

### 10.2.1  *Writing counter test script*

In this section, you'll learn about an approach to writing the test scripts using the commands provided by the Truffle JS test framework. Writing a test function script involves these three steps:

- Identifying functions and modifiers to test
- Writing the test script that will exercise each of the functions and ensure that these functions work as expected
- Writing the test script for exercising each of the modifiers and making sure that they work

How do you write these test scripts? What support structures do you have to write these tests? Truffle testing framework provides structures that facilitate writing the tests. Some common and useful test structures are

- beforeEach()—This function specifies the preconditions for other tests. It allows you to specify the code that will be executed before every test defined by it() and describe() test specifications. The beforeEach() function initializes the contract and establishes the base condition for the execution of a test command.
- it()—This function is a standalone test of a function; you can think of it as an *independent test* or a unit test.

- describe()—This function is a composite test structure, and it specifies a group of related it() tests. The Mocha framework supports these test functions. Inside the test functions (it, describe, and so on), you'll also use a few other declarations:
  - async()—Allows for the asynchronous execution of functions, especially because transactions on a blockchain takes variable run times
  - await()—Waits for a callback from the function invoked using async() mode
  - assert()—Specifies the condition to assert; typically, it helps match the actual result of a statement execution with expected results. If the match fails, the assertion fails.

Now let's examine how these items (beforeEach(), it(), describe(), async(), await(), and assert()) are used in writing the test script for the counter smart contract. Listing 10.2 is the JS code for testing the counter smart contract. How do you develop the test code?

First, define the smart contract to be tested. Also declare that you are using the Truffle assertions framework and that a module is required. Then write the code to deploy and initialize the contract, using the beforeEach() function. Before execution of every it() test, the beforeEach() function is executed. Listing 10.2 provides a model test script to get you started.

The listing shows the independent tests (it()) for each function and each modifier in the smart contract. This simple test script consists of one it() function for each item to be tested. Each it() test has an assert() or truffleAssert() statement to check whether the test succeeded. This approach is simple, but a good starting point.

**Listing 10.2  counterTest.js**

```
const Counter = artifacts.require('../contracts/Counter.sol')      ◁──────┐
const truffleAssert = require('truffle-assertions');

                                                        Start definition of test function;
contract('Counter', function () {                       identify smart contract tested
  let counter
  const negativeCounterError = 'Counter cannot become negative';
  const negativeValueError = 'Value must be greater than zero';

  beforeEach('Setup contract for each test', async function () {     ◁──────┐
    counter = await Counter.new()
    await counter.initialize(100)          This code executes before each test;
  })                                       deploy and initialize the contract.

  it('Success on initialization of counter.', async function () {  ◁──┐ Test
    assert.equal(await counter.get(), 100)                             │ function for
  })                                                                   │ initialize()

  it('Success on decrement of counter.', async function () {  ◁──┐ Test function
    await counter.decrement(5)                                    │ for decrement()
```

```
    assert.equal(await counter.get(), 95)
  })

  it('Success on increment of counter.', async function () {      Test function
    await counter.increment(5)                                    for increment()
    assert.equal(await counter.get(), 105)
  })

  it('Failure on initialization of counter with negative number.',
                                      async function () {
    await truffleAssert.reverts(
      counter.initialize(-1),
      truffleAssert.ErrorType.REVERT,
      negativeValueError,
      negativeValueError
    )
  })

  it('Failure on underflow of counter.', async function () {
    await truffleAssert.reverts(
      counter.decrement(105),
      truffleAssert.ErrorType.REVERT,              Tests for a modifier
      negativeCounterError,                        that controls the
      negativeCounterError                         value of the counter
    )                                              to be >=0
  })

  it('Failure on increment with negative numbers.', async function () {
    await truffleAssert.reverts(
      counter.increment(-2),
      truffleAssert.ErrorType.REVERT,
      negativeValueError,
      negativeValueError
    )
  })

  it('Failure on decrement with negative numbers.', async function () {
    await truffleAssert.reverts(
      counter.decrement(-2),
      truffleAssert.ErrorType.REVERT,
      negativeValueError,
      negativeValueError
    )
  })
})
```

Before running each test function, the counter is set to 100 by the function before-
Each(). For the tests, each it() test performs an operation, awaits the results, and
asserts (checks) whether the results match the expected outcome. The it() for decrement shows these aspects. Observe the meaningful string parameter that describes the
test: 'Success on decrement.' It decrements by a value of 5 the counter value that
has been set to 100 by the beforeEach() function. Then it awaits completion of this

operation and checks if it is 95 using the `assert.equal(…)`. Use this syntax as a pattern for writing `it()` test scripts:

```
it('Success on decrement of counter.', async function () {
    await counter.decrement(5)
    assert.equal(await counter.get(), 95)
  })
```

Observe the syntax of the `it()` test. It has a description string for the test, and the function to be executed. Because the function is an `async()` function (asynchronous), the next line is the code to await completion of the decrement function, followed by the `assert` statement that compares the result to check whether it is correct. That's it. Now you're all set to write test scripts with simple independent tests defined by `it()`, using the test script in listing 10.2 as a guide.

### 10.2.2 Positive and negative tests

Recall the idea of positive tests and negative tests described in chapter 3. Here are some suggestions for developing a testing scheme so that you can identify the negative and positive tests when developing and running the scripts:

- *Positive tests*—Make sure that the smart contract performs correctly and as expected when given a valid set of inputs. In the test script, all these tests have their description begin with the phrase `'Success on'`. This string is also output when you run the script.
- *Negative tests*—Make sure that the smart contract catches the errors during verification and validation and that functions revert when given invalid inputs. In the test script, all these tests have their description begin with the phrase `'Failure on'`. This string is also output when you run the script.

### 10.2.3 Running the test script

Now it is time to run the test script and check whether the tests passed. The script shown in listing 10.2 captures the testing concepts discussed so far. Save this script as counterTest.js in the test directory of your application's contract directory. (Recall from chapter 4 that this test directory was created automatically when the `truffle init` command executed.) The general directory structure is shown in figure 10.1. The test directory houses the test.js script (in this case, counterTest.js), which will be run to test the contract automatically.

First, we need to start our Ganache test network on which the contract to be tested will be deployed. Double-click the Ganache icon and then click Quickstart, and you'll see the Ganache UI. (You can also start the Ganache by using the command-line interface.) Then enter these commands (the `npm install` command is for installing testing modules of Truffle):

```
npm install
truffle test
```

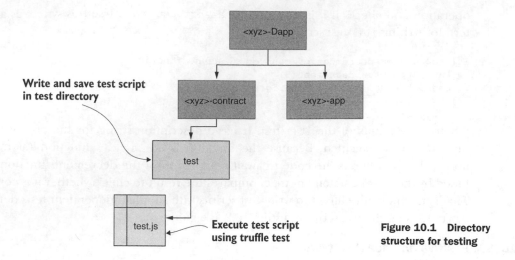

**Write and save test script in test directory**

**Execute test script using truffle test**

Figure 10.1   Directory structure for testing

That is it. Automatic execution of the test scripts begins, and you will observe that the tests pass, as shown in figure 10.2. The `truffle test` command initiates the execution of the test script, compiles and deploys the contract, and then runs the test script. The response screenshot is shown in figure 10.2.

```
Contract: Counter
  ✓ Success on initialization of counter. (55ms)
  ✓ Success on decrement of counter. (116ms)
  ✓ Success on increment of counter. (132ms)
  ✓ Failure on initialization of counter with negative number. (83ms)
  ✓ Failure on underflow of counter. (71ms)
  ✓ Failure on increment with negative numbers. (65ms)
  ✓ Failure on decrement with negative numbers. (69ms)


7 passing (1s)
```

**Figure 10.2   Test outputs for the counter smart contract**

You can observe three tests for the three functions, and four tests for the modifiers work as expected, verified by the assertions at the end of the test script functions. The output messages for the positive tests begin with `'Success on'`, and those for negative tests begin with `'Failure on'`. Follow this best practice in your design of test scripts to identify the test type. The check before the test outcomes indicates that the test has passed. The time shown in parentheses indicates the time it took to perform the test. Times greater than 100ms are displayed in red, in case you want to reduce the time and cost of execution of a certain test. These times are a concern when you test this smart contract on a real network such as an Ethereum mainnet. For now, you don't need to worry about that number, because your goal is to test the functional characteristics of the smart contract, not the timing issues.

Next, let's explore additional testing features and reinforce the testing approach introduced with the simple counter smart contract.

## 10.3 Testing ballot smart contract

This section tests another smart contract discussed in chapters 3 and 4: the ballot smart contract. Let's review its functions: registering the voter, voting, requesting the winner, and advancing the phase of voting. Review the smart contract for the ballot and its functions, and then you're ready to learn to write the test script. This contract requires more-involved testing than the counter smart contract. Besides the test primitives `beforeEach()` and `it()`, a new composite test primitive, `describe()`, is introduced.

### 10.3.1 Writing the ballot test script

Let's examine how you can automate testing of the familiar ballot smart contract. An abbreviated test script is shown in listing 10.3. The condensed version of the test scripts shows the structure of the tests, such as how a new composite test, `describe()`, is structured with many `it()`s. Observe that `describe()` is a combination of `beforeEach()` and `it()` tests. This occurs because you have to set up the conditions for voting before you can vote, you have to complete voting before you can test the winner function, and so on.

---

**Listing 10.3  ballotTest.js**

```
...
contract('Ballot', function (accounts) {

  let ballot

  beforeEach('Setup contract for each test', async function () {      ◄──── Before each test, deploy the smart contract ballot.
    ballot = await Ballot.new(3)
  });

  it('Success on initialization to registration phase.',
                                     async function(){      ◄──── A standalone it() test to check balloting state/phase
    let state = await ballot.state()
    assert.equal(state, 1)
  });

  describe('Voter registration', function() {      ◄──── A composite test describe() with three it()s for testing registration
    it('Success on registration of voters by chairperson.',
                                   async function () {...

    it('Failure on registration of voters by non-chairperson entity.',
                                   async function () {     ...

    it('Failure of registration of voters in invalid phase.',
                                   async function () { ...

  });
```

```
describe('Voting', function() {       ⟵   A describe() test with
  beforeEach() {}                          beforeEach() and five
  it() { }                                 it()s for testing voting
  it() { }
  it() { }
  it() { }
  it() { }   });
                                          A composite test
                                          describe() with three it()s
describe('Phase change', function() {  ⟵  for testing phase change

  it() { }
  it() { }
  it() { }   });
                                          A describe() test with
                                          beforeEach() and six it()s
describe('Requesting winner', function() {  ⟵  for testing request winner
  beforeEach() {}
  it() { }
  it() { }
  it() { }
  it() { }
  it() { } });
})
```

Now let's examine the first describe() composite test for voter registration. For a voter to be registered, the registration

- Has to be performed by the chairperson
- Has to be done during the registration phase
- Cannot be done by nonchairperson voters

These test conditions are coded as three it() test cases within the describe() test. I've chosen to introduce the testing of the ballot smart contract because it is ideally suited for illustrating the composite test cases defined by describe(), as you see three more of them in listing 10.3.

Testing the vote() function of the ballot smart contract requires a setup before each it(), described, of course, by a beforeEach() script. Similarly, testing a reqWinner() function requires a combination of beforeEach() and it() scripts. Testing the phase change function of the ballot smart contract requires three it() tests. You can use these tests as examples when designing and defining your test scripts.

Now let's run the test script, using Ganache and Truffle, and examine the output.

### 10.3.2 *Executing the ballot test script*

Download the code ballot-contract from the codebase of the chapter. Start the Ganache test chain by clicking its icon and then clicking Quickstart. Then navigate to the ballot-contract directory. Install the node modules required, using the npm command. Then run the test command, using truffle test. This command picks up the JS test file ballotTest.js from the test directory and runs it. Figure 10.3 shows the test output after you enter these two commands:

```
npm install
truffle test
```

```
Contract: Ballot
  ✓ Success on initialization to registration phase. (55ms)
  Voter registration
    ✓ Success on registration of voters by chairperson.
    ✓ Failure on registration of voters by non-chairperson entity. (69ms)
    ✓ Failure on registration of voters in invalid phase. (281ms)
  Voting
    ✓ Success on vote. (189ms)
    ✓ Failure on voting for invalid candidate. (155ms)
    ✓ Failure on repeat vote. (195ms)
    ✓ Failure on vote by an unregistered user. (56ms)
    ✓ Failure on vote in invalid phase. (184ms)
  Phase Change
    ✓ Success on phase increment (99ms)
    ✓ Failure on phase decrement. (51ms)
    ✓ Failure on phase change by non-chairperson entity. (217ms)
  Requesting winner
    ✓ Success on query of winner with majority. (346ms)
    ✓ Success on query for the winner by a non-chairperson entity. (357ms)
    ✓ Success on tie-breaker when multiple candidates tied for the majority. (595ms)
    ✓ Failure on request for winner with majority vote less than three. (281ms)
    ✓ Failure on request for winner in invalid phase. (126ms)


17 passing (6s)
```

**Figure 10.3  Test outputs for the ballot smart contract**

The output of the test run shows five sets of outputs resulting in 17 test cases. Voter registration, voting, phase change, and requesting the winner are composite `describe()` test scripts representing the four main functions of the ballot smart contract. You can identify the positive and negative tests by using the output messages coded in the test script. In the output, the leading messages (Voter registration, Voting, and so on) output by the `describe()` in your test code. Next, you examine the code for one of the `describe()` structures in detail to understand the steps in writing one.

### 10.3.3  Describe() and it() test functions

Let's analyze the syntax of part of the `describe()` function, which has these elements:

- A `beforeEach()` function
- A positive test coded as `it()`
- A negative test coded as another `it()` test.

First, make sure that you're able to identify these elements in the following code snippet. Then note that each `it()` is an asynchronous function, so you wait for its complete execution and return before testing the outcome, using an `assert` statement. The first `it()` demonstrates a positive test case, that of a successful vote by a registered account holder, and the second `it()` demonstrates a negative test case in which a voter account votes for a nonexistent proposal number. Hence, the latter should revert. Now study the code to understand the concepts of testing so that you can write your test script for your smart contract:

```
describe('Voting', function() {
    beforeEach('Setup contract for each voting test', async function () {
        // register two accounts
        await ballot.register(accounts[1], { from: accounts[0]})
        await ballot.register(accounts[2], { from: accounts[0]})
    });

    it('Success on vote.', async function () {
        //Registration -> Vote
        await ballot.changeState(2)
        let result = await ballot.vote(1, { from: accounts[1]})
        assert.equal(result.receipt.status, success)
        result = await ballot.vote(1, { from: accounts[2]})
        assert.equal(result.receipt.status, success)
    });

    it('Failure on voting for invalid candidate.', async function () {
        //Registration -> Vote
        await ballot.changeState(2)

        //number of proposals is 3: must fail when trying to vote for 10.
        await truffleAssert.reverts(
            ballot.vote(10, { from: accounts[1]}), wrongProposalError
        )
    });
```

## 10.4  *Recap writing of test script*

Now that you've seen two examples, let's recap the structure of the test scripts and an approach to coding one. The general structure of the test script is shown in figure 10.4. Let's apply the concepts to yet another smart contract, blind auction, and get familiar with the test script writing skills.

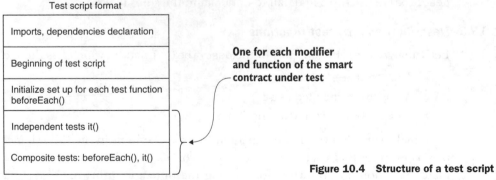

**Figure 10.4   Structure of a test script**

## 10.5  *The blind auction test script*

You have seen two examples of coding test scripts. Also, you got a review of the structure of the test script and the items that may be used to code it. Now let's reinforce the concepts with another example: the familiar blind auction example. This smart contract is a more involved smart contract with equally complex test scripts. Use figure

10.4 as a guideline to understand the test script. The required dependencies for this test script are as follows:

```
const BlindAuction = artifacts.require('../contracts/BlindAuction.sol')
const truffleAssert = require('truffle-assertions');
```

The next step is initializing the numerous variables of the blind auction. You need to set up a minimum number of bidders and the bid amounts:

```
const success = '0x01'
let blindAuction
const onlyBeneficiaryError = 'Only beneficiary can perform this action'
const validPhaseError = 'Invalid phase'
const badRevealError = 'Not matching bid'

// Bidding amount placeholders in ether for fast modification.
let BID1 = 1
let BID2 = 2
let BID3 = 3

// Account placeholders for user accounts for testing
let BEN = accounts[0]
let ACC1 = accounts[3]
let ACC2 = accounts[4]
let ACC3 = accounts[5]
```

After these data definitions, you're ready to code the test functions (listing 10.4). Be warned, these functions are much more complex than those for the counter and ballot smart contracts; blind auction represents a practical application, including encryption and hashing.

---

**Listing 10.4   blindAuctionTest.js**

```
beforeEach('Setup contract for each test', async function () {

describe('Initialization and Phase Change.', async ()=>{
   it('Success on initialization to bidding phase.',async function() {…
   it('Success on phase change by beneficiary.', async function() {…
      it('Success on change from DONE phase to INIT phase.',
                                                    async function()
      …}

   describe('Bidding Phase.', async ()=>{
it('Success on single bid.', async function () { …
it('Failure on bid in invalid state.', async function () { …
}

   describe('REVEAL Phase.', async ()=>{
       it('Success on refund of difference when sent value is >
                                                    bid amount.',
      it('Success on refund when sent value is less than bid amount.',…{
      it('Success on refund if bid amount is less than highest bid.', …{
```

```
      it('Failure on incorrect key for reveal.', async function () {
      it('Failure on incorrect bid value for reveal.', async function () {
      it('Failure on reveal in invalid state.', async function () {
… }

describe('Withdraw.', async ()=>{
      it('Success on withdraw on loosing bid.', async function () {
…}

describe('Auction end.', async ()=>{
it('Success on end of auction on single bid.', async function () {
it('Failure on end of auction in invalid phase.', async function () {
…}

describe('Full Auction Run.', async ()=>{
it('Success on run with 3 accounts.', async function () {
…}
```

Let's examine the test script for the blind auction in listing 10.4. This test script has the usual `beforeEach()`, which allows the blind auction contract to be deployed before every test described by `describe()`. By now, the `describe-it` combination should be quite familiar to you from the examples of counter and ballot smart contracts. Each `describe()` function has many `it()` test cases, and each test case tests the success or failure of a certain condition. The aspect is described in the string message of the `it()` test, beginning with a `'Success on'` condition for a positive test and a `'Failure on…condition'` for a negative test. Five of the six tests in listing 10.4 defined by `describe()` are for testing the status of blind auction functions:

- Initialization and phase change
- Bidding phase
- Reveal phase
- Withdraw
- Auction end

Each `describe()` is further defined by several `it()`s based on the individual operations and the corresponding tests. A sixth `describe()` in listing 10.4 walks through the complete end-to-end operation of the blind auction.

There could be two more tests for the `withdraw()` function: one for the failure of the winner of the bid trying to withdraw, and one for failure of `withdraw()` from an incorrect state. These tests are left as exercises for you to try on your own.

### 10.5.1 *Analysis of describe() and it() code*

Download the blindAuctionTest.js from the codebase of this chapter, and examine its content. Let's examine one `it()` of the `describe()` for the bidding phase to understand how to define and code the `describe()` test:

```
describe('Bidding Phase.', async ()=>{
    it('Success on single bid.', async function () {
        // Before bidding
    let balanceBefore = Number(web3.utils.fromWei(await
                (web3.eth.getBalance(ACC1), 'ether'));
        // Bidding
    let bidInWei = web3.utils.toWei(String(BID1), 'ether');
    let valueInWei = web3.utils.toWei(String(BID1+1), 'ether');
    let hashValue = web3.utils.keccak256(..);
    await blindAuction.bid(hashValue, {from: ACC1, value: valueInWei});
            // After bidding
    let balanceAfter = Number(web3.utils.fromWei(await
                    web3.eth.getBalance(ACC1), 'ether'));
    assert.isAbove(balanceBefore - balanceAfter, BID1+1);
    assert.isBelow(balanceBefore - balanceAfter, BID1+2);}});
```

There are three parts to this bidding function:

1  Set up or initialize before bidding.
2  Enter statements for bidding.
3  Await completion of bidding, and check the results.

Actual code snippets for these operations can be extracted from the blind auction code. Note the initialization performed by the `let` statements. The bidding operation itself is asynchronous because the transactions need time to run and be recorded on the blockchain. So you await the completion of the bidding operation. When the bidding is complete, you can evaluate the results by using assert statements—in this case, `assert.isAbove()` and `assert.isBelow()`.

### 10.5.2 *Executing the blind auction test script*

Now you are ready to run the test script and observe its operation. The commands for running the test script are the same as the ones that you used for counter and ballot smart contracts. Download the code blindAuction-contract from the codebase of the chapter. Start the Ganache test chain by clicking its icon and then clicking Quickstart. Then navigate to the blindAuction-contract directory. Use these commands to execute the test script:

```
npm install
truffle test
```

The output of the test run shows six sets of outputs resulting in 16 test cases: initialization and change phase, bidding, reveal, auction end, withdraw, and full auction run. Each of these test items is represented by `describe()`. Every `describe()` has a `beforEach()` setting up the tests and several `it()` tests. Every `describe()` has a meaningful string parameter that specifies the nature of the test, and that string is output as shown in figure 10.5, identifying the tests.

```
Contract: BlindAuction
  Initialization and Phase Change.
    ✓ Success on initialization to bidding phase.
    ✓ Success on phase change by beneficiary. (177ms)
    ✓ Success on change from DONE phase to INIT phase. (233ms)
    ✓ Failure on phase change by a non-beneficiary. (64ms)
  Bidding Phase.
    ✓ Success on single bid. (1049ms)
    ✓ Failure on bid in invalid state. (117ms)
  Reveal Phase.
    ✓ Success on refund of difference when sent value is greater than bid amount. (215ms)
    ✓ Success on refund when sent value is less than bid amount. (170ms)
    ✓ Success on refund if bid amount is less than highest bid. (297ms)
    ✓ Failure on incorrect key for reveal. (165ms)
    ✓ Failure on incorrect bid value for reveal. (171ms)
    ✓ Failure on reveal in invalid state. (108ms)
  Withdraw.
    ✓ Success on withdraw on loosing bid. (349ms)
  Auction end.
    ✓ Success on end of auction on single bid. (272ms)
    ✓ Failure of end of auction in invalid phase. (49ms)
  Full Auction Run.
    ✓ Success on simulated auction with 3 bidders (accounts). (754ms)


16 passing (6s)
```

**Figure 10.5   Test output from blind auction testing**

### 10.5.3  *Full auction run*

The test script for the blind auction smart contract includes a complete full auction test run. This automatic test script is equivalent to manual testing of the single run through the deployed smart contract. You can open the blindAuctionTest.js and follow along with the description provided here. The code represents these tests:

- The blind auction full test run involves a simulated auction among three bidders' accounts. The beneficiary deploys the smart contract. Before the start of the bidding process, the balances of all three bidders are saved for later checking.
- In the Bidding phase, each bidder decides on a bid value. A string representation of this value and the hex value of the secret word are hashed, using the keccak256 function and a one-time password. Deposit values in the bid are 1 ETH greater than the actual bid amount. The beneficiary advances to the Reveal phase.
- In the Reveal phase, all bidders send their bid amounts and secret keys to the smart contract. The contract evaluates the validity and provenance of the bids. The auction now moves to the Done phase. The beneficiary ends the auction and transfers the winning bid amount to their account. The result of the auction is fetched.
- The bidders can withdraw the bidding amount. This amount is returned if the bid was not successful.

- The balances of all accounts are fetched again. The result of the auction contains the address of the winner (ACC3, in this case) and the winning bid amount (BID3). The ending balances are checked. The account balances of bidders who lost are close to the starting balances because only Txs cost is used up. The winner of the auction balance is reduced by the bid amount plus any Tx cost.

In this fully integrated run, the script exhaustively exercises the functions of the blind auction in a single test and verifies that the smart contract works as expected.

## 10.6  Retrospective

In all three cases, the smart contract testing was successful. This situation may not be the case in the development stages as a team is developing the functions of the smart contract. Change some number value in any of the smart contracts discussed in this chapter, and you'll get one or more tests failing (X instead of a check in the test output). I recommend that you try this now.

In a test-driven development, the test script is written first; then the smart contract is developed to meet the requirements specified in the test. Testing can be used as a means of maintaining the integrity of a codebase when multiple developers are contributing to its parts. In this scenario, test scripts can be used to make sure that the code committed meets the requirements.

The test scripts looked complex, but these test programs are the executable scripts capturing the manual input testing you did in earlier chapters. The testing introduced in this chapter is also a formal process that you need to complete before launching smart contracts into the production environment.

## 10.7  Best practices

Testing is an important phase in the development of the blockchain-based decentralized application. Here are some best practices:

- Decide on the functions to be tested.
- Decide on the modifiers to be tested.
- Write positive test code that should be successful for correct inputs.
- Write negative test code that fails or reverts (typically, on a modifier or `require` statement)
- Use meaningful and concise descriptions for the tests, and note that these descriptions are output during testing.
- Use `'Success on'` and `'Failure on'` as prefixes for the positive and negative tests to identify the type of testing.
- Use a standard naming convention for the test file (<name of the smart contract>Test.js).

## *10.8   Summary*

- Three test scripts discussed in this chapter—counterTest.js, ballotTest.js, and blindAuctionTest.js—illustrate how to write test scripts for smart contracts.
- The main building blocks or coding elements for a test script are `beforeEach()`, `it()`, and `describe()`.
- The `beforeEach()` function is defined by code for establishing the preliminary conditions (before execution) of each test.
- `async()`, `await()`, and `assert()` help in managing execution of functions during testing. The commands for completing the test setup are simple: initializing the Ganache test chain, installing the required modules using `npm install`, and executing the test code using `truffle test`.

# 11

# A roadmap to
# Dapp development

**This chapter covers**

- Navigating end-to-end Dapp development guided by
  a roadmap
- Designing and developing an educational credentialing
  application
- Developing a test-driven prototype on a local test chain
- Configuring and transforming the prototype Dapp for
  public deployment
- Creating a distributable web app to enable
  decentralized participants

This chapter provides a roadmap for Dapp development from beginning to end. In
the preceding chapters, you learned how to design, develop, deploy, and test smart
contracts and decentralized web applications (Dapps). You learned the core idea of
blockchain technology and its application. You explored a wide variety of applications, from a simple counter to asset tokenization. You studied a new language, Solidity, for programming smart contracts, and tools such as Remix and Truffle to process

and test them. Blockchain programming is not meant for data-intensive image processing; neither is it for computationally intensive scientific computation. In the case of a smart contract, for example, it is not good practice to use a smart contract for storing multidimensional image processing or for long-running, complex computations.

In this chapter, let's put all these concepts together, not only to reinforce the concepts discussed, but also to comprehend how and why blockchain programming is different from traditional web application development.

Blockchain programming is not about porting a program in any high-level language, such as Java, to a smart contract written in Solidity or a similar language. It is about carefully choosing the data and transactions to be recorded and the rules for validation and verification. This chapter will demonstrate the importance of choosing appropriate data structures, control structures for verification, and notification. You'll investigate a real educational certificate application. You can apply the knowledge and skills learned in earlier chapters to design, develop, test locally, deploy publicly, and interact with a decentralized solution. End-to-end development is summarized using a real-world use case. The treatment in this chapter will provide an A-to-Z path for Ethereum-based decentralized application development guided by a roadmap. You can download the completed codebase that illustrates all the steps and follow along with the instructions.

Let's begin with the motivation for the scenario I chose for this chapter.

## 11.1   *Motivating scenario: Educational credentialing*

Educational credentialing is a vast problem domain of high interest to many all over the planet. It has diverse stakeholders at all levels, from government agencies to online education providers, traditional universities, and student enrollees. Such a large problem is typically composed of many smaller problems, some of which can benefit from a blockchain solution. The blockchain-based solution you'll explore in this chapter works within a large, conventional system, improving the scalability and efficacy of a particular subsystem.

You may wonder what educational credentials and certificates have to do with blockchain. A lot. You are fortunate to be able to enjoy online lessons on many subjects and skills through a variety of digital media and in classrooms. Although the methods of educational delivery have diversified vastly in the past decade, most methods of evaluating these credentials for certification and degree auditing are still performed manually or by a legacy application, using the records stored in traditional student databases. What we want is an independent application. Students and other key stakeholders (advisers) should be able to verify credentials without the help of the centralized databases, such as to keep track of students' progress through a certificate or a degree program.

You could write a traditional web application that addresses this problem by using the data from a central student database. But imagine this situation:

- The participants in the program are decentralized.

- The courses or credentials originate from many educational settings (such as online courses and work experiences).

- The participants are not associated with any traditional institution, such as a university.

These characteristics are the motivations for a decentralized application that independently verifies that students have fulfilled degree or certificate requirements. This application is a self-help tool for key stakeholders in a degree or certification pathway to monitor progress through a program.

The use case in this chapter is a real certificate program at the University at Buffalo. This certificate program is for data-intensive computing; the detailed requirements are at http://mng.bz/4Bja. I am using this scenario to motivate you to look for issues in your environment that can be addressed by blockchain solutions and can benefit from the blockchain-based approach. That's an essential goal of the problem discussed in this chapter.

## 11.2 The roadmap

Chapters 2–10 covered pieces of the puzzle in the development of a blockchain-based Dapp. In this chapter, all these pieces are assembled to solve a single problem. It is a challenge to view the concepts together, so here is a roadmap to guide you through the chapter and the Dapp development process. Figure 11.1 closely maps the sections of this chapter, each section demonstrating a task in the roadmap. Review this roadmap before starting the next section.

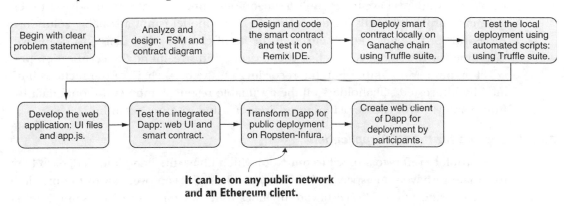

**Figure 11.1  A roadmap to developing Dapps for Ethereum blockchain**

Figure 11.1 shows the roadmap from local deployment on the Ganache test chain to the public implementation involving the public network Ropsten with Infura as web3 provider. Although Ropsten is the network used in this chapter, you can choose to work another public Ethereum network, including mainnet, simply by configuring your deployment. The roadmap will help you can navigate this chapter as well as your future Dapp development.

## 11.3    Problem description

Let's begin by articulating a clear statement for the problem to be solved.

> **PROBLEM STATEMENT**    An undergraduate data-intensive computing certificate (hereafter referred to as DCC) program requires an enrollee to complete four categories of courses and an average grade-point average (GPA) of at least 2.5 in these courses. Although the details of this program are stated in an undergraduate catalog page, there is no traditional tool implemented for verifying the fulfillment of a certificate. The objective of this project is to build an independent blockchain-based tool so that any student interested in this certificate program can use this tool. A student enrolled in the certificate program can self-check their progress through the program from anywhere.

In other words, any student in the undergraduate program can evaluate their

- Eligibility to enroll in the certificate and to plan their future courses
- Progress through the certificate program as they complete courses
- Certificate fulfillment status, including the GPA requirement, on completion of all the course requirements

> **NOTE**    Students in this situation do not violate Family Educational Rights and Privacy Act (FERPA) law or any other regulations because they are dealing with only their own grades and do not access the central student database.

Currently, students have to schedule a one-on-one appointment with an adviser to verify their fulfillment status for the certificate. This model is not a scalable solution if thousands of students want to enroll in the certificate program. This DCC-Dapp will save time for the students as well as the advisers, and streamline the certification process for some. More important, the recording on the blockchain of transactions initiated by interested stakeholders will be a valuable resource and institutional data for future analytics for course planning, advisement, and resource planning.

### 11.3.1    Context for the DCC application

This problem refers to a specific context of which I have firsthand knowledge, so I am fortunate to have some specific details. Figure 11.2 gives an overview of the problem under consideration. The certificate includes four categories of courses and a minimum GPA in these courses. Any stakeholder, student or adviser, can register by using a decentralized identity the first time, and then log in at subsequent times, add the courses, and request verification. If the courses entered fulfill the requirements, the GPA is computed and verified. This DCC system is different from the university's central database, so it does not pose any security or legal threat to that system.

Review figure 11.2 and imagine a user (say, a student) using this self-serve tool independent of the central system. This tool puts the decision-making process in the

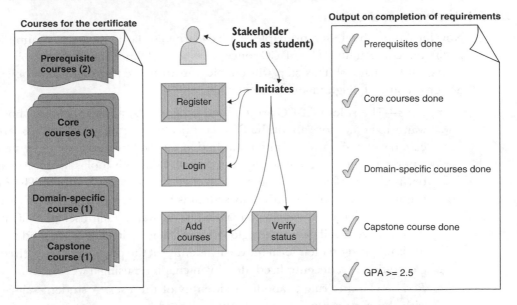

**Figure 11.2   DCC concept: certificate courses, stakeholder functions, and output**

hands of the student, eliminating the middle person (the adviser). This situation encourages more participation because the information is readily available to potential participants. The blockchain recording provides valuable additional data, including timeline and transaction details. This data can be used for data analysis of the operations originated by many decentralized users, perhaps to provide better service.

Let's design the solution for this problem, referred to hereafter as DCC-Dapp (Data-intensive Computing Certificate Dapp).

### 11.3.2  Design choices

You have many choices of application to address this problem:

- A standalone mobile app independent of the central system
- A web or enterprise application integrated with the central student management system
- A blockchain-based decentralized application independent of the central system

The first two choices are traditional; the last one offers the independence of a mobile app and at the same time keeps track of the transactions on the immutable ledger of the blockchain. That's the design you'll explore in the following sections.

## 11.4  Analysis and design

Now let's apply the design principles you've learned so far to design a solution for the problem. Using figure 11.2, DCC-concept, as a guideline, identify the roles, rules, assets, and functions. This step will enable you to think through the problem and design a contract diagram and its elements:

- *Roles*—The roles of DCC are defined by students, advisers, and anybody who wants to know more about the DCC certificate program. These people are associated with the university and identified in the student management system with a person number. In particular, it is expected that this tool is meant for and will be used by students interested or enrolled in the DCC program. The person-number identity of the university system is the tether linking the DCC application to the larger university management software. Each user of DCC holds a decentralized (self-generated) globally unique identity of 256 bits, and this identity is mapped on their local university identity of the person number. (Recall the generation of a decentralized identity in chapter 8 using a web tool.)
- *Rules*—The first rule is about the identity of the user. A student self-registers with the person number, an identity assigned by a university system. This rule enables the decentralized blockchain identity of an enrollee to be mapped onto the person number of the centralized system. The second rule is that only a registered user (validStudent) can add courses to the DCC application.

**NOTE**   The msg.sender attribute of a blockchain transaction holds the 256-bit decentralized identity of the sender of the transaction.

- *Assets*—Assets are the course categories, allowed courses in each category, and GPA. Each student user with a (blockchain-based) decentralized identity has their own set of data:
  - An efficient structure of courses and grades
  - A mapping of their 256-bit address to corresponding person number
- *Events*—Fulfillment of requirements of the categories of courses by a user is indicated by emitting an event. Events emitted are logged in the block. These logs are used as notifications to users as well as for analysis. Events can be emitted on completion of each category of courses and also on completion of the certificate. The emitted events can be displayed as notifications in the UI as certificate status.

### 11.4.1  Operation flow and finite state machine

Let's examine the DCC operations and their flow by using a finite state machine (FSM) diagram (figure 11.3). This figure also gives you a rough idea of the sequence of interactions by a user.

This DCC-Dapp is a long-running program because the completion of the required courses may take as long as four years. More important, the university may want a

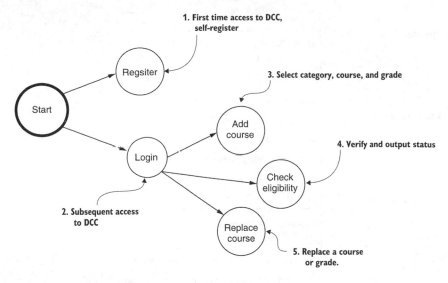

**Figure 11.3   FSM for user operations of DCC-Dapp**

historical ledger of DCC timeline and engagement. Users may use this DCC-Dapp as their progress sheet through the certificate program. With this context, here are the numbered functions, as shown in figure 11.3:

1 *Register.* A user identified by a 256-bit decentralized account address registers their person number associated with the university or institution. This operation is done only once, at the beginning of the process.

2 *Log in.* For subsequent access to the DCC-Dapp, login with the person number and a matching decentralized identity is required; otherwise, the login will be rejected.

3 *Add a course.* To add a course to be considered for the certificate program, the user enters the category, course, and grade in the course.

4 *Check eligibility.* This function determines the user's standing in the certificate program in five criteria: four course categories and overall GPA.

5 *Replace a course.* This function replaces a course in the certificate program. The user probably will add a different course to improve their GPA or update their grade after retaking the course.

These operations will guide the design of the smart contract for the DCC-Dapp. Other support functions may be required to complete the design of the smart contracts.

### 11.4.2  *Contract diagram*

Consider the functions depicted in figure 11.3 and the discussion of the roles, assets, and events to obtain the contract diagram, as shown in figure 11.4. A contract diagram lists the data structures, events, modifiers, and function headers of the contract.

Using the details from the problem statement (section 11.3), design the DCC contract diagram.

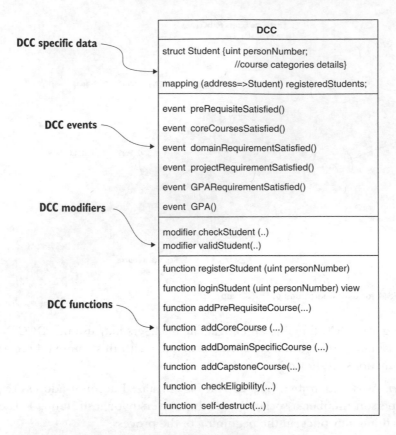

**DCC specific data**

**DCC events**

**DCC modifiers**

**DCC functions**

```
                        DCC
struct Student {uint personNumber;
                //course categories details}
mapping (address=>Student) registeredStudents;

event  preRequisiteSatisfied()
event  coreCoursesSatisfied()
event  domainRequirementSatisfied()
event  projectRequirementSatisfied()
event  GPARequirementSatisfied()
event  GPA()

modifier checkStudent (..)
modifier validStudent(..)

function registerStudent (uint personNumber)
function loginStudent (uint personNumber) view
function addPreRequisiteCourse(...)
function  addCoreCourse (...)
function  addDomainSpecificCourse (...)
function  addCapstoneCourse(...)
function  checkEligibility(...)
function  self-destruct(...)
```

**Figure 11.4   DCC contract diagram**

## 11.5   Developing the smart contract

Use the contract diagram, develop the smart contract, and do a quick test in the Remix IDE. After a successful test in Remix, open the DCC-Dapp codebase to review the smart contract in the DCC-contract directory. I explain these steps in detail next.

### 11.5.1   Data structures

Listing 11.1 shows the data structure that stores the data about a student's courses, the modifiers, the events, and the functions. The names of the items are self-explanatory, and they follow camel-case notation.

### 11.5.2   Events

There are six event definitions, one for each category of courses. An event is emitted when the courses in a category are completed. The code also includes two more events: one emitted when the GPA is satisfied and one that shows the current GPA value.

### 11.5.3 Modifiers

There are two modifiers. checkStudent allows a student to register only once, and validStudent enforces that only a valid student is permitted to add courses. In other words, before a student adds any courses, their person numbers (identity in the university system) and identity in the decentralized system (a 256-bit account number) should be registered in the DCC system.

### 11.5.4 Functions

You can also observe in listing 11.1 that the contract diagram has functions to add courses, not remove them. The purpose of removing a course would be

- To replace the current grade with the better grade for prerequisite and core courses.
- To replace the current course with another course with a better grade. The grade replacement is applicable to any category; the case of course replacement is applicable only to a domain-specific course and the capstone course.

The function to add a course can itself be reused to carry out the remove and replace operation. That is, if a user adds a course in the category that already has an existing course, it is overwritten. This operation accomplishes the removal and replacement of a course. When you're implementing solutions, you ought to be thinking about the possibilities for reusing functions in the manner shown here. Also note the inclusion of the self-destruct function, which is useful for undeploying the contract, especially during the testing phases on public networks.

Among the functions, code for addCoreCourse() is shown in listing 11.1. It is simple: If the value of the parameter course is 115 or 116 (core courses), the grade for the course is updated. The variables for courses 115 and 116 do not hold any data except for the grade, thus minimizing storage. Storage needed for each student is about nine words.

#### Listing 11.1  DCC.sol

```
contract DTCCertification{
    uint constant private MINIMUM_GPA_REQUIRED = 250;

    struct Student {              Data structure for each
        uint personNumber;        student participant

        uint prereq115;
        uint prereq116;

        uint core250;
        uint core486;
        uint core487;

        uint domainSpecificCourse;
        uint domainSpecificGrade;
```

```
        uint capstoneCourse;
        uint capstoneGrade;

    }

    mapping(address => Student) registeredStudents;   ◁──┐ Mapping from account
                                                          address to student structure

    event preRequisiteSatisfied(uint personNumber);
    event coreCoursesSatisfied(uint personNumber);          ┐
    event GPARequirementSatisfied(uint personNumber);       │ Event
    event projectRequirementSatisfied(uint personNumber);   │ definitions
    event domainRequirementSatisfied(uint personNumber);    │
    event GPA(uint result);

//-------------------------------------------
// Modifiers
//-------------------------------------------                ◁──┐ Modifier definitions
    modifier checkStudent(uint personNumber) {
        require(registeredStudents[msg.sender].personNumber == 0,
                                "Student has already registered");
        _;}

    modifier validStudent(){   //#D
        require(registeredStudents[msg.sender].personNumber > 0,
                                "Invalid student");
        _;}

//-------------------------------------------
// Functions
//-------------------------------------------
    function registerStudent(uint personNumber) public
                            checkStudent(personNumber) {          ◁──┐ Functions
        registeredStudents[msg.sender].personNumber = personNumber;    for adding
    }                                                                  a student
                                                                       user
    function loginStudent(uint personNumber) public view
                                        returns (bool){         ◁──┘
        if(registeredStudents[msg.sender].personNumber == personNumber){
            return true;
        }else{
            return false;
        }
    }

    function addPreRequisiteCourse(uint courseNumber, uint grade)
                                    public validStudent {   ◁──┐ Functions
                                                                for adding
                                                                courses
        if(courseNumber == 115) {
            registeredStudents[msg.sender].prereq115 = grade;
        }
        else if(courseNumber -= 116) {
            registeredStudents[msg.sender].prereq116 = grade;
        }
        else {
```

```
            revert("Invalid course information provided");
    }

    ...    }

    function addCoreCourse(uint courseNumber, uint grade) public
                                        validStudent {
{ ...}

    function addDomainSpecificCourse(uint courseNumber, uint grade) public
                                validStudent {
```

**Functions for
adding courses**

```
    ...}

    function addCapstoneCourse(uint courseNumber, uint grade) public
                                validStudent {

    ...    }

    function checkEligibility(uint personNumber) public validStudent
                                        returns(bool) {


    ...
// courses in each category are examined and event emitted if satisfied
// overall GPA computed if all course requirements are satisfied
  if(registeredStudents[msg.sender].prereq115 > 0 &&
        registeredStudents[msg.sender].prereq116 > 0) {
```

**Function for
determining
certificate
eligibility**

```
        preRequisitesSatisfied = true;
        emit preRequisiteSatisfied(personNumber);
        totalGPA += registeredStudents[msg.sender].prereq115 +
                    registeredStudents[msg.sender].prereq116;
...
...
        }}
```

### CODING THE FUNCTIONS

Download the DCC.sol from the codebase, and review it. Observe the simplicity of the data structures and the functions. I'll discuss just two snippets:

- Adding a prerequisite course (115 or 116)
- Checking the eligibility of the prerequisite course requirement of the DCC

Here is the function for adding a prerequisite course:

```
function addPreRequisiteCourse(uint courseNumber, uint grade) public
    validStudent
{
        if(courseNumber == 115) {
            registeredStudents[msg.sender].prereq115 = grade;
        }
        else if(courseNumber == 116) {
            registeredStudents[msg.sender].prereq116 = grade;
        }
```

```
    else {
        revert("Invalid course information provided");
    }
```

In the header of the function, the modifier validStudent enforces the condition that the caller of this function (sender of the Tx: msg.sender) must have a registered identity. The parameters passed to the function are the course number and the grade for that course. The body of the functions checks the course number and updates the course grade—as simple as that. The code is for the addition of a new course (115 or 116) and replacement of grade for a course. The revert statement at the end is to handle any exceptional or invalid input.

The code for adding courses in other categories is similar. Here is the snippet for testing fulfillment of the core courses:

```
if(registeredStudents[msg.sender].prereq115 > 0 &&
        registeredStudents[msg.sender].prereq116 > 0) {


        preRequisitesSatisfied = true;
        emit preRequisiteSatisfied(personNumber);
        totalGPA += registeredStudents[msg.sender].prereq115 +
                    registeredStudents[msg.sender].prereq116;
```

In this case, the code checks to see whether courses 115 and 116 are present by checking whether the grade recorded is greater than 0. If so, it sets the flag preRequisite-Satisfied to true, emits an event indicating that fact, and adds up the grades to compute the overall certificate GPA. Also, note that the emitted event has the person number as a parameter, enabling external applications to access emitted events.

#### DESIGN CHOICES

There are choices in the data structures and approaches used in the design of the smart contract. Consider the choices and choose the optimal ones for the current design. Here are some design choices made for the DCC smart contract:

- *On-chain data structure for student data*—The structure representing that data can be defined as off-chain data, and only the hash of this data structure is stored on-chain for security and immutability of the DCC data. If the data is off-chain, the rules that verify the data will have to be off-chain operations, and verification will not be recorded on the blockchain. So the choice is keeping the minimal data about the certificate courses on-chain. This data is a small (nine words) subset of the student's data in the external database of the larger system.
- *Person number versus 256-bit account number as parameter in events*—The parameter for all the emitted events is the person number versus the 256-bit account address, because the larger system outside the university identifies the user by person number. Although both options may serve as markers of the Tx issuer, a person number is a typical identifier in the university system. From a nondeveloper point of view, if they are shown the transaction details, people in the context

of the university would understand person numbers better. That is the reason for the design choice of person number as a parameter for the events emitted.

- In theory, we should be creating the test cases first before coding the contract, but we've chosen to focus on the smart contract design first to understand the DCC concept. So the formal testing with scripts is performed after the exploration with Remix IDE. This is another design choice we made to enable better understanding of the DCC problem.

### INCREMENTALLY ADD CODE

Incrementally add the code for other categories of courses by adapting the function to add a prerequisite course discussed earlier in this chapter. Also, add the code in the `checkEligibility()` function for verifying the fulfillment of the category of courses, emitting events, and computing the GPA by following the pattern discussed in the second snippet in the same section.

### TESTING IN REMIX IDE

Load the smart contract DCC.sol into the Remix IDE's editor, and debug any compile errors. Deploy the smart contract in the JavaScript VM, and observe the UI that appears after deployment (figure 11.5). You can see an interface with a one-to-one mapping to the functions in the contract diagram and the code that followed it. Simulate a single student registering, logging in, and adding courses and checking eligibility to make sure that all the functions work as expected. This UI of the Remix IDE for DCC.sol will serve as a guideline for the web UI design later.

Observe that the `loginStudent()` function is like a gatekeeper that allows only registered students to add courses. It is a `view` function, so it is not recorded on the chain. It might be interesting for audit purposes to keep a trace of login activities. In that case, you can remove the keyword view from the function header definition.

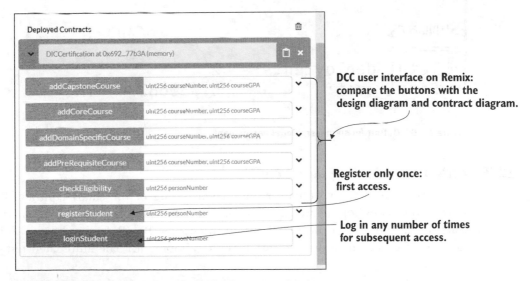

**Figure 11.5   UI on Remix IDE for the DCC.sol smart contract**

## 11.6  *Local deployment*

The next step in the roadmap is navigating from the Remix IDE to test the DCC.sol on the local.Ganache test chain. By now, you should be familiar with the sequence of these steps. Click the Ganache icon, and click Quickstart. Wait for it to start. Download the codebase for DCC-Dapp-local.zip from the chapter's codebase. Unzip it. Then navigate to DCC-contract.

The commands

```
cd DCC-contract
truffle migrate --reset
```

compile and deploy the contracts in the contracts directory. There are two contracts: DCC.sol and Migrations.sol. As they are compiled and deployed, you'll see several messages, ending with the final message that two contracts were deployed, as shown in figure 11.6. These messages indicate that two smart contracts—DCC.sol and Migrations.sol—were deployed successfully. Recall that the migration process itself is written as a Solidity smart contract. The next step is testing this DCC.sol deployed on the Ganache test chain.

```
> Saving migration to chain.
> Saving artifacts
---------------------------------------
> Total cost:            0.02545488 ETH


Summary
=======
> Total deployments:    2
> Final cost:           0.03068274 ETH
```

Figure 11.6   Output for successful local deployment

## 11.7  *Automated testing using truffle*

The next step in the roadmap is automated testing of the smart contract. Before moving on to develop the web application of the DCC-Dapp, test the DCC smart contract, using the JavaScript tests discussed in chapter 10. (Refer to chapter 10 if you need a refresher on automated test-driven development.) The automated test script

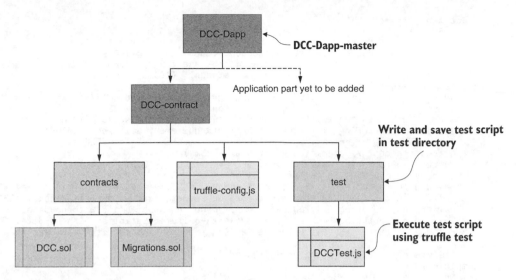

**Figure 11.7  Directory structure for the smart contract part of DCC**

for DCC.sol is provided in DCCTest.js in the codebase for this chapter. Review the directory structure and contents of the test directory. At this step, the directory structure should be as shown in figure 11.7.

Now you are ready to run the test. Navigate the DCC-contract directory. Make sure that the Ganache test chain is ready. Then run the `truffle test` command. The commands are repeated here for review:

```
cd DCC-contract
npm install
truffle test
```

The output shows positive and negative tests. Figure 11.8 shows only a partial list of 38 tests, some positive and some negative, for the category capstone project. DCCTest.js also contains scripts for the other three categories (prerequisites, core, and domain-specific courses). Just imagine running these 38 tests manually!

Recall from chapter 10 that the messages for the positive test begin with `'Success on'` and the output messages for negative tests begin with `'Failure on'`. Review the extensive DCCTest.js provided in the test directory, and use it as a model for your future test scripts. The script includes individual tests as well as a complete run testing the entire flow through the smart contract. It is good practice to test the smart contract before coding the web application and UI. Refer to chapter 10 for more details about writing the test script.

```
Capstone Project
  ✓ Success on adding grade for a capstone course. (52ms)
  ✓ Success on adding grades for 2 different capstone courses. (104ms)
  ✓ Success on adding grade for a capstone course twice. (100ms)
  ✓ Failure on adding grades for invalid capstone course. (96ms)
  ✓ Failure on adding grades for invalid student. (185ms)
Events and Eligibility
  ✓ Success on capturing emitted event preRequisiteSatisified. (154ms)
  ✓ Success on capturing emitted event coreCoursesSatisfied. (225ms)
  ✓ Success on capturing emitted event domainRequirementSatisfied. (100ms)
  ✓ Success on capturing emitted event projectRequirementSatisfied. (107ms)
  ✓ Success on capturing emitted event GPARequirementSatisfied. (526ms)
  ✓ Success on capturing emitted event GPA. (485ms)
  ✓ Success on capturing emitted event GPA even if GPA < 2.5. (466ms)
  ✓ Success on eligibility criteria. (447ms)
  ✓ Failure on capturing emitted event preRequisiteSatisified with partial data. (158ms)
  ✓ Failure on capturing emitted event coreCoursesSatisfied with partial data. (251ms)
  ✓ Failure on capturing emitted event domainRequirementSatisfied with no data. (49ms)
  ✓ Failure on capturing emitted event projectRequirementSatisfied with no data. (42ms)
  ✓ Failure on capturing emitted event GPARequirementSatisfied with GPA lower than 2.5. (
ms)
  ✓ Failure on eligibility criteria. (254ms)
Complete runs
  ✓ Success on run with 3 concurrent users. (1461ms)


38 passing (12s)
```

**Figure 11.8   Output for autotesting DCC.sol**

## 11.8   *Developing the web application*

Now that you have the smart contract coded and tested, you are ready to develop the DCC-app. Review chapters 6–10 for details on developing the web application part of the Dapp. The Dapp has files for installing the required modules (package.json) and setting up the web UI (index.js, src). The web3 API calls and code that connect the web UI to the smart contract are in app.js, available in the DCC-app code provided with this chapter. You can review these files and use them as a base for your web application development. Compare the diagram in figure 11.9 with the directory structure of the codebase.

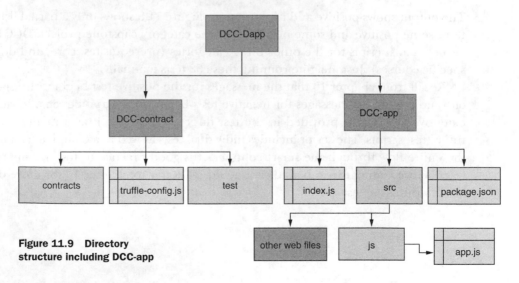

**Figure 11.9   Directory structure including DCC-app**

The UI design and the smart contract functions determine the coding of the app.js. The smart contract details are discussed in section 11.5. Now let's discuss the UI design followed by the app.js code.

### 11.8.1 UI design

The opening screen of the DCC-app has two functions—Register and Login, as shown in figure 11.10—and both have the same names as the corresponding smart contract functions. A first-time user uses the Register function by providing the person number in the box provided. For the subsequent access, a user uses the Login function once again with the person number as a parameter. This parameter value entered should have been registered. Otherwise, Login will revert.

**Figure 11.10   Opening screen, DCC-Dapp**

Successful registration and login will open the interface for adding courses, as shown in figure 11.11. These screens are the only two UI screens. Keep the UI design simple and intuitive.

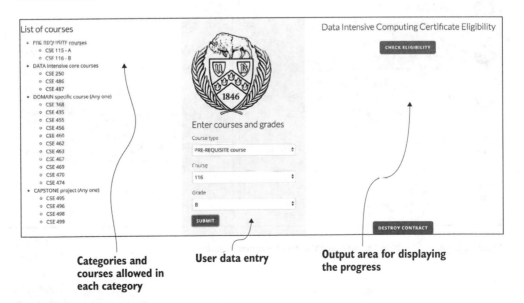

**Figure 11.11   UI for adding courses**

The UI for adding courses has three panels:

- The first panel lists the categories of courses and list of allowed courses in each category—prerequisites, core courses, domain-specific courses, and capstone project courses.
- The second panel shows the university logo, below which are drop-down boxes for selecting the category of courses and courses in each category.
- The third panel shows the button for checking eligibility and another button (Destroy Contract) for undeploying the contract. Destroy Contract is only in the test version and will not be featured in the production version of the UI.
- The blank space in the third panel of figure 11.11 is for displaying the fulfillment status of each category of courses and the GPA requirement for the DCC program.

Now if you click the Check Eligibility button before adding the courses, you'll see the screen shown in figure 11.12, which shows that none of the criteria for the certificate is satisfied. Initially, when no requirement is satisfied, all the items have X marks against them, as shown in figure 11.12. When all the requirements are met, you see check marks against them. When only some of the requirements are satisfied, the panel shows a combination of X and check marks. If all the course requirements are met, the GPA is computed, verified, and displayed. These details are shown in figure 11.12.

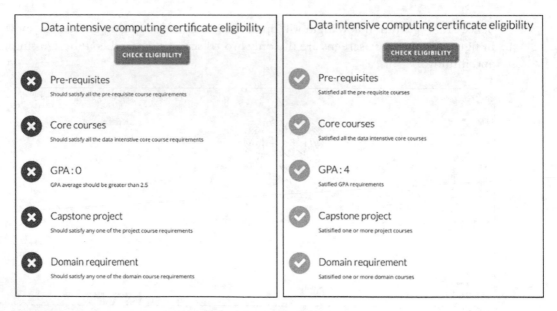

**Figure 11.12   UI with none and all of the course requirements satisfied**

### 11.8.2  *Coding the app.js*

You can add code for the structural elements of the UI and code app.js to link the user requests to the smart contract functions. The UI operation of adding a course and course category together decides the smart contract function to call from app.js. The two inputs to add a course are passed as parameters to the function called. Review this logic in the code snippet of app.js:

```
...
else if (course_type == "core") {
      App.contracts.Certification.methods.addCoreCourse(course, grade)
         .send(option)
         .on('receipt', (receipt) => {
          App.courseGrades(course, grade);
         })
         .on('error', (err) => {
           console.log(err);
         });
      }
```

The snippet shows the call to addCoreCourse of the smart contract with course number and grade as parameters. When this transaction is confirmed, the grade is saved in the web context for updating the UI. This snippet is the pattern for coding the other three categories of courses. Two data files support the app.js code: the data.json file maintains the user grades for display, and grades.json maps the numeric values of the letter grades. Locate and review these files. You can use JSON format for keeping any data local to the web; this format also maps well with many databases, such as Mongo DB.

## 11.9  *Testing the DCC-Dapp*

The smart contract was already deployed when we tested it earlier, but you can redeploy it for completeness. Make sure that the Ganache local test chain is running. Now deploy the DCC-app on the Node.js server and test the integrated system. By now, you should be familiar with these steps:

```
cd ../DCC-app
npm install
npm start
```

Open a Chrome browser (localhost:3000), and use MetaMask to restore the accounts, using the seed phrase of the Ganache test chain. Restart the browser, and execute these operations:

1  Register with 13567890 as the person number.
2  Log in with the same number as a parameter.
3  Then add courses and grades for each category in the interface (middle panel).
4  Check eligibility by clicking the Check Eligibility button at any time as you add courses.

5  You can add a course again. The previous entry is overwritten. This is how the replacement of a course is implemented.

6  Check eligibility after entering all the courses.

7  For another person, you can register, login, and enter grades of C or lower for the courses. Observe GPA eligibility failing.

That completes minimum testing. I am sure that student users will find creative ways to use this tool to plan their courses when you leave the information at their fingertips through this DCC-Dapp. You can exercise the Dapp for other combinations and improve on the basic UI design provided in this chapter.

## 11.10  *Public deployment*

So far, you've completed deploying and testing the Dapp on a local test chain. Now it's time to move to the next step in the roadmap: deployment on a public chain. We discussed the details of public deployment in chapter 8. The public chain you'll use is Ropsten, and the deployment infrastructure (web3 provider node and gateway) is hosted on Infura. Here are a few steps you'll need to complete before you begin the public deployment process. If you have all these items ready from chapter 8, you can reuse them. Refer to chapter 8 for details on the Ropsten and Infura public infrastructures:

- You'll need a Ropsten account address and seed mnemonic to restore this account (chapter 8). Save the 256-bit account number and the mnemonic in a file (such as DCCEnv.txt) for use during deployment and interaction.

- You must have an ether balance in the Ropsten account, which you can get through a Ropsten faucet (chapter 8).

- You must have an Infura account. Sign up at Infura, and create a project. Note the Ropsten endpoint number. Save the endpoint in the DCCEnv.txt file. Figure 11.13 shows a sample Infura endpoint.

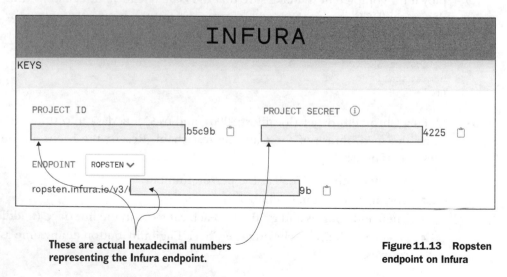

These are actual hexadecimal numbers representing the Infura endpoint.

Figure 11.13  Ropsten endpoint on Infura

### 11.10.1 Deployment on Ropsten-Infura

In this section, you'll learn to transform a Dapp tested in a local test environment for deployment on public infrastructure. In this case, the Dapp is DCC-Dapp, and the web3 provider and the blockchain network are Infura and Ropsten, respectively. Download the codebase for DCC-Dapp-public.zip from the code base. Here are the steps for deployment on Ropsten. Unzip or extract all the files of DCC-Dapp-public.zip. Navigate to the DCC-Dapp master, and use DCC-contract and DCC-app for these steps:

1 In the DCC-contract directory, update truffle-config.js to include an HDWallet-Provider for account management and Ropsten endpoint value on the Infura project (shown in figure 11.13). Save the account seed phrase mnemonic for your Ropsten account in a file called mnemonic.secret. You can download the truffle-config.js in listing 11.2, review the changes, and update it with values specific to your deployment. You'll have to change two items: the mnemonic and the `ropsten-infura` endpoint.

Listing 11.2 truffle-config.js

**HDWalletProvider of the truffle for account management**

```
const HDWalletProvider = require('@truffle/hdwallet-provider');
// file mnemonic.secret contains the ropsten mnemonic
//for connecting and deploying.
const fs = require('fs');
const mnemonic = fs.readFileSync("mnemonic.secret").toString().trim();

module.exports = {

  networks: {
    ...

    ropsten: {
      provider: () => new HDWalletProvider(mnemonic,
                          `https://ropsten.infura.io/v3/...`),
    ...
```

**Obtain mnemonic from a secret file**

**Fill in the ropsten-infura endpoint here.**

2 Navigate back to DCC-contract, and run the command to deploy the contract on the Ropsten network:

```
npm install
truffle migrate --network ropsten
```

You should observe messages with the deployed smart contract address highlighted (figure 11.14). Be patient; the deployment of DCC smart contract will take some time because it has to contend with all the other Txs on the public Ropsten network. Save the smart contract address generated in the DCCEnv.txt file (or any location of your choice) for use in the next step.

```
1cbe9fe4e101
    > Blocks: 1              Seconds: 4
    > contract address:      0x08E20bf72087aCb5a8F59e8E52d3638DE526e490
    > block number:          7114375
    > block timestamp:       1578857671
    > account:               0x02812c612a84ACbc6EF82878d8645112964843A9
    > balance:               44.000187612995945396
    > gas used:              2513062
    > gas price:             20 gwei
    > value sent:            0 ETH
    > total cost:            0.05026124 ETH


    > Saving migration to chain.
    > Saving artifacts
    -------------------------------------------
    > Total cost:            0.05026124 ETH


Summary
=======
> Total deployments:   2
> Final cost:          0.0547271 ETH
```

Figure 11.14   Output of deployment on Ropsten

3   Now that the smart contract has been successfully deployed, navigate to the web application part DCC-app, and update the app.js. The app.js accesses the smart contract function, using the address of the deployed smart contract and the application binary interface (ABI). Locate the smart contract address at the top of the app.js file, and replace it with the newly deployed smart contract address. I've already added the ABI for the DCC smart contract in the app.js code.

4   Execute the commands to deploy the web application to access the smart contract. The web application will be on your local machine but will access the smart contract on the Ropsten network:

```
npm install
npm start
```

5   Now you are ready to interact with the application, using your web page, MetaMask, and the Ropsten account. Make sure that you restore your Ropsten network account in your MetaMask, using the mnemonics from the DCCEnv.txt file. Reset the accounts and reload the web page before you start testing the public deployment. After this, the interaction with the Dapp will be the same as before with the local deployment. Refer to the UI diagrams (figures 11.10 and 11.11) as guidance when interacting with the DCC-app.

6 It is important to note that transactions will take time to confirm. Be patient. Your transactions coexist on the network with the transactions of many other public Dapps on Ropsten and their participants. You can observe the status of the transaction you initiated by clicking MetaMask, which will indicate whether the Tx is pending, confirmed, or failed.

That completes the testing of the public deployment by the administrator, deployer, or a tester. But the student, a user, or a decentralized participant does not have to worry about deploying the smart contract (as shown in steps 1–3). All they need to deploy is the web application Dapp-app part of the Dapp. That's what you'll do in the next section.

### 11.10.2 Create web-client for distribution

The smart contract is deployed only once, by the administrator, but used by many. These participants and student users need to deploy only the web application interface to interact with the deployed contract. Think about this for a few minutes. This client module is located in the DCC-Dapp-app-only.zip file. Unzip or extract all its components. It has only DCC-app. When you develop a blockchain application, you'll distribute only this part to the users, who may not be even aware that this is a blockchain-based decentralized application. They need to install the required modules and start the web client and interact. The prerequisite for executing the DCC-app is having Node.js and npm installed:

1 Download the DCC-Dapp-app-only, and unzip it. In src/js/app.js, update the smart contract address to the newly deployed smart contract address from the DCCEnv.txt file, and save it. (The smart contract should have been deployed by the administrator as described in section 11.10.1, so you should know the smart contract address.)

2 Navigate to DCC-app, and execute these commands to install the `requires` node modules and start the Node.js server:

```
npm install
npm start
```

3 Interact with the smart contract deployed in section 11.10.1. Try distributing this codebase (only the DCC-Dapp-app-only.zip) to your friends, and let them interact with the smart contract you deployed.

You can use these steps to work with the web client of the other applications you may have developed or may develop in the future. Also, you distribute only the app part of the Dapp—in this case, DCC-Dapp-app—to the decentralized participants.

## 11.11 Retrospective

The code for this blockchain-based project requires development of many parts, with proper use of techniques, tools, and configurations. It is complex, so you need a roadmap with clear directions for navigating the various parts. This chapter provided that roadmap as well as sample code to illustrate the waypoints in the roadmap. It took you all the way from a problem statement to local deployment of a prototype, testing, public deployment, and finally a distributable client application. It captured the concepts discussed in chapters 2–10 in a single application. This chapter may serve as a one-stop model for your Dapp development projects.

## 11.12 Best practices

This chapter allowed you to review best practices to follow when you are developing Dapps:

- Carefully examine the problem, evaluate the context, analyze the traditional solutions, and discuss any alternatives, if available.
- Design before you start developing the solution. Use standard diagrams such as a contract diagram and state diagram to represent the design.
- Use the FSM diagram and contract diagram as guidelines for developing the smart contract and user interface.
- Use standard directory structure and locations for the critical files. For XYZ-Dapp, use XYZ-contract, XYZ-app, XYZ.sol, and app.js.
- Use modifiers for representing rules. Modifiers revert transactions that don't meet the rules, so they help prevent the unnecessary recording of transactions on the blockchain.
- Use and emit event definitions to indicate significant milestones. These events emitted are recorded on the block and can be used for UI notification as well as postdata analysis.
- Design the smart contract with only the required data structures and operations. The smart contract has to be concise and precise, with simple, straightforward logic. Avoid loops and complex computations by creatively moving these operations to the nonblockchain components of the Dapp, such as to app.js.
- Use the Truffle and Ganache test environments to test the smart contract's operation before deploying the Dapp on a public network such as Ropsten.
- Deploy the Dapp on the blockchain client node in a cloud-environment such as Infura.
- Design a simple, intuitive UI for development purposes. This design will enable and guide the team later to develop a production-quality UI (a topic that is beyond the scope of this book).
- Test the integrated Dapp thoroughly before distributing it to stakeholders. Distribute only the client application part to the peer participants, who may be using a lightweight web client or mobile client.

## 11.13 Summary

- The blockchain-based solution is typically part of a larger system. In this chapter, DCC-Dapp for facilitating a certificate program is part of a larger university system.
- A roadmap is helpful for analyzing, designing, and developing a blockchain-based decentralized application solution for a problem.
- Analyzing a problem for its roles, rules, data structures, functions, and events emitted guides the development of a smart contract.
- A single complex off-chain operation for adding courses is split into four smaller smart contract functions (add prerequisite, add core, and so on) for simpler transactions to be recorded on-chain.
- JavaScript testing scripts and the Truffle test tool help in automating smart contract testing.
- Dapp development begins with smart contract development, its local deployment, and testing; migrating it to a production infrastructure; and creating a deployable module for the participants.
- Techniques such as events, off-chain and on-chain data and operations, and modifiers for verification and validation help in designing effective blockchain-based solutions.
- Tools such as Remix IDE, Truffle suite, Node.js-based package management, Infura web3 provider, Ropsten public network, and MetaMask wallet help in organizing the codebase and configuring it for standard deployment and testing.
- The DCC-Dapp codebase provides a one-stop model illustrating tools, techniques, and best practices for your Dapp development projects.

# Blockchain: The road ahead

## This chapter covers

- Exploring decentralized identity management
- Understanding consensus among decentralized participants
- Reviewing scalability, privacy, security, and confidentiality
- Analyzing public, private and permissioned blockchain networks
- Capturing the scientific research behind blockchain concepts

Any emerging technology will experience challenges as it is maturing. Blockchain is no exception. This field is churning with activities and initiatives in a quest for continuous improvement in technology. Although blockchain is a brilliant technology for trusted transactions, social interaction, and commerce, it is also open and decentralized. Openness and inclusivity of decentralized participants are two of the many impediments to the ready adoption of the technology. Dapps deployed on the blockchain address these concerns by enabling trusted transactions. Now that you are armed with the knowledge from earlier chapters, I encourage you to examine the challenges at all levels of the blockchain stack, from decentralized application development to contribution to protocol improvements.

In this chapter, you'll learn about some nonfunctional attributes that are relevant to blockchain applications. You need to pay attention to these attributes while designing and developing Dapps. This chapter will provide a high-level view of these attributes, challenges, existing solutions, potential opportunities, and the road ahead.

## 12.1 Decentralized identity

What is your name? How are you identified? Identity is a fundamental requirement for interacting with any system, computing or noncomputing. You need an instrument such as a driver's license to identify you for many of your routine activities, such as cashing a large check or taking an airline flight. You use a student ID card to avail yourself of the services of a university. But these identities are issued by a central authority after verification of your credentials, such as your Social Security number. For decentralized applications, there is no central authority for assigning identity for the participants. A decentralized system is made up of unknown participants who are potentially from anywhere in the world. In such a system, the challenge is how to

- Define a unique identity for participants
- Create and assign it to the participants
- Make it unique for every participant
- Manage (restore and remember) it

In addressing these concerns, blockchains rely on two fundamental concepts: cryptographic algorithms and larger address space (256 bits versus 64 bits). As you'll recall from chapter 5, the Ethereum identity of a participant is 160 bits. It is derived from a private-public key pair of 256 bits, using hashing algorithms for uniqueness, and can be self-generated. This kind of self-managed identity is an important distinction between traditional centralized applications and blockchain-based decentralized applications.

## 12.2 Self-managed identity

To understand the concept of self-managed identity, let's create it and do some blockchain operations with it. You'll also collect test Ethereum cryptocurrency with it. First, you'll generate a private-public key pair, generate a mnemonic for it, and use that mnemonic to extract account addresses to populate a MetaMask wallet. This mnemonic represents a deterministic set of account addresses for your digital wallet, such as MetaMask. (*Deterministic* means that the same unique set of accounts is generated for a given mnemonic representing a private key.) You performed these steps within the context of developing Dapps in chapters 5 and 8:

1   Open your Chrome browser.
2   Link to the website https://iancoleman.io/bip39.

    Figure 12.1 shows the screenshot of the web page. You can see that this web tool can generate addresses for other coins (cryptocurrencies) too.

3   Make these three choices, as indicated in the figure:
    –   Generate a 12-word mnemonic.
    –   Choose English as the language for the mnemonic, and press the Return key.
    –   Choose ETH (Ethereum) as the coin or cryptocurrency.

4   The mnemonic appears in the BIP39 mnemonic box. Copy it, and keep it safe and secure. The mnemonic generated for me was *later dirt alert wear exotic hotel nasty thunder comfort powder alarm build.*

    You can retrieve accounts and their balances by using this mnemonic. Next, let's obtain a seed phrase.

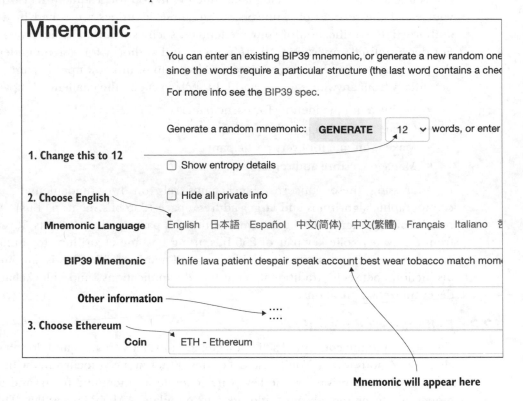

**Figure 12.1   BIP39 interface to generate a seed phrase/ mnemonic from a private key**

**SECURE YOUR SEED PHRASE**   The seed phrase represents your private key. If the seed phrase is compromised (stolen or given away), the loss is equivalent to losing a credit card from your wallet. The person who gets hold of the seed phrase can restore the accounts on their wallet and divert the funds there.

In the next steps, you'll create an account address to represent your decentralized identity. With this identity, you'll be able to collect test Ethereum cryptocurrency for transactions on the Ropsten network.

5  Click the MetaMask icon in your Chrome browser.

6  Choose the Ropsten network as shown in figure 12.2

7  You may choose other networks for your later explorations.

8  Click Import Account Using Seed Phrase at the bottom of the MetaMask dropdown box.

9  In the screen that appears in figure 12.2, enter the mnemonic you generated earlier.

10  Enter a password, repeat it to confirm, and click Restore. You see your account number in the MetaMask drop-down box.

My account address after this exercise was 0xCbc16bad0bD4C75Ad261BC8 593b99c365a0bc1A4. Here, 0x indicates that what follows is hexadecimal, followed by 20 bytes or a 160-bit address. This address is your decentralized identity; you can share it with any application to interact with it. You can give out the account numbers but not the mnemonic representing the private key. You can create many account numbers similar to the numbers of your checking, savings, college, and home accounts, and so on.

11  In MetaMask, click the Account 1 logo, and in the drop-down box that appears, select Create Account to create different accounts or identities for yourself. The MetaMask drop-down box will be similar to the one in figure 12.2, but with account details.

The MetaMask wallet shows that your account balance is 0. You need test ether to transact on the Ropsten Ethereum test network. Let us start collecting ether from a cryptocurrency faucet meant for this purpose.

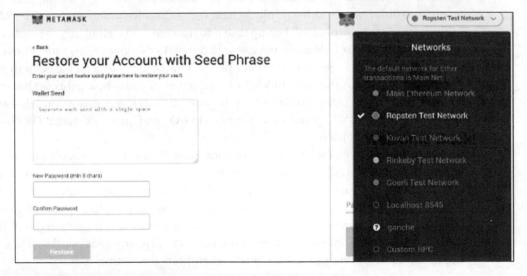

Figure 12.2   Restore account using seed phrase in MetaMask wallet

12  Copy your account address, as shown in MetaMask. You need this address to collect test ether for your account.

13  Open a Ropsten faucet (https://faucet.ropsten.be) to receive 1.0 test ether.

14  In the box that appears, enter your testnet account address from step 10, and click the Send Me Test Ether button. You'll have to connect the account to the Ropsten faucet using the connect option on MetaMask account.

   You should see a 1.0 ETH balance added to your account. You can view this balance in the MetaMask wallet.

   You can collect 1.0 ETH every 24 hours. Keep collecting ether to support the explorations of the various Dapps you may create.

The mnemonic you generated earlier in this section defines a unique set of accounts for your wallet. You can access these accounts from anywhere with the MetaMask-enabled browser and the mnemonic. The solution discussed in this section is for a single user self-generating the identity.

   The account addresses generated can be used as identities on any Ethereum-based blockchain networks. The challenge is to teach users that they must keep the key phrases safe and secure, as they do with their Social Security numbers. Thus, managing identities is a crucial concept in production environments. To manage identities, the Sovrin organization has defined a complete, self-sovereign identity framework that provides an open identity management framework (http://mng.bz/QxWw) by using digital credentials you own. Sovrin uses an issuer-verifier-owner model for managing identity and trust.

## 12.3   *Consensus and integrity*

The consensus model is a hotly debated topic in blockchain technology. Participants enabled by the self-assigned identity can send transactions, and these transactions are collected into different blocks by the blockchain (miner) nodes, as shown in figure 12.3. One of the many blocks formed will be appended to the chain. The challenge is to add a block about which the stakeholders in the network agree. Let's explore this aspect next.

   *Consensus* means agreement among peers. This consensus is an agreement among the full nodes about the next block to be added to the chain, a process that ensures the integrity of the chain. To address this issue, different consensus models—such as proof of work (POW), proof of authority (POA), and proof of stake (POS)—have been proposed and tried.

   Bitcoin uses proof of work (POW) for consensus. Figure 12.3 shows a high-level depiction of POW consensus. The figure shows that miners compete (by solving a computation puzzle) to add the next block to the chain. POW is computationally intensive and results in enormous power consumption in the massive racks of specialized computers used in solving the POW puzzle for the right to mine the next block. It is estimated that Bitcoin mining consumes as much as energy as the country of Ireland uses per day. Therein lies the problem. Let's discuss the POW method and two alternatives to it.

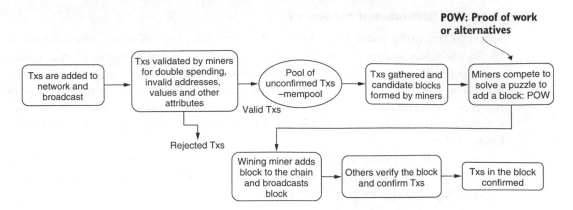

**Figure 12.3   Block creation and transaction confirmation with POW consensus model**

### 12.3.1   *Proof of work*

The POW algorithm has been working in Bitcoin since its inception more than ten years ago; Ethereum has used POW since its release. POW is the baseline for many consensus algorithms that are being proposed, so it is good to review POW in this section. POW works like this. Compute the hash H of block header elements (fixed) and a nonce (variable):

1  `H = hash(header, nonce) //nonce is variable parameter in the header`
2  `If H <= function(difficulty) for Ethereum, the miner has solved the puzzle, jump to step 4. //difficulty is a variable parameter in the header`
3  `Else change the nonce and repeat steps 1 and 2.`
4  `Puzzle has been solved.`

Although it is difficult to find the combination (header, nonce) that solves the problem in step 2, it is easy to verify. How do you verify that a hash $H <= 2^{128}$ assuming $2^{128}$ is the `function(difficulty)` in the steps? Check whether the leading (256-128= 128) 128 bits of H is zero. Note that all data and computations are in 256 bits. In the newer version, Ethereum Istanbul, the plan is to use proof of stake (section 12.3.2).

### 12.3.2   *Proof of stake*

In proof of stake (POS), the full node with the most at stake or most coins in its account chooses the next block to be added to the chain, which is why it is called proof of stake. The idea is that the node with the most at stake will not act maliciously and risk its stake by forking the network. A round-robin policy is used to avoid monopoly by the node with the most at stake. The transaction fees pay the minter (yes, *minter*, not *miner*) fee, and there is no miner fee, such as in POW. The POS approach is expected to be environment-friendly and efficient.

### 12.3.3 *Byzantine fault-tolerant consensus*

Practical Byzantine Fault Tolerance (PBFT) has been proven to tolerate random or Byzantine node failures (including malicious nodes). In PBFT, nodes elect a leader, and that leader adds the next block to the chain. The nodes exchange messages. The messages, along with the saved state, are used to reach a consensus in the presence of random independent faults or bad nodes. The chosen node adds the next block of validated transactions. PBFT is popular in permissioned blockchains such as Hyperledger Fabric.

As you can see, consensus is a core component of a blockchain protocol, and an efficient algorithm is essential for both the integrity and scalability of blockchain. Scalability is the next challenge I'll discuss.

## 12.4    *Scalability*

Scalability is a bottleneck preventing the broader adoption of blockchain for business applications. The question many businesses ask is whether blockchain protocol, infrastructure, network, and nodes can successfully deliver a transaction rate on par with that of credit card transactions. Average transaction confirmation time depends on the average block time—the time required to confirm a block. As shown in figure 12.3, transactions are packed in a block, and the block is appended to the chain. All the transactions in a confirmed block have the timestamp of the block. You must be aware of this fact when using transaction confirmation times for verification in your application.

> **DEFINITION**    *Scalability* is the ability of a system to perform satisfactorily at all practical levels of load. Load, in the context of the blockchain, could be transaction times, transaction rate, number of nodes, number of participants and accounts, number of transactions, or other attributes.

In the case of blockchain, practitioners are concerned about the transaction rate, or transactions per second. This metric is critical for many applications, from payment systems to supply chain management, so let's focus on transactions per second as the metric for scalability.

Blockchain has taken on the responsibilities of the intermediaries, including validation, verification, and recording of the transaction. The consensus process for the integrity of the chain is another time-consuming function. All these functions take time and result in significant overhead in Tx confirmation time compared with that of a centralized system. The transactions execute sequentially. The full nodes store the entire chain. Thus, transaction rates are not satisfactory compared with those of centralized applications, which affects scalability. In this section, let's examine some solutions that address scalability.

Figure 12.4 shows average transaction time from etherscan.io from January 2016 to July 2020, the average block time, ranging from 12 seconds in 2020 to a maximum 30 seconds in 2017. A credit card transaction can be confirmed in less than a second,

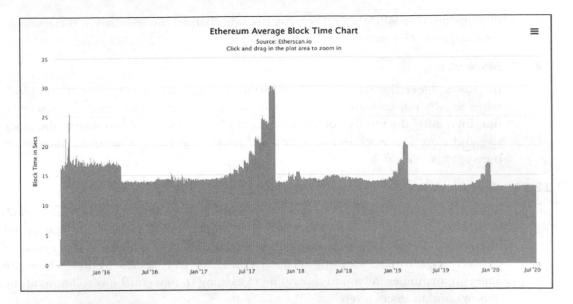

**Figure 12.4  Ethereum average block time chart**

whereas it takes an average of 10 seconds for Ethereum. It is expected that in the latest version of Ethereum, transactions per second will improve to 3,000. But the Visa credit card network is capable of handling a load of 65,000 transactions per second. Thus, scalability is an area that requires a lot of attention, and this is an opportunity for you to contribute creative solutions.

## 12.5  Scalability solutions

Many solutions have been proposed, and quite a few of them have been in operation in production networks. The Ethereum community is working hard to address the scalability issues. The proposed solutions are across all levels of the stack.

### 12.5.1  Side channel

Side channel is a solution at the blockchain application level. The state channel of Ethereum and the lightning channel of Bitcoin are examples. The idea is to keep only relevant transactions on-chain for confirmation and recording. Other transactions between trusted parties are offloaded to a side channel, thus reducing the transaction load on the main channel. Periodically, the gist of the off-chain happenings are synchronized with a transaction on the main channel. The transactions of off-chain channels take place at much higher speeds than on the blockchain networks because no consensus or recording on the blockchain distributed ledger is required.

Recall that you used a side channel in the MPC-Dapp in chapter 7. This Dapp addresses scalability to a certain extent at the application level. At this point, you have the knowledge and skill to apply the side channel concept when developing Dapps, as demonstrated in MPC-Dapp. Try using the side channel model where it is relevant in your Dapp development.

### 12.5.2 Block size

Increasing block size is a protocol-level solution. Transaction time depends on block time. So why not increase the size of the block to accommodate more transactions, thus increasing the number of transactions per block? The idea is to double the block size and store the block header data segregated (Segwit2X) to accommodate more transactions in a block.

### 12.5.3 Network speed

Improving network speed is a network-level solution. Researchers believe that scalability is a network-level problem, and increasing the bandwidth at the level that of the internet will help. The idea is that higher network speed may lead to a faster relay of transactions and block, leading to faster consensus and block selection. There are many opportunities for you to contribute to existing or new scalability solutions at the network and protocol levels.

## 12.6 Privacy

When I introduce blockchain to any audience, the most frequently asked question is about privacy. A public blockchain is an open network that anybody can join and leave, so how do you keep it private? I often reply with another question: How do you keep something private in real life? By not allowing others to see it.

The first-line solution for addressing privacy is restricting and controlling who is allowed to join and transact on the blockchain. That's been the solution for blockchain too. Consider a democratic voting system on the blockchain. There is no need for the country's voting blockchain network to be open to the entire world; you want this network to be private to the legal or permitted citizens of that country. Hence, we have permissioned blockchain, which leads to the first line of defense supporting privacy, the three major models for blockchain networks: public, private, and permissioned.

## 12.7 Public, private, and permissioned networks

Bitcoin (also called the permissionless blockchain) is a working example of a public blockchain. The primary purpose of the Bitcoin blockchain is to support a decentralized, peer-to-peer payment system. It's meant to be a transparent, permissionless *public* system that anyone can join and leave as they wish, as in any other bearer payment system, such as transacting cash. If you pay cash for an item you purchase in a store, for example, nobody asks you for your signature or needs you to authorize the payment. Similarly, Bitcoin enables a peer-to-peer digital payment system without any intermediaries.

When the use cases for blockchain expanded beyond the simple payment system into business areas such as personal health care systems and financial systems, privacy and restricted access became necessary. Even in the public payment systems, it became apparent that the whole chain may not be relevant to all the participants. Business transactions in a Buffalo school district may not be relevant to the Nairobi tourism board, for example. Such thoughts and ideas resulted in the creation of permissioned blockchain (figure 12.5), in which only permitted participants can transact and take part in the blockchain operations.

The permissioned blockchain is also known as a consortium blockchain based on its everyday use cases in specific vertical business domains, such as the auto or food services consortiums. Chapters 2 and 6 introduced the ASK airline consortium, which is a suitable Dapp for a permissioned blockchain. In the case of the micropayment channel in chapter 7, a public chain is appropriate.

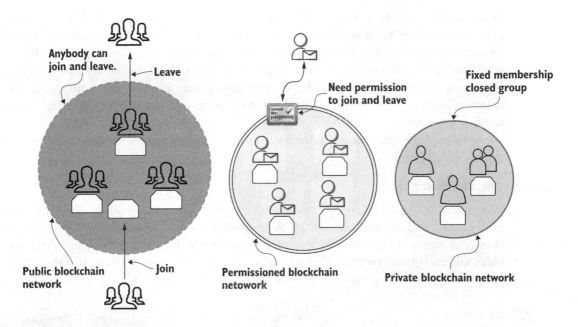

**Figure 12.5   Public, permissioned, and private blockchain networks**

The third type, *private*, is an extreme case of permissioned network in which membership is highly selective and often limited and permanent. Although experts claim that a private blockchain is no different from a centralized system among known participants, it still has potential for useful applications. Sometimes, trust is a significant issue even among known or related peers, such as members of a family, the board of directors of a company, or a group of researchers working on sensitive matters of national security. You could develop a private blockchain among a closed set of entities to record deliberations and decisions, to be used later for discovery and in some cases for litigation. The significant issue with a smaller membership and consequently with private blockchain is the 51 percent attack. In this case, it is potentially easier for a few members to collude and make the chain inconsistent.

All three types of public blockchains—permissionless, permissioned, and private—are relevant in the blockchain application domains. They differ mainly in the way membership is determined. With closed membership, it is possible to implement a more efficient consensus mechanism than the POW of Bitcoin, which consumes an enormous amount of power. But in a closed, private system, you are reverting to trusting a few designated participants, as in a centralized system. You must weigh these facts when deciding which type of blockchain is appropriate for a given problem. Whether the blockchain is public, private, or permissioned, you need security mechanisms to protect the data.

## 12.8    Confidentiality

Many people equate privacy with confidentiality. Confidentiality is different from privacy; it is about keeping details (or metainformation) about the transaction closed. In some situations, transactions have to be confidential. Consider a patient–doctor relationship. If there were ten transactions between a patient and healthcare provider in a day, this information might convey something, even if the content of the transactions is kept private. The fact that ten transactions occurred between the parties implies something.

Let's explore how open the transactions are in the Ropsten network you used to deploy your Dapps.

### 12.8.1    Open information

Whether it is a public chain or a private chain, you can search the blockchain ledger with an account number to find all the transactions associated with this address, as shown in figure 12.6. You can also search by transaction hash, block number, and other filters. If you have an account number, you can try it for by yourself at the Etherscan for Ropsten site (https://ropsten.etherscan.io).

**Figure 12.6   Searching the blockchain records by a certain filter**

If I want to know all the transactions that originated from a certain identity, for example, I can search for it by using its account address, as shown in figure 12.7. You realize that you can secure all the data by using encryption, but the fact that the transaction happened is not confidential. It shows the transaction from account 0x28... along with other details. Even if the contents of transactions are encrypted, the transactions

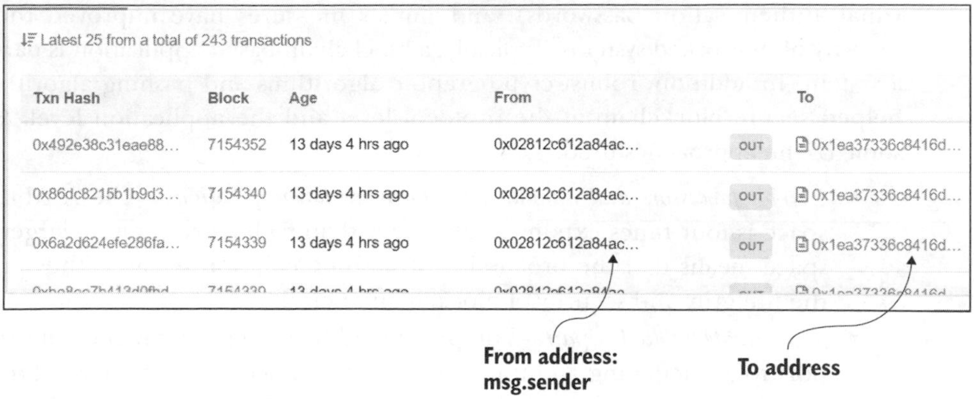

**Figure 12.7   Transactions from account 0x2812c... on Ropsten public chain**

themselves are not confidential. If this is my address, you know that I have been frequently invoking a smart contract at the address 0x1e... This information conveys some intelligence to you. If the smart contract were my stockbroker, you might infer that I have been considering some financial moves. In other words, although my transactions were secure, they were not confidential.

### 12.8.2  *A solution*

How do you achieve confidentiality in blockchain applications? To protect the confidentiality of data, a novel concept called zero-knowledge-proof has been proposed. Zcash (https://z.cash/technology) is a working solution for realizing confidentiality in cryptocurrency transfers. It achieves confidentiality by implementing a novel type of Txs called shielded transactions or z Txs. In this realm, unshielded Txs are referred to as t Txs. Zcash is well-founded in a strong scientific background. It offers four types of Txs:

- Both sender (z) and receiver (z) are shielded (fully private).
- Only sender (z) is shielded, not the receiver (t).
- Only receiver (z) is shielded, not the sender (t).
- Both receiver and sender are not shielded (public).

In this case, z refers to shielding or hiding, and t refers to a regular nonshielded entity. Although this solution is available only for digital currency such as that offered by Zcash, a similar solution can be adapted to other application domains, such as health care, financial, and military.

## 12.9   *Security*

Security is a challenge for any computing system and network, especially in an open and decentralized system of typically unknown participants. Over the years, security at the network level (http:// to https://), infrastructure level (firewalls), system level (dual authentication passwords), and similar measures have improved the overall security of networked systems. Typically, a blockchain-based application is part of such a system. In addition, robust cryptographic algorithms and hashing algorithms have helped secure blockchain at the protocol level and the application level. Here are some of the approaches used:

- *256-bit processors and computations for blockchain operations*—The 256-bit address space is four times exponentially larger than 64-bit space, and a larger address space means that the probability of hashing collision is lower, thus preserving the integrity and security of blockchain operation.
- *The private-public key pair*—The private-public key pair is the metaphorical passport to participating and transacting on the blockchain. Similar to the way you use, secure, and protect a credit card, you need to protect the private key and the mnemonic representing it for the security of your assets.
- *Elliptic curve cryptography (ECC)*—At the protocol level, blockchain protocol uses the ECC family of algorithms instead of the traditional RSA (Rivest-Shamir-Edelman) algorithm. Why ECC, not RSA? ECC is stronger than RSA for a given number of bits. A 256-bit ECC key-pair is equivalent in strength to about a 3072-bit RSA key pair.
- *Tx and block hashes*—Tx hashes and block hashes are computed at the time of their creation. Any modifications (even a single bit) to a Tx or a block will result in a mismatched hash, resulting in rejection of the Tx and the block securing the integrity of the chain.
- *Off-chain data security*—Application data off-chain can be secured by hashing the data and storing *only* the hash value on the chain. This concept is discussed in chapters 2–6, in which the airline data off-chain can be secured by a hash on the chain.
- *On-chain data security*—At the application level, a combination of encryption, hashing, and one-time-password helps secure the data transmitted in a Tx. You used hashing and encryption with a one-time password to secure the bid in the MPC-Dapp in chapters 7 and 8.

Thus, a combination of hashing and cryptography plays a critical role in the blockchain creation process, as well as the integrity of transactions and the security of data. A developer will routinely use cryptography and hashing algorithms in their development. As you learned in chapter 9, the web3 API provides Keccak and SHA3 functions to facilitate security in Dapps.

Do you wonder about the role of cryptocurrency in a typical Dapp? Do you wonder whether you can develop without the use of cryptocurrency and focus solely on business logic on the blockchain? That's what you'll explore next.

## 12.10 *Securing it with cryptocurrency*

Another important consideration in blockchain applications is the cryptocurrency aspect that is not prevalent in your regular network computations. The genesis of blockchain is cryptocurrency transfers with the advent of Bitcoin. As you may have realized through your explorations in this book, ETH cryptocurrency is required for deploying a Dapp, transacting, and executing smart contract functions. The cryptocurrency, miner fees, transaction fees, gas points, and incentives all ensure proper operation and enable trust. In other words, these expenses incurred are the cost of trust. Blockchain platforms use cryptocurrency as well as protocol logic to implement trust. This aspect leads to the classification of platforms based on their primary purpose. Bitcoin, Ethereum, and Linux Foundation's Hyperledger (figure 12.8) are three different platforms based on their primary purpose. Many other platforms are available, and I urge you to explore appropriate ones for your application domain.

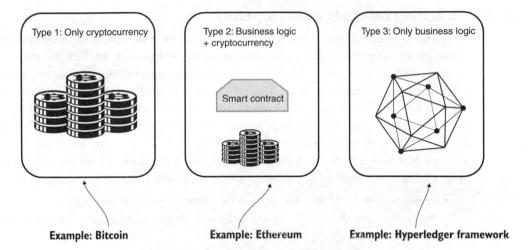

**Figure 12.8   Types of blockchain, from pure cryptocurrency to pure logic**

Here are a few prominent platforms to consider for your applications:

- Bitcoin is meant for cryptocurrency transfer and does not support arbitrary logic in such instruments as a smart contract. Bitcoin protocol does support a minimal script for conditional transfer of cryptocurrency.
- The Ethereum mainnet is a public network, but Ethereum can be used for private, public, and permissioned networks. Enterprise Ethereum Alliance (EEA) was created to support the need for consortium or permissioned as well as private Ethereum networks. Ethereum supports cryptocurrency as well as computational logic in smart contracts.

- The Hyperledger framework focuses on computation logic and currently does not support cryptocurrency. The Hyperledger framework has many implementations, including Iroha, Intel's Sawtooth, Fabric, Indy, Burrow, and IBM's Fabric (version 2). Currently, these platforms are purely business-logic-based. No cryptocurrency is involved.

Thus in figure 12.8, you can see the two ends of the spectrum of blockchains, from real cryptocurrency enablers to pure business logic enablers. When you are designing blockchain-based solutions, you must consider cryptocurrency to be an integral part. Blockchain may not be only for sending and receiving value. You can create incentive models involving participants, fees for various activities, creative solutions for planetary-level problems (such as MPC discussed in chapter 7), and new economic models centered on a working digital currency. The cryptocurrency incurred is the cost of trust for the decentralized blockchain-based application.

## 12.11 *Accessing off-chain data (Oracles)*

Have you wondered how a smart contract can access external data? A smart contract operates in a sandbox. It cannot call an outside function or link to an external resource. Why can't a smart contract access outside sources? Depending on the source called, external data access from a smart contract may affect the global consistency of the blockchain. The results of any operation on the blockchain have to be deterministic. These issues limit the applicability of smart contracts in many real-world applications that may involve obtaining facts, data, and assets from external real-world sources. Moreover, data may have to be obtained at the time of execution and may not be available at the time of deployment of the contract. Let's look at some examples:

- *Temperatures on Mount Kilimanjaro on a given day*—The temperatures are universal facts, but they have to be obtained from an authentic external weather source.
- *Stock market data*—This data may be the high and low prices of a stock on a particular date on the NASDAQ market. This condition ensures that all the participants on the chain get the same consistent outcome for a smart contract operation.

How do you get access to external resources? Accessing data sources external to the smart contract is addressed by a concept called *oracles*. An oracle service fetches external data for a smart contract. Merriam-Webster defines *oracle* as "an authoritative or wise expression or answer." This definition closely defines the role of the oracle service in smart-contract development.

> **DEFINITION** An oracle service is a data carrier between web resources (APIs and URLs) and a smart contract. An oracle service is located outside the blockchain protocol.

An oracle is a useful component that facilitates the availability of real-world facts needed for the functioning of certain smart contracts. Provable (https://provable .xyz/index.html) is an implementation of an oracle service for getting outside data into a smart contract. Chainlink (https://chain.link/features) is a more recent oracle service for smart contracts to access external data feeds, APIs, and payments.

Oracle service is implemented as a smart contract that provides a query function to access external sources. The oracle smart contract is imported into the calling smart contract and inherited. Then a query is used to access the oracle with the required data. The data requested is returned through a callback function because accessing data and verification may take some time. Figure 12.9 shows a simple class diagram relating a smart contract, oracle services, and an external data source.

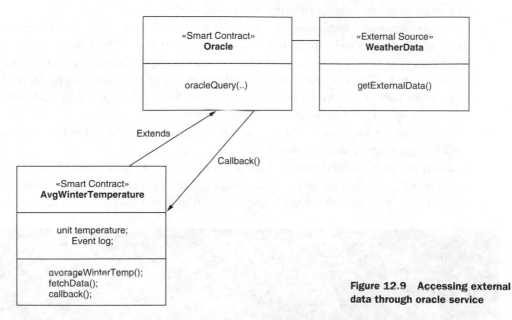

**Figure 12.9   Accessing external data through oracle service**

When the smart contract AvgWinterTemperature is deployed, it calls `fetchData()`, which in turn invokes the oracle service's query with the URL for the data source. It may take time to fetch the data, so a callback function is provided that can be invoked when the required data has been fetched. The oracle service accesses the external data source, authenticates the requested data, and sends it to the originating smart contract. Additionally, the service may offer methods to verify the authenticity of the data fetched.

## 12.12 *From foundations to practical systems*

Blockchain is based on nearly 40 years of scientific research in cryptography and math algorithms. The butterfly effect is defined as a little perturbation of an initial state that culminates in significant outcomes. This concept is defined in the context of chaos theory. The advent of Bitcoin has had a butterfly effect on technology. It has creatively synthesized scientific research results from the past four decades to release an innovative working model for a peer-peer digital payment system, as shown in figure 12.10. It shows how foundational research in public-key cryptography and security has led to the discovery of the internet and secure distributed systems. These discoveries, along with hashing and cryptographic algorithms, enabled Bitcoin and the underlying foundation of blockchain. All these concepts culminated in blockchain's distributed ledger, disintermediation, smart contracts, decentralized apps, and planetary-level inclusive systems.

The smart contract concept in figure 12.10 is enabled by blockchain. A smart contract represents a token. In other words, a smart contract can provide an elegant representation of an asset in the physical world or digital world: a stock, a piece of real estate (as discussed in chapter 9), or a digital game bounty. This tokenized asset can be traded, discounted, divided, archived, and destroyed. The tokens (or their fractions) can be used for incentivization, such as shopping coupons and participatory remuneration. The entire history, since the creation of the asset, can be recorded in a trusted distributed immutable ledger that can facilitate audits and authentication. These features have the potential to spawn a new token economy.

You can see from figure 12.10 that this single idea of blockchain is ushering in a technological and a social revolution. You are witnessing the transformation from centralized to decentralized applications enabled by blockchain technology and cryptocurrencies. These emerging technologies are expected to culminate in new applications that transcend demographics and national barriers. As explained in this

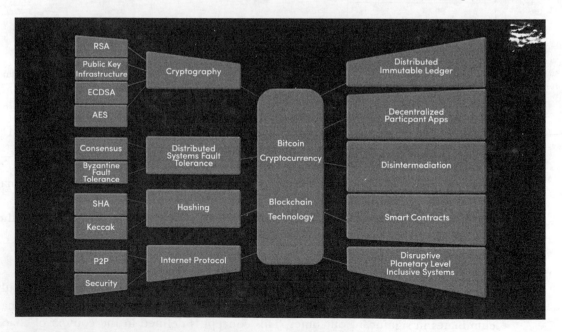

**Figure 12.10   The blockchain butterfly: foundations to contributions**

chapter, this area is in flux, and a lot more needs to be done. Transforming this strong foundational knowledge into practical and useful Dapps will require reimagining traditional applications to include the trust component. You can play an important role as a participant, collaborator, and contributor to this revolution.

## 12.13 Looking ahead

At the global level, organizations such as the United Nations have an opportunity to serve as a test bed for many blockchain applications, such as verifiable disaster relief, vaccine distribution, maintaining international peace through trust, and enforcing democratic processes. Chapters 7 and 8 demonstrate a massive global plastics cleanup problem.

Within any country, government officials and policymakers can take up policies and regulations to ease the adoption of blockchain. U.S. states such as New York and Delaware are considering regulations that will help in the widespread adoption of blockchain solutions. Unlike with other traditional technologies, the government can host a full node or nodes to facilitate decentralized operations. This feature offers the additional benefit of full nodes storing a completed timestamped ledger of Txs. The information on the ledger can be used for audit and review purposes. The Department of Education, for example, may play a vital leadership role in the adoption of blockchain for educational purposes such as countrywide credentialing. (Chapter 11 discusses the credentialing prototype DCC-Dapp.)

At the application level, autonomous vehicles and robots on shop floors and in home care have become a reality. Augmenting these innovations with blockchain can develop a layer of trust for monitoring autonomous actions. Enabling a cryptocurrency capability for these autonomous entities, you can design self-paying and self-managing machines. You can send cryptocurrency to pay these machines for their services in cryptocurrency, and they can use their cryptobalances to self-schedule repairs, replenishments, and payments.

Have you wondered about the data that gets stored on the distributed immutable ledger of blockchain? This timestamped data is indeed a valuable resource for post-analysis to discover patterns, actionable intelligence, and anomalies.

More developers and practitioners are wanted to focus on many of the challenges discussed in this chapter. More tools, frameworks, and test beds are needed for rapid prototyping and testing. Educating stakeholders at all levels and training users and developers in the proper use of blockchain technology is an important step. Thinkers and designers who are knowledgeable about blockchain are needed to use blockchain to solve problems creatively.

## 12.14 Best practices

Here are some best practices for what you learned in this chapter:

- Choose the type of blockchain based on the membership requirements of the application: private, public (permissionless), or permissioned (consortium).
- Determine the blockchain platform for your environment, depending on whether you need cryptocurrency.
- Carefully review the problem; it may not require blockchain involvement.
- To support Dapp development, choose the language for the smart contract, frameworks for the frontend, tools such as Remix and Truffle, test bed (Ganache), cloud support (Infura), and test plans.
- Design before you develop. Use a test-driven development approach (as discussed in chapters 4, 6, and 10).
- Make sure to pay attention to the best practices discussed throughout this book for developing Dapps.

## 12.15 Retrospective

Blockchain is here to stay. Bitcoin is an excellent example of what has been running autonomously and supported by a developer community. Blockchain, such as Ethereum discussed in this book, has added execution logic to make it viable for solving business problems. Blockchain is not without its share of challenges, as it is evolving and growing its ecosystem.This book covered quite a range of decentralized applications and supporting concepts. The seven worked-out examples are

- A versatile counter (Counter-Dapp)
- A digital democracy (Ballot-Dapp)
- A marketplace for unused airline seats (ASK-Dapp)
- A blind auction framework (BlindAuction-Dapp)
- An incentivization model and side channel for micropayments (MPC-Dapp)
- A token model for real estate transactions (RES4-Dapp)
- An educational credentialing model (DCC-Dapp)

These Dapps provide application models with instructions to support your learning and development efforts. The book also covered relevant concepts that support the development of these Dapps, including

- Trust and integrity
- Security and privacy
- Off-chain and on-chain data
- Local and public deployment
- Automated testing

All the concepts are supported by code to illustrate their application in the development process. I hope you find them useful for understanding and developing with blockchain technology.

## 12.16 Summary

- Decentralized identity, consensus, and cryptocurrency are unique issues related to blockchain that you do not find in traditional networked systems.
- Scalability is a major challenge in blockchain networks. Innovative solutions are needed to address scalability and to encourage broader adoption of blockchain.
- Privacy, confidentiality, and security are critical in systems supported by blockchain because no central authority polices or manages them.
- Blockchain has a deep, strong foundation in nearly four decades of mathematical and scientific research.
- Blockchain provides a trust layer to enable autonomous applications. These applications will usher in a new wave of innovations that is sure to lead us to another revolution in internet technology.

# appendix A
# UML blockchain
# design models

Software application development should always begin with a clear problem statement that describes a problem to be solved, including its requirements, scope, limitations, exceptions, and expected outcomes. You analyze this problem statement to come up with a design representation. The design representation of an application is like the blueprint that is created before the construction of a home or the engineering design created before a product is machined.

Software application developers are often eager to jump into coding before they design, but this is not good practice. The best practice is to analyze and design the solution to a problem in a standard format so that all the parameters can be discussed with the stakeholders in an implementation-independent fashion, using visual representations of the design components. Unified Modeling Language (UML) (https://www.uml.org) offers multiple diagram models for design representation.

The UML design methodology was introduced about three decades ago to address the development challenges that arose as the scale and complexity of software increased, with small-scale systems being replaced by large, multimodule systems. UML modeling has been widely adopted by many organizations, and UML diagrams have become a standard for visual models for designing software. The UML models and documentation are maintained by the not-for-profit Object Management Group (OMG). The latest version, UML 2.0, has 13 types of diagrams categorized in 3 groups: structural, behavioral, and interaction diagrams. There is a good chance that you are currently using one or more of these diagrams in your environment. This appendix reviews a selected set of UML diagrams that are used in the design of decentralized blockchain applications in this book. Many UML tools, free and paid, are available for drawing UML diagrams. One of the freeware options, draw.io (https://app.diagrams.net/), was used to develop the designs for the applications in this book.

## A.1    *Problem analysis and design*

Would you ever launch into building a house without a blueprint? No way! Not only do you need a plan, but you also need a plan in a standard format that can be reviewed, understood, and approved by the authorizing agency. Similarly, UML diagrams are a set of diagrams that help you visually represent the design of your solution to a problem so that stakeholders can understand, discuss, and approve it before you start developing and coding the solution.

Let's take a look at the behavioral, structural, and interaction diagrams that are put to use in this book for designing decentralized applications.

## A.2    *Behavioral diagrams*

In this book, we employ two UML behavioral diagrams: use case diagrams for requirement gathering as one of the first steps in the design process, and finite state machine (FSM) diagrams later in the design process for defining state transitions of the executable code (smart contracts) on the blockchain.

### A.2.1    *Use case diagrams*

Use case models help you analyze a problem statement, identify the actors or users of the system defined by the problem, and determine how these actors will use the system. The actors need not be only humans; they can be humans, applications, and devices, for example. The actors are anything or anyone that provides the stimulus for activation of one of the use cases identified by the problem statement. The use case diagram, therefore, defines three items, as shown in figure A.1:

- The actors of the system
- The use cases of the system
- The stimuli provided by the actors

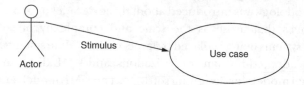

Figure A.1    Actor, use case, and stimulus

An *actor* is someone or something that interacts with the system you are designing. A *use case* provides some value to the actor. Let's analyze a problem and design the use case diagram for it to clarify this process.

> **PROBLEM STATEMENT**    Design a vending machine: a customer inserts coins and chooses a drink that is delivered. For simplicity, consider only the case with no exceptions and with the exact amount of coins required deposited.

The use case diagram for the vending machine coin counter and drink dispenser is shown in figure A.2. It has four use cases at the first level—insert coins, see drinks, select drink, and pick up drink—which are direct stimuli or operations invoked by the customer. The insert coins operation in turn invokes the count coins use case, see drinks requires display drinks, and select drink results in deliver drink. These secondary use cases are not directly invoked or used by the customer. An important note is that a use case diagram is not like a traditional flow chart. It simply lists the operations in the elliptical use case symbols. The operational flow is not defined here.

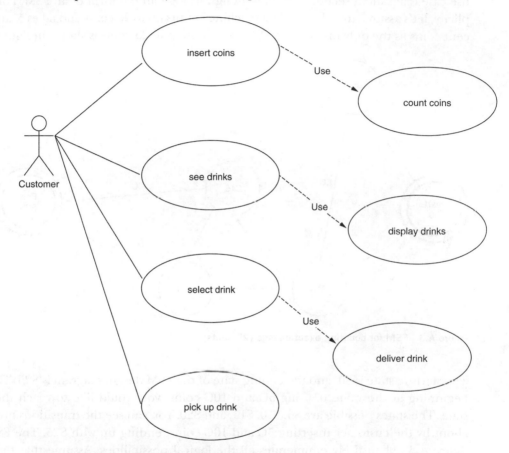

**Figure A.2   Use case diagram for vending machine**

Try using draw.io, Microsoft Visio, or another tool of your choice to create the use case diagram and get some practice.

## A.2.2   *Finite state machine diagrams*

FSM diagrams define the states that define the operational flow on execution of code and the transitions among them, a classic type of diagram from the theoretical foundations of mathematics and computer science. In the context of blockchain, an FSM diagram is used to define the states and state transitions when a smart contract executes; it's a convenient tool for expressing the behavior of a smart contract.

**DEFINITION**  A *finite state machine* is made up of a set of states (an initial state and one or more terminal states), transitions from one state to another, and the events that bring about those transitions.

Let's explore the elements of the FSMm using an example problem and its finite state machine representation. We'll use the count coins use case from the vending machine use case diagram in section A.2.1 and design its logic in the form of an FSM. For simplicity, let's assume that the vending machine counts up to 25 cents and takes 5- and 10-cent coins as the only inputs. The FSM for counting to 25 cents is shown in figure A.3.

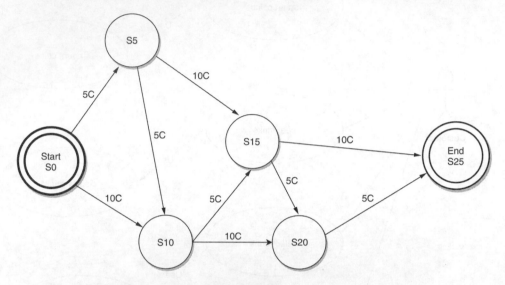

**Figure A.3    FSM for counting exact change (25 cents)**

The starting state is S0, and the ending state of the FSM design diagram is S25. That is, beginning at the value 0, using 5C and 10C coins, you would like to reach the S25 state. The states possible are S5, S10, S15, and S20. You can see the transitions brought about by the customer inserting 5C and 10C coins, ending up with S25. The FSM in figure A.3 exhaustively enumerates all the logical possibilities. Assume that the customer is aware of the requirement to insert exact change.

You can draw this diagram with any tool of your choice. The version here was created with the widgets provided by the draw.io tool; draw.io does not explicitly provide an FSM diagram, but you can use the circles and arrows from the general template.

## A.3  *Structural diagrams*

This category of UML diagrams helps you define the static structural design of your solution. We will study only one of them: the class diagram. You will learn to represent multiple classes and their relationships, using standard notations. Class diagrams are useful for defining the overall structure of a module or a smart contract solution.

## A.3.1  *Class diagrams*

The class diagram was introduced to represent a class in an object-oriented design of a solution, but it can be used to represent any class of object in a problem. You discover classes in your problem statement by underlining the nouns in the statement and making a list of these nouns. Then you examine the complexity of the nouns to decide whether a noun or object is complex enough to be a class or should be a structure within a class or a simple scalar variable.

A class diagram has three compartments, as shown in the template in figure A.4: the name of the class, the data area with a field and type for each data item, and the functions area. This template is from the draw.io tool, but you can create a class diagram using any UML tool or drawing package you are familiar with.

| Classname |
| --- |
| + field: type |
| + method(type): type |

**Figure A.4   Class diagram template**

Let's define a simple class diagram, using the automobile as an example.

PROBLEM STATEMENT  Design a class diagram representing a generic automobile.

Choose a simple name, Auto, for the class and then design the other parts of the class diagram. A rule of thumb for discovering data items is to ask and answer these questions: "What are the characteristics of this class of object? What data defines an automobile?" Imagine yourself in an auto dealership, and try to enumerate all the characteristics you desire in the automobile you want to buy. There can be many, but for this example, choose color, miles per gallon, and year of manufacture. You can see these characteristics in the first compartment of figure A.5.

Next, add the functions. The question to ask this time is "What are the behaviors of this class of objects?" Once again, you can imagine many answers to this question, and they may vary depending on whether you are a simple user of the automobile or a mechanic who repairs it, who may know about fuel injection and other inner details. The simple functions of the automobile are enumerated in the second compartment in figure A.5; again, these are a few representative examples.

| Auto |
| --- |
| color autoColor; |
| make autoMake; |
| float mpg; |
| accelerate() |
| brake() |
| startEngine() |

**Figure A.5   Class diagram for an automobile**

The data fields of the class can be obtained by answering this question: What are the properties of the objects of this class? The functions can be obtained by answering this question: What can the objects of this class do?

Next, we'll look at associating many types of objects in relationships.

## A.3.2   *Classes and relationships*

A problem design can be defined by different types of classes in relationships such as

- Inheritance (generalization/specialization)
- Composition
- Association

Other relationships are possible, but these will be useful in the context of smart contracts and blockchain-based decentralized applications.

### INHERITANCE

Generalization and specialization of classes, known as *inheritance hierarchy*, is used for representing a hierarchical structure of classes, as shown in figure A.6. Continuing with the automobile example, we can specialize the basic design by using various characteristics and behaviors. In this case, you can see the specialization of the `Auto` class into `Sedan`, `Truck`, and `Van` classes. Here, only one item has been added to the data field of each class (parameters for the number of doors, presence of a cargo bed, and number of passengers), but you may be able to think of other features that specialize these classes. The relationships are clearly indicated. These classes extend the basic `Auto` design, as shown by the Extends arrows in the diagram. (An unfilled triangle shape is used for the arrowhead in this kind of relationship.) `Sedan`, `Truck`, and `Van` are said to have the same characteristics as the base class `Auto` and to inherit them from the `Auto` class, but they also have special features that qualify them to have their own class definitions.

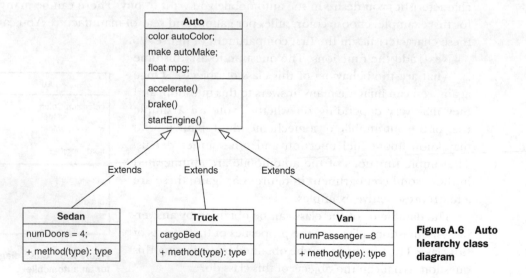

**Figure A.6   Auto hierarchy class diagram**

### COMPOSITION

Composition or aggregation relationships are used when a class is composed of one or more other classes of objects. Using the same example, an `Auto` is composed of many other classes of objects or aggregations of objects, as shown in figure A.7. (The solid

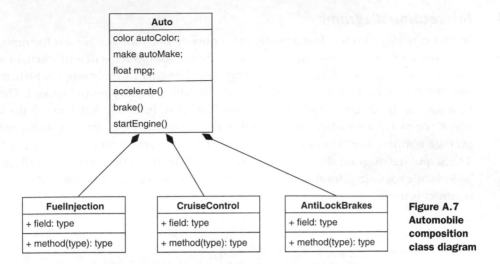

**Figure A.7
Automobile
composition
class diagram**

diamond shape at the head of the arrow indicates this type of relationship). These classes include FuelInjection, CruiseControl, and AntiLockBrakes. Note that I haven't filled in any fields or functions in the class definitions because I'm not an expert in this domain. If your team doesn't contain a domain expert, it will need to collaborate with one to fill in these kinds of details.

### ASSOCIATION

An association relationship among classes is used when a class needs to use the functions of another class. Consider the example of a Teacher class and a GradingSheet class, as shown in figure A.8. The association between these two classes is that a Teacher uses a GradingSheet. This relationship is not inheritance because a Grading-Sheet is not a type of Teacher, and obviously, a Teacher cannot be composed of Grad-ingSheets. So the relation is association. In this case the association is *uses*, as indicated in the diagram in figure A.8. Also observe the one-to-many designation (1..n) on the arrow connecting the two classes, indicating that a Teacher may have many GradingSheets.

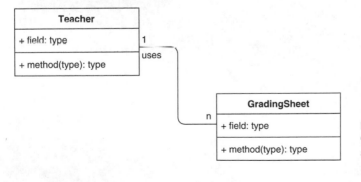

**Figure A.8
Teacher–GradingSheet
association diagram**

## A.4    *Interaction diagrams*

In this category, you will learn about the sequence diagram as a means for designing and analyzing interactions among various software components of a blockchain application. The sequence diagram adds temporal elements to the design, which means that it lets you specify the time and the order in which functions are invoked. The vertical line in the diagram indicates timeline/progress. In figure A.9, you see the interaction between a weather station and a data source in the field to compute the average temperature. The two classes shown are WeatherStation and WeatherSource. The sequence diagram shows the interaction and the timeline. This type of diagram is useful for explaining the sequence of operations with reference to time when a smart contract is used.

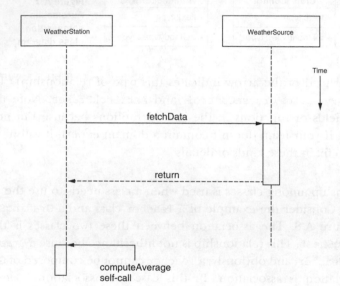

**Figure A.9   Weather sequence diagram**

# appendix B
# Design principles

**DESIGN PRINCIPLE 1**   Design before you code, develop, and deploy a smart contract on a test chain, and thoroughly test it before you deploy on a production block-chain, because when the smart contract is deployed, it is immutable. (Chapter 2)

**DESIGN PRINCIPLE 2**   Define the users of and use cases for the system. Users are entities that generate the actions and the input and receive the output from the system you'll be designing. (Chapter 2)

**DESIGN PRINCIPLE 3**   Define the data assets, peer participants, and their roles, rules to be enforced, and transactions to be recorded for the system you'll be designing. (Chapter 2)

**DESIGN PRINCIPLE 4**   Define a contract diagram that specifies the name, data assets, functions, and rules for execution of functions and access to the data. (Chapter 2)

**DESIGN PRINCIPLE 5**   Use a finite state machine UML diagram to represent system dynamics such as state transitions within a smart contract. (Chapter 3)

**DESIGN PRINCIPLE 6**   Implement the verification and validation needed for trust intermediation by using modifiers specifying the rules and conditions in a smart contract. Typically, verification covers general rules about participants, and validation covers conditions for checking application-specific data. (Chapter 3)

**DESIGN PRINCIPLE 7**   Ensure the privacy and security of function parameters by secure-hashing the parameters along with a single-use secret password. (Chapter 5)

**DESIGN PRINCIPLE 8**   Design smart contracts with only the functions and data needed for enforcing rules, compliance, regulation, provenance, logs for real-time notifications, and timestamped footprints and messages about offline operations. (Chapter 6)

**DESIGN PRINCIPLE 9**    Use a UML sequence diagram to represent the sequence(s) in which functions within a smart contract may (and can) be called. The sequence diagram captures the dynamic operations of a system. (Chapter 6)

**DESIGN PRINCIPLE 10**    An important design decision in blockchain applications is to determine which data and operations are to be coded on-chain and which data and operations are to be implemented off-chain. (Chapter 7)

# *index*